SARTRE
A PHILOSOPHIC STUDY

SARTRE
A PHILOSOPHIC
STUDY

ANTHONY MANSER

OXFORD UNIVERSITY PRESS

NEW YORK

PREFACE

In this book I have tried to give a full survey of Sartre's thought, though the sub-title 'A Philosophic Study' indicates the main area of my interest. Sartre is a complex and many-sided figure; my interpretation often differs from that of other writers. Indeed, it was dissatisfaction with what had been said about him that first drove me to start writing. My central concern has been to show the hard core of philosophic argument which runs through all his works, for this, more than any other single feature of his writings and in spite of the exaggeration of which he is sometimes guilty, is what marks him as one of the great figures of our time. In some ways his philosophic background and methods are far removed from those in which I was educated, yet often I have found the difference to be one of terminology rather than of thought. Consequently I feel that the effort to understand him will prove worth while to those whose first impulse is to reject.

I have tried to justify my statements by quotations. In general these are my own translations; where I have used another's version I have indicated this in the notes. Sartre's major works are referred to by abbreviations, a list of which is given on page x.

There are many people to whom I owe a debt of gratitude for their assistance in different aspects of this book; I cannot possibly list and thank them all individually. Three, however, must be mentioned here: Mr J. N. J. Palmer, with whom I have had many helpful discussions on Sartre's plays and other topics; Professor J. Cruickshank of the University of Sussex, who generously gave me both time and advice; and above all, Mr David Cook of Makerere University College, Kampala, whose encouragement and help made this book possible. They, as well as my colleagues and students of the University of Southampton, are no doubt also grateful that the book has been completed.

Southampton, England A.R.M.
College Park, Maryland
1965

CONTENTS

ABBREVIATIONS

The following abbreviations have been used in the text for works by Sartre:

AdeR	*L'Age de raison*
B	*Baudelaire*
CRD	*Critique de la raison dialectique*
EN	*L'Etre et le néant*
EP	*Entretiens sur la politique*
In	*L'Imagination*
Ire	*L'Imaginaire*
LM	*Les Mots*
LS	*Le Sursis*
MdA	*La Mort dans l'âme*
ME	*Marxisme et existentialisme*
N	*La Nausée*
QJ	*Réflexions sur la question juive*
S.I–S.V	*Situations I – V*
StG	*Saint Genet*
TE	*La Transcendance de l'égo*
TM	*Les Temps modernes*

Full details of these and of Sartre's other works are given in the Bibliography. Page references, unless otherwise stated, are to the original French editions.

I

The Novel as Philosophy:
La Nausée

TO START a book which is primarily a philosophic study by talking about a novel is not gratuitous eccentricity. Rather would the eccentricity seem to be Sartre's, for in 1938, the year of publication of *La Nausée*, it seemed clear that he was a professional philosopher intending to make his way up the normal French educational ladder. To this end he had published two philosophical articles and a book, taught philosophy in various Lycées, and spent a year in Germany studying Heidegger's philosophy. If he had been killed in the war, after the publication of *L'Etre et le néant* (1943), it is possible that *La Nausée* and the volume of short stories *Le Mur* (1939) would have been forgotten and Sartre remembered only as a philosopher. A comparison between the pre- and post-war literary works will also reveal an important difference; the latter are much more consciously 'literary' and less 'philosophical' than the former. This difference reflects a difference in his attitude to the act of writing itself, as he has hinted. Simone de Beauvoir states that *La Nausée* corresponded to Sartre's intentions, which were to "express in literary form metaphysical truths and feelings".[1] This could not be said about *Les Chemins de la liberté*, which is much less philosophically dense. Even on a superficial level it is remarkable that Mathieu, the philosopher-hero of the trilogy, thinks much less philosophically than does Roquentin, explorer and historian, in *La Nausée*. Before the publication of Simone de Beauvoir's memoirs there was current a story that

[1] *La Force de l'age*, 293.

I

Sartre had originally written *La Nausée* as a piece of pure philosophy, and had only been persuaded to make it into a work of fiction by his publisher, who thought it could not be sold as an academic work. Though it seems to be untrue, the story is revealing; it could not have been told of *L'Age de raison*. I have noticed that philosophy students, even those ignorant of 'existentialism', find much less difficulty in making sense of *La Nausée* than do students of literature; to the former it has a naturalness precisely because it is so stuffed with philosophic references which they can appreciate.

There has been little discussion of the place of philosophy in literature, though there seems to be a general assumption that its presence is an intrusion, that literature has a different task to philosophy. Further, it would seem to be agreed that, though it might be possible to *extract* a philosophy from a work of art, such a philosophy should normally remain implicit, not obtrude itself. The final word of the critic might well be that unless such succesful integration takes place, unless the philosophy is only an underlying part of the novel, it will fail from a literary point of view because the majority of its readers will not be philosophers and hence will miss the point of the book. A recent writer[1] has called *Candide* a philosophic novel because Voltaire sets out to demolish Leibnizian optimism. But most of those who enjoy the work are virtually unaware of Leibniz's views and would not be qualified to say how far Voltaire had succeeded in what he set out to do. His intentions are largely irrelevant to the success of the book. On the other hand, the philosopher is liable to complain that what he is given is example in place of argument, and, in this case, a not very convincing example. Very little knowledge of Leibniz is needed to bring one to realise that his views are untouched by the sufferings of Candide, Cunegonde, Pangloss and the others; nothing Voltaire says actually conflicts with the doctrine that this is the "best of all possible worlds". Any alternative might be much worse. The danger of trying to combine philosophy and fiction is that the product is liable to be attacked from

[1] Morris Weitz in *Philosophy in Literature* (Wayne State University Press, 1963).

both sides, that of the critic and that of the philosopher. If it is held to be obvious that the function of literature is to represent and that of philosophy to argue, then there is no place for a 'philosophic novel'; the two have been defined mutually exclusively. But there seems no reason why this rigid division should be accepted; the novel is not a closely defined art-form. Indeed, its only criterion would seem to be its success in finding readers; a piece of prose fiction which is read for its own sake can properly be called a novel. It is clear that this is true of *La Nausée*. Also it is too simple to assert that philosophy must consist of long trains of argument. The recent cult of the striking example in England has shown that argument is sometimes superfluous. There are few long arguments in the works of Wittgenstein, though he certainly succeeds in producing changes of philosophical view in his readers. Here again success would seem to be a legitimate criterion; if Sartre succeeds in what he has set out to do, then his technique is legitimate.

The literary value of *La Nausée* has been the source of some controversy. One point on which there has been a measure of agreement is that the book has no genuine conclusion, it merely finishes. There is no reason to suppose that Roquentin, the hero, will behave any differently in the future, that what has happened to him in the course of the novel will have any real effect on him. What has been missed by those who use the inconclusive ending to give an adverse judgment is that this is the effect that Sartre intended: "In order that the most ordinary event should become an adventure, it is only necessary that it should be *recounted*. That's what deceives people: man is always a story-teller, he lives surrounded by his own and others' stories and sees all that happens to him through them; he tries to live his life as if it were a story he was telling. But you must choose: Live or recount. . . . When you live, nothing happens. The scene changes, people come in and go out, that's all. There are never any beginnings" (*N*, 57). And, of course, no endings either. This passage is an ironic comment on Roquentin's way of escape from his impasse by writing a novel, which might be *La Nausée* itself. But there is no escape in that direction. Sartre's irony should never be forgotten in reading any of his works. Many of the errors made by critics in discussing him are due to a failure to notice his irony, or even in some cases his jokes at the expense of philosophy. One of his plays, *Nekrassov*, is extremely funny, but even his purely philosophical books contain witty remarks, and sometimes puns. In this case the irony is partly at Sartre's own expense, because he cannot bring the book to a successful conclusion in the terms in which it has been written. At this stage of his thought he was unable to see a way of life which would be appropriate to the insights he had given Roquentin. Indeed, the purpose of the novel was destructive only; in it Sartre was clearing his own mind of certain philosophical views that seemed to him wrong, but as yet he had nothing to put in their place.

Sartre was, in fact, attacking the philosopher he had earlier hailed as master, Edmund Husserl. Husserl's phenomenology had seemed to him the way out of a philosophical impasse. What had seemed most attractive in phenomenology was its attack on metaphysics, which accorded well with Sartre's sceptical temperament. The Husserlian motto, "Back to the things themselves", seemed a recall to reality after so much idealist metaphysics, an attempt to bring philosophy back into contact with the real world. Unfortunately the phenomenologists failed to live up to their claims; Husserl, in his interminable and almost unreadable analyses, attempted to describe only what is given, the phenomena themselves. This apparent realism led him into an ultimate idealism, to such statements as "We shall never know if there is a world." This was because in order to contemplate the actual phenomena, Husserl found it necessary to ignore what we ordinarily think about the world, to describe only the material of consciousness itself. Only in this area could he find true certainty, and from this basis all else was to be constructed. The method is clearly akin to Descartes' methodological doubt, the attempt to discover certainty by doubting everything that could be doubted. Husserl formalised this method by his famous *epoché* or reduction, which he described as a "bracketing off" of all our normal attitudes to the world. Descartes found that, in order to reconstruct a certain external world after he had corroded away the uncertainties by doubt, he had to introduce God to guarantee the reality of external objects. But Descartes' doubt was only methodological; he never really doubted the existence of things; he was no sceptic. Husserl wanted to do the same as Descartes without invoking a *deus ex machina*, to construct a "transcendental science" which was both certain and free from all presuppositions. But having cut human consciousness off from a real world, he found no satisfactory means to bring it back into contact with it. In this way his attempted realism became idealism.

Such an analysis raised the further question of what it was that had the experiences, that gave unity to the contents of a single consciousness. Descartes had, in fact, been convinced of the existence of a divinely created soul, so no problems about the unity of the self were raised in his mind; hence he could write that "The soul is more easily known than the body". Husserl, trying to avoid any such metaphysical assumptions, nevertheless had to fall back on the notion of a "transcendental ego", an "I" essentially involved in any possible act of consciousness. This was a metaphysical notion very like Kant's transcendental ego, a means of guaranteeing the unity of consciousness. Once such a notion is introduced it is easy to proceed on Kantian lines. But this notion seemed to Sartre a reintroduction of the metaphysical ideas that it had been the object of the whole exercise to avoid. He began to part company with Husserl, at first on the specific point about the existence of a transcendental ego, and later, as a result of his first criticisms, on the whole reduction of the real world. The break on the question of the self is marked by the publication of the article 'La Transcendance de l'égo' in 1936. When this appeared he was working on *La Nausée*, though the novel was not published till two years later. It is in the context of the latter work that Sartre first formulates his own 'existentialist' views. It is worth noting that one of the results of Sartre's criticism of Husserl was a change in his use of the term 'phenomenology'; henceforth Sartre means by it something more like the meaning given by Hegel. The attack in the article starts by denying the existence of anything resembling a transcendental ego: "I would like to show here that the ego is neither formally nor materially *in* consciousness: it is outside, *in the world*. It is a being in the world, like the ego of another" (*TE*, 31).[1] He illustrates this point: "When I run after a street-car, when I look at the time, when I am absorbed in contemplating a portrait, there is no *I*. There is consciousness *of the streetcar having to be* overtaken, etc. . . . In fact, I am then plunged into the world of objects; it is they which constitute the unity of my consciousnesses; it is they which present themselves with values, with attractive and repellent qualities—but *me*, I have disappeared. . . . And this is not a matter of chance, due to a momentary lapse of attention, but happens because of the very structure of consciousness" (*TE*, 48–49). This passage is very reminiscent of Hume:

For my part, when I enter most intimately into what I call *myself*, I always stumble on some particular perception or other, of heat or cold, light or shade, love or hatred, pain or pleasure. I never catch *myself* at any time without a perception, and never can observe anything but the perception.[2]

Sartre's point here, as so often at this stage of his career, is very like Hume's; the many similarities between the two philosophers have been insufficiently noticed.

The point is like Hume's, but it is not quite the same. The Scottish philosopher found it impossible to produce any explanation of the 'unity of the self' on his principles, though this fact did not greatly worry him. But once the problem has been stated in such terms it is very natural to claim that the unity is given by the very fact that "all my *experiences* are *my* experiences", by the existence of some unifying factor in the structure of consciousness itself, though this factor is only detected by the existence of the unity. Sartre's solution is more radical; 'I' is not the name of anything, real or transcendental, it is rather a grammatical necessity. The unity which I appear to experience depends ultimately

[1] Tr. F. Williams and R. Kirkpatrick, *The Transcendence of the Ego*, 1957.
[2] *Treatise of Human Nature*, Bk. I, pt. iv, sect. vi.

on the nature of the world and my body's relation to it, though Sartre did not develop this point fully until *L'Etre et le néant*. If I were not a being who moved about in the world and acted on objects in it, as well as being acted on by it, there would be no such thing as self-consciousness. If it were possible to 'bracket off' the external world, then the self would also have disappeared. Hence it is impossible to study the self by *a priori* procedures as Husserl tried to do; we must literally go back to the things themselves, to the real world: "That is to say precisely the one in which we live, with its countries, its men and its history of men. We are here in the presence of an irreducible primary fact. . . ." (*Ire*, 227–8). It seems to me that one of the chief aims of *La Nausée* was to illustrate this point, to stress the *existent* qualities of things in the world and the impossibility of an *epoché* which would attempt to ignore them. And, by the same token, Sartre wished to bring out the actual nature of the self, its particular mode of existence. This part of his enterprise has given rise to many misunderstandings; Roquentin is represented as a solitary individual because only through such a person can the sorts of question that Sartre wishes to raise be illustrated. There is no suggestion that he is living a kind of life that all men do, or should, experience.

The first prong of the attack on Husserl is best illustrated by the famous "chestnut root" passage, which is quoted in most discussions of Sartre. It puts the point so well that I shall repeat it here.

"Just now I was in the park. The root of a chestnut tree buried itself in the earth just under my seat. I could no longer remember that it was a root. Words had disappeared, and, with them, the meanings of things, their uses, the feeble bench-marks that men had scratched on the surface. I was sitting down, bent over a bit, my head down, alone and face to face with this raw black knotty mass which terrified me.

"It took my breath away. Never, before these last few days, had I understood what 'to exist' meant. I was like the others, like those who walk by the sea in their summer clothes. Like them I said 'the sea *is* green; that white dot up there *is* a sea-gull', but I didn't feel that it existed, that the sea-gull was an 'existing sea-gull'; ordinarily, existence hides from us. It is there, around us, in us, it is *us*, you can't say two words without talking about it, and, lastly, you can't touch it. When I tried to think about it, I thought nothing, my head was empty, or there was just a word in my head, the word 'Being'. . . . Even when I looked at things, I was miles away from thinking that they existed. . . . If I had been asked what existence was, I would have replied in good faith that it was nothing, just an empty form added to things from the outside, without changing their nature. And then there it was; suddenly it was there, it was as clear as day; existence had suddenly been unveiled. It had lost its inoffensive manner of being an abstract category; it was the very stuff of things; this root was made of existence. . . . But in the presence of this gross ruddy paste, neither knowledge nor ignorance were important; the world of explanations and of reasons is not the world of existence. A circle is not absurd, it can be explained perfectly well by the rotation of a segment of a straight line round one of its extremities. But in addition a circle does not exist. But this root, on the other hand, existed in so far as I could not explain it. Knotty, inert, without name, it fascinated me, it filled my eyes, it kept on bringing me back to my own existence. I tried to repeat 'It's a root'—that did no good. I could see that it was impossible to pass from its function as a root, a pump, to *that*, to that hard compact skin like a seal's, to that oily, horny, stubborn aspect. Its function explained nothing; it allowed you to understand in general what a root was, but not *this*. This root, with its colour, its shape, its fixed movement, was . . . beyond all explanation" (*N*, 161–4).

The contrast here and in many similar passages in the book is between the 'thinginess' of things and the abstract perfection of ideas, geometrical figures, tunes and so on. There is no difference between *thinking* of a root and of a circle; in Husserl's terminology both are the 'intentional objects' of my thought. But when I actually *see* the root or any other physical object there is a vast difference; I am confronted with something alien which exists in its own right and which cannot be disposed of by any 'reduction'.

THE NOVEL AS PHILOSOPHY: *LA NAUSÉE*

Normally this sense of the brute existence of things is masked from us, because we see the external world through a screen of intentions and activities. Things are regarded either as utensils or as obstacles or as mere backgrounds; they are not contemplated for their own sakes. Even works of art which are also physical objects are not really looked at for their own sakes, but as paintings or sculptures. The strange appearance of the physical objects in *La Nausée* is due to the fact that Roquentin contemplates them, looks at them rather than through them as we normally do. An analogous example with words will illustrate the point; normally we use words without being conscious of them, expressing what we want to say *through* them, hardly aware of the word as such. But if for some reason we repeat a word over and over again to ourselves it becomes a sinister thing, it begins to exist in the same way that the chestnut root did for Roquentin. In the case of the word our language is, as it were, idling; similarly in *La Nausée* the perceptions and emotions of Roquentin are idling. Sartre has taken care to put him into a position where such a process is possible, cut off from any real contact with those who surround him, with no need to work for his living, in fact not at all involved with the everyday world of normal men. To the latter the world does not appear in this guise, and, I think, Sartre makes it clear in his later works that it should not often do so. The attack on the Husserlian *epoché* is thus twofold; first it can only be performed by cutting oneself off from normal human life. Second, even if this is done, brute existence will reassert itself; existence cannot be avoided or ignored.

The second prong of Sartre's attack on Husserl is concerned with the individual's awareness of his own existence, which is to be seen as very different from that imagined by Husserl or Descartes. The whole of a long passage in the centre of the novel (*N*, 126–33) can be considered as a sort of argument against the Cogito, Descartes' attempt to prove his own existence by arguing "I think, therefore I exist". Husserl developed Descartes' argument, and Sartre is attacking both versions. I have called it 'a sort of argument', for it consists in a series of images strung together in the style of the stream of consciousness novel. But there is an important difference from the typical example of this style of writing; the images that Sartre uses are *philosophic* images, and the connecting links between them are ones that a philosopher, and probably no one else, would make. It is for this reason that philosophers find less difficulty in following the train of thought that Sartre is representing here and in other places in the novel. Before tackling the major passage, I will illustrate this device where Sartre is using a well-known set of philosophic arguments, so that the technique, which plays such an important part in the book, can be easily seen. Roquentin is looking down on Bouville, thinking about the narrow lives of the inhabitants, their fixed ideas, their belief that "the world obeys fixed and immutable laws. Unsupported bodies always fall at the same speed, the park is closed every day at 4 o'clock in winter, at 6 in summer, lead melts at 335°, the last tram leaves the town hall at 11.5 p.m." (*N*, 198.) The townsmen believe in the "Law of Uniformity of Nature", that the universe is a law-abiding place. They are so philosophically unsophisticated that they fail to distinguish between natural and man-made regularities. But Roquentin is a good Humean: "I know that she [Nature] is not governed by laws; . . . there are only her habits and those could be changed tomorrow" (*N*, 199). He realises that there are no ultimate laws, only regularities to which we are accustomed, which we accept as laws because we are accustomed to them. Hence he goes on to imagine what it would be like if they did change: "A mother will notice her child's cheek and ask him: 'What's that, a pimple?' and she will see the flesh swell a little, crack, open up; and at the bottom of the hole a third eye, a laughing eye, will appear. Or people will feel a gentle tickling all over their bodies, as they feel water-weeds when swimming. And they will discover that their clothes have become alive. Or someone will find that he has something scratching the inside of his mouth. When he looks in a mirror he will find that his tongue has become an enormous living centipede" (*N*, ibid.). The reference to the controversy over the uniformity of nature is essential to grasping the point of the long passage of horrors; it is not brought in merely to shock, but to get the reader to reflect on induction. Of course, it is also true that Roquentin would like something of this sort to happen, to have the bourgeoisie shocked out of their complacent attitudes and realise that the world is not a comfortable place in which to live. The hatred of the bourgeoisie that Sartre expresses through the character of Roquentin was not, at this period, in any sense a political attitude. Rather it was part of the typical way in which French writers and artists thought about them, the serious-minded people who were uninterested in ideas; similar thoughts were expressed by many other Frenchmen in the half-century preceding Sartre. Indeed, it sometimes seems as if the Marxism of Sartre's later years were a product of his dislike of the bourgeoisie rather than the other way about.

The passage I have just quoted merely refers to a set of arguments; the anti-Cogito passage is more radical in that it is an attempt to destroy an argument by producing a state of feeling in which the kind of pure intellection demanded by Descartes and Husserl is seen to be impossible. "I exist. I think that I exist. Oh, the long coil, this sensation of existence—and I unwind it, gently. . . . If I could stop myself thinking! I try, I succeed; it seems as if my head is filled with smoke . . . and then it all begins again: 'Smoke . . . do not think. . . . I don't want to think. I must not think that I don't want to think. Because that is another thought. Will it never end?' " (N, 129). But thoughts by themselves are not enough to give a real sense of existence; the body is more important. Roquentin cuts into the train of thought by stabbing himself in the hand; he becomes fully aware of his body: "My body of flesh which lives, flesh which crawls and sweetly turns liquors, turns cream, flesh which turns, turns, turns, the sweet and sugary water of my body, the blood of my hand, it hurts, sweet to my bruised flesh which turns, walks, I walk, I flee, I am an unworthy individual with bruised flesh, bruised by existence at these walls" (N, 131). "Existence takes my thoughts from behind, takes me from behind, forces me to think from behind, and therefore to be something" (N, 132).

"I think, therefore I exist" should rather run "I am forced by my body to think and feel, therefore I exist". The Cogito is not performed by a disembodied (or potentially disembodied) intellect, but by this only-too-embodied being. Existence cannot be understood by the mind; it can only be apprehended by the feelings and bodily sensations which I cannot help experiencing, which force themselves on me sometimes in spite of my wishes. I can even taste the flavour of my existence, an insipid taste in the mouth, "une espèce d'écoeurement douceâtre", a sweetish sort of disgust, nausea itself. In spite of the fact that Sartre originally wrote the book under the title *Melancolia*, with the Dürer engraving in mind, some critics have maintained that the notion of nausea is central to his thought. In *L'Etre et le néant* he writes of it as follows: "This perpetual experience of an insipid and ever-present taste which remains with me even when I try to get rid of it and which is *my* taste is what I have described elsewhere under the name of *Nausea*. A dull and inescapable nausea perpetually reveals my body to my consciousness. . . . Far from it being the case that we should understand this term *nausea* as a metaphor drawn from our physiological disgust, it is on the contrary on its foundations that all actual concrete nauseas, which make us vomit, (nausea in the presence of rotten meat, fresh blood, excrements, etc.) are produced" (*EN*, 404). Incidentally, Sartre's use of the notion in his later work is more sophisticated and less central; in the sixty-two pages of his discussion of the body it merely occupies a single paragraph, almost the whole of which I have quoted.

On the basis of this and other passages in *La Nausée* the charge has been levelled that Sartre actually finds existence sickening and revolting. If he himself thought so, then his only logical course would be to commit suicide, rather than to lead the active life which he has led. Further, it is always dangerous to assume that a fictional character's statements actually represent the views of the author. But if my argument is correct, then it is possible to see that nausea has an important role to play in a kind of argument, and hence that there is no need to assume that it represents an attitude of the author. Philosophers have talked as if "the soul is more easily known than the body"; Sartre wants to show that bodily existence has primacy. He tries to do this by getting his readers to enter into the experiences of Roquentin and hence to reflect on their own. They will then realise that the consciousness of the body is primary, that it is inescapable. But, just as normally the existence of external objects is hidden from us because we think of them only as instruments or obstacles, so our bodies are normally 'transparent'. It is through them that we act, and action is the main preoccupation of the normal man. Whilst I am typing this I am not conscious of my fingers, but only of what I want to say. My fingers are not even the instruments I use to write with. Of course, whilst I was learning to type I had to pay attention to them, was aware of their movements. I can now become aware of them, but only at the cost of not concentrating on what I am doing. When the body is working efficiently it is not noticed.

But the philosopher is not using his body or his thoughts; he is looking at them reflectively, and thus they are idling. It is at such moments that nausea is experienced. One remedy for such a feeling would be to go out and do something in the real world, to get on with a job of work. There is even a hint in Sartre's novel that philosophy is, as Wittgenstein almost thought, a disease to be cured rather than a legitimate occupation for the intellect. But since philosophers have put forward arguments of a certain type, these have to be refuted first by similar methods. Philosophers try to establish their points by relying on pure thought, by thinking about bare existence, not about any particular thing. Sartre feels he must defeat them by showing that at this level their position is untenable, that it is impossible to contemplate bare existence. The only real objects of contemplation are existent things which, whether they be objects external to me or my own body, are resistant to my thoughts, and which cannot be got rid of by any phenomenological reduction. The form of Roquentin's experience depends on the doctrines that Sartre is trying to expose. I say 'expose' rather than 'refute' because there is no place in the novel for a triumphant *Q.E.D.*; but someone who has really experienced the feelings of Roquentin in the course of the book can never accept Husserl's views in quite the same way as he might have done before. He will have a 'metaphysical feeling' which turns him against such a position even though he has no coherent *arguments* against it. The constant impact of the violent images of *La Nausée* has, I think, the effect that Sartre intended.

Sartre further implies that philosophers have shown a kind of bad faith in trying to conceal from themselves that they do have bodies; they have done this by locating perfection in the realm of abstract ideas, of mathematical objects and other non-existent things. They have used these notions to cleanse themselves of such corruptions as sexual desire; Roquentin says to himself "I need to cleanse myself with abstract thoughts, as transparent as water" (N, 77). Logic can function as a kind of liver-pill against nausea. Ideal objects, for instance those dealt with in mathematics, can be defined by pure thought even if no physical example can be found or constructed. In this lies their superiority to things to be discovered in the world. These latter, as Plato thought, are necessarily inferior, and this inferiority is shown by their resistance to the pure intellect, the fact that they cannot be deduced from first principles. Roquentin expresses this in almost textbook fashion: "The essential thing is contingency. I want to say that existence is the opposite of necessity by definition. To exist is simply *to be there*; existing things appear, are met with, but they can never be *deduced*. Some people, I think, have realised this. Only they have tried to get round this contingency by inventing a necessary being who is his own cause. But no necessary being could explain existence; contingency is not an outward show, an appearance which can be got rid of; it is the absolute itself and consequently perfectly gratuitous" (N, 166). (This is, in fact, the conclusion he draws from his contemplation of the chestnut root.) Sartre makes his final attack on the notion of ideal objects existing in a timeless world by means of irony, though the fact has been missed by those who have taken the conclusion of the book perfectly seriously. For the one example of perfect being that he discusses at length is the tune 'Some of these days'; the choice of a sentimental and slightly banal air is deliberate. But Roquentin is not looking for an aesthetic consolation; as he himself says: "There are some imbeciles who get consolation from the fine arts. Like my aunt Bigeois: 'Chopin's *Préludes* were of great assistance to me on the death of your poor uncle.' And the concert rooms disgorge humiliated and injured people, who, with closed eyes, try to transform their pale faces into sensitive antennae. They think that the captured sounds flow into them, sweet and nourishing, and that their sufferings become music, like those of Werther; they think that beauty is compassionate. *Les cons*" (N, 217). He realises that the air is trivial: "It is an old *rag-time* with a sung chorus. I had heard the American troops whistling it in the streets of La Rochelle in 1917. It must date from before the war. But this recording is much more recent. Still, it's the oldest record in the pile, a Pathé record for sapphire needle" (N, 35–36).

What attracts Roquentin is the nature of a piece of music as manifested in this (or any other) tune. "It [the tune] doesn't exist. In fact this is in itself annoying; if I got up and snatched the record from the turn-table and broke it in two, I wouldn't have touched the tune. It is beyond—always beyond something, beyond a voice, beyond the note of a violin. Across the thicknesses and thicknesses of existence it revealed itself, slender and firm, and, if you tried to catch it, you only struck existing things, you stumbled on meaningless existents. It lies behind them; I don't even hear it, I hear only sounds, vibrations of the air which reveal it. It doesn't exist, because there is nothing *de trop* in it; everything else is *de trop* with respect to it. It *is*" (N, 218). The contrast in this passage between 'is' and 'exists' is hard to bring out in translation. Ideal objects 'are', physical objects 'exist' merely. God replied to Moses "I am that I am". The being of the tune, compared with the existence of things, lies in its changelessness, in the fact that it is untouchable, that it cannot be affected by the accidents of the world. In fact, Roquentin does not think about his example with full philosophic rigour; even though the tune does not consist in this particular series of notes, nor even in the printed score, nor even in the original score jotted down by the composer, it is still not an ideal object in the sense that a geometrical figure is. If all records and all human memories were destroyed, it would be odd to say that the tune still was, and there was clearly a time before it was. But in this sense a circle (or the circle) cannot be created or destroyed.

Still, it serves Roquentin's purpose, which is to make him realise that what he really wanted was being, not existence. His feeling of nausea at his contingent body arose from his desire to escape from contingency; there is a hint that nausea may be the result of this desire for being in most cases. In the passage from *L'Etre et le néant* quoted above, it is the most blatantly contingent things of all which are the sources of actual vomiting. "And I also wanted to *be*. That was even the only thing that I wanted, the aim of my life; behind all these apparently unconnected attempts lay the same desire, to drive existence from me, to empty the moments of their fat, to wring them out, to dry them up, to purify myself, harden myself, so that at last I gave out a sound as clear and precise as the note of a saxophone" (N, 218). By a train of thought that is clearly intended to be fallacious as an argument, Roquentin transfers the characteristics of the tune itself to the composer and singer: "For me they are rather like the dead, rather like the heroes of a novel; they are cleansed of the sin of existence. Not completely, obviously—but as much as a man can be. This thought suddenly struck me, because that was all I wanted" (N, 221). For Sartre the desire to be rather than to exist as a finite human being is one form of 'bad faith'. The irony which he is now using in suggesting this solution for Roquentin is manifested in the fact that what Roquentin is now seeking, being, is that very object for which he has criticised the bourgeois throughout the book; they, too, seek being and this is what is wrong with them. This is brought out well in the conclusion to the short story 'L'Enfance d'un chef', written about the same time as *La Nausée*: "Rights! Things of the same kind as triangles and circles, which were so perfect that no specimen existed. Thousands of figures could be drawn with a compass without achieving a single circle. Generations of workers could, in the same way, scrupulously obey Lucien's orders without ever exhausting his right to command. Rights were beyond existence, like mathematical objects and religious dogmas."[1]

If the bourgeois are wrong in thinking that they can achieve being, rather than existence, then so is Roquentin. Sartre makes the illusory nature of this escape route still more evident; what has saved the singer and composer from existence, and what will save Roquentin, is not something in their lives but the mere fact that others will think of them in a certain way. Roquentin states this explicitly: "A book. A novel. And then there will be people who will read the novel and say: 'Antoine Roquentin wrote that; he was a red-headed chap who spent his time in cafés', and they will think about my life as I think about the singer's, as something precious and half-legendary" (N, 222). The goal is not the achievement of writing the novel, nor the effect this will actually have on his life, but only the fact that others will think of him. Roquentin does not say how this will save him from nausea. Miss Murdoch suggests that the fault lies in Sartre's lack of interest in the conclusion of the novel: "The interest of *La Nausée* does not lie in its conclusion, which is merely sketched in; Sartre has not developed it sufficiently for it even to pose as a solution to the problem."[2] It seems to me that Sartre rather intended Roquentin's suggestion to be seen as no remedy for his difficulties. In fact, it bears a resemblance to Hume's remedy for an impasse in his own thought. He recommended "carelessness and inattention"; "I dine, I play backgammon, I converse, and am merry with my friends; and when after three or four hours' amusement, I would return to these speculations, they appear so cold, and strain'd, and ridiculous, that I cannot find it in my heart to enter on to them any farther."[3] In many ways Roquentin is an up-to-date Hume, an existentialist version of the Scottish philosopher. Roquentin's novel is likely to be as important (or as unimportant) as Hume's game of backgammon. The two solutions are alike in that they seek a way out of a philosophical impasse by giving up philosophising, Hume

[1] *Le Mur*, 243 (Collection Pourpre).
[2] *Sartre*, 16 (Bowes & Bowes, 1953).
[3] *Treatise of Human Nature*, Bk. I, pt. iv, sect. vii.

temporarily and Roquentin probably permanently. For he has seen, in his criticism of the inhabitants of Bouville, that the search for being is not a way out and yet he intends to make it. Sartre, I am sure, was quite aware at the time of writing the novel that the solution was only to be found by going through the difficulty. It is probable that he did not know what the solution was and so could not incorporate it; the negative part of his philosophy had been done, the attempt to be positive only came later.

La Nausée is thus that rare thing, a genuinely philosophic novel, though it cannot be called entirely successful. Firstly this is because it does not stand on its own feet; to appreciate it fully a considerable amount of outside knowledge is needed, knowledge which is not available to the average reader. No doubt it succeeds in creating a powerful impression, but this is due to the strikingness of the imagery rather than to the structure of the whole; the connections between different sections are liable to be missed. Sartre himself evidently did not find the experiment wholly successful, for he did not use the same form again. His subsequent works are either more conventional pieces of philosophising or more like normal novels; the thought in them is spread much more thinly. Nevertheless, the attempt is interesting; Sartre clearly learnt the need for striking examples which he uses in his subsequent works. But in using such examples he was proceeding in a way very similar to that of contemporary British philosophers. As one of them has written:

What do you find in reading Ryle or Wittgenstein? Lots of examples with little or no logical bone in between. Why so many examples? They speak for themselves; they are usually more transparent than the trouble maker; each one acts as an analogy; together they light up the whole linguistic background with the effect that the case before us is seen in the light they produce. Indeed, examples aptly arranged are often more convincing than an argument which is anyhow spidery. Not that the 'proofs' offered are valueless: a *reductio ad absurdum* always points to a knot in thought, and so does an infinite regress. But they *point* only. The real strength lies in the examples. All the proofs, in a good book on philosophy, could be dispensed with, without its losing a whit of its convincingness. To seek, in philosophy, for rigorous proofs is to seek for the shadow of one's voice.[1]

In *La Nausée*, Sartre seems to have done precisely this, to have dispensed with the proofs and left us the examples. We in England may find it hard to assess the effectiveness of his procedure, the value of his examples, because we were never caught in the particular fly-bottle which he was showing us the way out of.

[1] F. Waismann, *Contemporary British Philosophy, 3rd Series*, 481-2.

II

The Imagination

SARTRE'S analysis of the imagination is the best introduction
to his philosophical work, firstly because the clarity and
originality of his thought is so manifest in this field, and
second because in the course of his study he elaborates some of the
basic features of his philosophy. He has written two books on the
cluster of problems which centre around the notion of the imagination, *L'Imagination* (1936) and *L'Imaginaire* (1940). The earlier
work consists mainly of exposition and criticism of the writings
of previous philosophers and psychologists; the second is a constructive attempt to produce a satisfactory account of the topic
from a philosophic point of view. For this reason it is unfortunate
that the first English translation of *L'Imaginaire* was given the title
The Psychology of the Imagination. The reason for this mistake is a
misunderstanding of the French sub-title *Psychologie Phénoménologique de l'Imagination*; the point of the use of the word 'phenomenological' in the title is to remove the impression of an empirical
approach to the subject, which might be given by the use of
'psychology'. Though the book makes use of psychological
investigations, it is clearly a work of philosophy throughout.

The conventional view of the imagination might be crudely
represented in the following way: there arise in the mind 'mental
pictures' which are in many ways like actual perceptions of external objects. These pictures are of two sorts, those of the reproductive imagination, exact copies of things seen in the past, and
those of the free imagination or fancy, combinations of fragments
from the reproductive imagination into new shapes. A person who
is good at the latter process has a 'good imagination', and is

likely to be an artist or writer. Hume may be taken as a typical representative of this view. He says:

Those perceptions, which enter with most force and violence, we may name *impressions*; and under this name I comprehend all our sensations, passions and emotions, as they make their first appearance in the soul. By *ideas* I mean the faint images of these in thinking and reasoning. . . . Everyone of himself will readily perceive the distinction betwixt feeling and thinking. The common degrees of these are easily distinguished; tho' it is not impossible but in particular instances they may very nearly approach to each other.[1]

The final sentence allows Hume to account for the occurrence of hallucinations and illusions; they are images which have been mistaken for genuine perceptions. An image is thus thought of as the same kind of thing as a perception, and as apprehended in the same way. Normally the two can be distinguished without difficulty, but in times of stress or inattention I may fall into error. This view inevitably leads to the belief that images are some sort of mental picture, a kind of internal analogue to a real picture or photograph. From these internal snapshots we can obtain information in the same way that we can obtain information from a real snapshot; memory consists partially in looking at our picture collection.

There are two major difficulties in such a view. First, the nature of the mental picture and the act of inner vision is unclear. Second, the ordinary use of the word 'imagination' and its cognates differs from this account and is wider than it allows. The imaginative ability of the artist is manifested in his works, not in what goes on in his mind. Similarly, pretending and imitating are things which can be done by people with good imaginations. Imagination is not a single notion, but a cluster of notions. The philosophers appear to have talked as if there were a central notion of mental picturing which had little or nothing to do with other things normally called imaginative. As a reaction to this view, some contemporary thinkers, such as Ryle in the *Concept of*

[1] *Treatise of Human Nature*, Bk. I, pt. i, sect. i.

Mind, seem to have denied the existence of mental images completely. Sartre tries both to do justice to the common belief in images and at the same time to account for the grouping together of several different human activities under the name of 'imagination'. To this end he makes use of the notion of *intentionality*, which was much discussed by earlier phenomenologists. The term itself was taken over from medieval discussions. "The conception of *intentionality* is needed to renovate our notion of the image" (*In*, 144). This means that mental contents point beyond themselves, generally to extra-mental objects; we need to know what images are *of*, not what they are like. Sartre and other French writers frequently use the word *viser*, to point to or aim at, in these contexts, but this is very like the English use of the phrase the 'image of' something. When we are thinking about a real problem it is the objects themselves we are concerned with, not what is going on in our minds. As long as there is a means of referring to objects in the world, the mechanism of reference is of little importance. We don't need to know what our images are *like*, only what they are images *of*. The term *intentionality* is only a convenient way of referring to this fact. Further, the quantity of imagery which different people experience varies without any corresponding variation in their powers of thought; this is another reason for attending to the referents of the images rather than the images themselves.

Some of the difficulties that philosophers have encountered in this area have arisen from trying to attend to the image as it is in itself, instead of looking at the way it actually functions in thought. Here, as so often, the attempt at introspection falsifies the very data it is trying to reach. If the effort is made to 'observe' the image, then it does seem to be something seen, like an object or a picture of the object. For this reason a denial of the existence of mental imagery is found shocking by many people. Further, certain questions which can be sensibly asked seem to stress the likeness between 'image' and 'mental picture', e.g. "How vivid is your mental imagery?" or "When you think of the colour of the cover of *Being and Nothingness*, do you just remember the name of the colour or does an image of it appear?" The idea that there *are* such things as mental images is not merely a creation of the philosophers but part of a very natural way of talking about what goes on in our minds. Nevertheless, it is not altogether clear what we are talking about when we give answers to questions like those above. For it is possible to talk about pictures without talking about what they are pictures of, for any picture in the normal sense of the word is also a physical object. It is not so obvious that we can talk about mental images in the same way.[1]

In everyday contexts it is the object of our images that interests us; only at the level of philosophy or psychology does the question of what images are really like arise. But, Sartre thinks, this kind of question only occurs because insufficient attention has been paid to the normal intentional way of talking about mental imagery. Hume's suggestion that there is a possibility of confusion between an image and a genuine perception was made because he failed to take care over this point. When I make a mistake in perception, for instance 'see' a tree or bush in the fog as a man, this may be reported by the sentence "No, there's nobody there; I must have imagined it". But the claim is not being made that an image was mistaken for a perception, merely that one existing object was 'taken for' another; nothing is really implied about the mechanism of the mistake. Sometimes, when listening to music on the radio, I think I hear the ringing of the telephone in the next room. Here again, the sound is 'imagined'. But there is no image of the sound of the telephone bell which competes with the actually heard music; what has happened is that a fragment of the music sounded like the ringing of the bell, and was taken to be such. Images cannot compete with reality; the suggestion is ridiculous. For normally perception is taken as being certain. Sartre illustrates this point: "I believe that my friend Peter is in America; I suddenly see him at the corner of the street. Do I say to myself 'It's an image'? ('I must be seeing things.') Not at all; my first reaction is to find out how it is possible he is already back; has he been

[1] cf. M. Shorter, 'Imagination', *Mind*, LXI, no. 244, 542.

recalled? Is someone ill at home? etc. . . . Far from rational motives making us doubt our perceptions, it is our perceptions which rule and direct our judgments and reasoning. It is to them that we constantly adapt our system of reference" (*In*, 106–7).

The possibility of experiencing a hallucination is often mentioned at this point of the argument. Here, it is claimed, are examples of what must be mental images which are believed by the victims of the hallucination to be real things. Merleau-Ponty, in his study of perception, gives several examples of actual hallucinations which count against such a view.

Another schizophrenic who said that he saw a man in the garden standing under his window, pointed out the place, and described the dress and the posture, was stupefied when somebody was actually placed in the garden at the indicated place, in the same clothes and position. He looked attentively; "It's true, there is someone, it's another person."[1]

This section of his book contains several interesting examples of the same kind, which lead him to conclude: "The sufferer from hallucinations does not see or hear them in the normal manner."[2] Sartre makes the same point more definitely: "The schizophrenic knows quite well that the objects with which he surrounds himself are unreal; it is for that very reason that he makes them appear" (*Ire*, 190–1). He treats this theme fictionally in the short story 'La Chambre', published in *Le Mur*. It would seem that many of those who use the possibility of hallucinations to establish philosophical points have not made the necessary empirical study of them, but have taken the accounts of the victims at their face value. But as the occurrence of a hallucination is evidence for some mental upset, such accounts need careful examination. Again, the experiences of people under the influence of drugs do not seem to reinforce the notion that images can be confused with perception. If the subject remains fully rational, as in some cases after taking mescaline, then he is aware that what he sees is unreal; if he is overcome by the drug, then he is in the same position as the

[1] *La Phénoménologie de la perception*, 385.
[2] ibid., 393.

mentally sick person, and what he says about his experience needs careful examination. Sartre quotes an example of an experiment designed to establish that there is a similarity between feeble perceptions and images: "If a subject is seated in a well-lighted room facing a ground glass screen behind which is a masked projector, it is often impossible for him to recognise whether the feeble colours which he sees on the glass come from the projector or from his own imagination. He is told: Imagine that there is an image of a banana on the screen. And, in a number of cases in which a very feeble band of yellow light is projected or that all actual light is suppressed, the result is the same; the perception of the yellow band is confused with the corresponding image" (*Ire*, 74). It is not at all clear what is supposed to have been confused with what. Nor is the instruction to "imagine an image of a banana on the screen" easy to carry out. Sartre comments: "I do not know who shows the greatest lack of understanding; the experimenter who asks such questions or the subject who replies docilely" (*Ire*, 75).

For if images and perceptions were of the same kind, then it would *never* be possible to be certain which confronted one. Our situation would be like that suggested by Descartes *vis-à-vis* dreams. If he were correct in claiming that only tests of coherence between our present experiences and our future ones will allow us to distinguish a waking state from one of dreaming, then it would be impossible to be certain of the present state; for there always exists the possibility that further tests will show that we had been mistaken. Similarly, if we start by assuming that images and perceptions are fundamentally the same, then we shall never discover any means of distinguishing between them (cf. *Ire*, 107–10). To assume that images are copies or reproductions of perceptions is to assume that the two types of thing are fundamentally the same, and that what can be done with one can be done with the other. For what makes one thing a copy of another is that the former will serve at least some of the purposes of the latter. Philosophers and psychologists sometimes talk as if images and perceptions were related as copy to thing copied; as if it were possible to discover by inspecting an image what could be discovered by inspecting the original object. This is not so; images are not, as Berkeley claimed, perfectly definite; they are frequently vague. It is impossible to go on extracting information from them as information can be continually extracted from a real object. An example will make this clear. Many people can imagine a building with which they are familiar, e.g. the façade of the British Museum. It may seem to them that they have a perfectly definite image of it. But if an attempt is made to count the number of columns which appear in the image, this will be found to be impossible. If the number is already *known*, then the image will have that number of columns; if it is not known, then the information cannot be extracted from the image, even though at first the image seemed to be of a definite number of columns. But it would be easy to count the number of columns in a very mediocre photograph or painting of the British Museum. A real object, on the other hand, is inexhaustible; the longer you look at it the more you can discover about it. An image gives all the information contained in it at once; it makes no sense to say that there was a feature of it that hadn't been noticed. As soon as a word like 'notice' is used, the difference between the image and the object is brought to light. There are a whole series of instructions that can be given to a person looking at an object (or even at the picture of an object), but cannot be given to a person contemplating an image. Such instructions could be included under the general heading of 'observation'. Sartre suggests that as the image cannot be observed we should talk of a process of "quasi-observation" in connection with it. He defines this: "We are, in effect, in an attitude of observation, but it is observation which tells us nothing. If I imagine the page of a book, I am in the attitude of a reader; I *look at* the printed lines, but I do not *read*. And, ultimately, I don't even look at them, for I already *know* what is written" (*Ire*, 21). Sartre stresses that there is no radical difference between memory images and pure figments of the imagination in this respect; in both cases nothing can be "extracted" from the image which was not already known.

The conventional picture of the process of memory seems to involve the appearance of an image which is a *reproduction* of the past, a kind of re-experiencing of the original event. This cannot be true, for then there would be nothing to distinguish a memory from a new experience. The suggestion that this image has a characteristic of 'pastness' or 'familiarity' which serves to mark it off from a fresh experience will not help, for no way in which such a characteristic can belong to the image can be suggested. What really is at issue is the fact that memory involves either the possibility of a verbal description of a past event, or a pictorial representation on paper, or an image of the event. The memory-image owes its existence to some knowledge which is possessed independently of the image, and it is this knowledge which is the important factor. The important consideration is the manner in which we verify our memories, which has nothing to do with the way in which those memories come to us.[1] If somebody is unable to remember a particular incident, it is no help to tell him to try to imagine it; if he cannot remember, he cannot imagine either. This account seems to involve the rejection of such things as Proust's imaginative re-creation of the past, of getting into contact with a past reality by means of memory. But Proust was making use of a literary device, not constructing a philosophical theory. It is true that a past event does sometimes 'rise up before the mind' with great vividness; Sartre would not wish to deny this. But it is precisely in its vividness that its imaginary quality lies. The actual event was not vivid, it just happened. Only copies, e.g. statues of human beings, can be lifelike, only images or pictures vivid. The point about such an experience is that it is known to be about the past from the first.

Sartre is not trying to give a merely empirical account of the imagination, basing himself on observations. The purpose of the doctrine of intentionality is to give his arguments general validity. It is because images always point beyond themselves, are images *of* something, that they cannot be copies, reproductions of sense-impressions. The normal attitude in the face of an image is

[1] cf. R. F. Holland, 'The Empiricist Theory of Memory', *Mind*, LXIII, 485.

not doubt but certainty. The object of which it is an image is *known* immediately, not discovered by looking at it in greater detail. The confusions on this point come from thinking of the 'mental picture' as if it were a real picture. It makes sense to talk of coming to see what a real picture is a picture of, by examining it or by comparing it. But there is nothing to compare in the case of the image; it would be ridiculous to expect that a physiologist could detect by an examination of the brain what an image was of. This is not to be discovered by any process. "At that word we both thought of him. . . . If God had looked into our minds he would not have been able to see there whom we were speaking of."[1] Because what we were speaking of was not something in our minds, but a person existing in the real world. Sartre stresses this point: "Really the expression 'mental image' leads to confusion. It would be better to say 'consciousness of Peter-in-image' or 'imaged awareness of Peter' ['conscience imageante de Pierre']. As the word 'image' has served for a long time, we cannot reject it completely. But, to avoid all ambiguity, we must remember here that the image is nothing other than a relation. The imaged awareness I have of Peter is not awareness of an image of Peter; Peter is directly reached, my attention is not directed on an image but on an object" (*Ire*, 17). An almost identical remark is made by an American philosopher:

Those philosophers who think that dreams are shadow-shows of imagery should be brought up short by the consideration that one's *brother* may appear in a dream. *Not* an image or vision of him (this too is a possible dream, but a different one) but one's actual brother—'the one who does surgery out in Long Beach, California'. The brother in one's dream may be 'in no way different' from one's brother. . . . There is *identity* in the one case as much as the other.[2]

It is interesting to see how two philosophers writing in different traditions express similar ideas; though the label 'intentionality' would not be used on this side of the channel, the notion behind it is one which any philosopher will arrive at if he is to deal satis-

[1] Wittgenstein, *Philosophical Investigations*, 217.
[2] N. Malcolm, *Dreaming*, 93.

factorily with these mental phenomena. Behind the difference in terminology often lies similarity of thought. "Whether I perceive or imagine this chair, the object of my perception and that of my image are identical; it is this wicker chair on which I am sitting" (*Ire*, 17).

It might be thought that the image that rises unbidden and unrecognised, say that of a human face, is an objection to this view. First, it should be noticed that there is immediate certainty that it is someone's face that is in question. Second, the process of recognition is not like that of recognising a species of insect or flower by noting the various characteristics that it possesses, but rather like that of fitting a name to a person we suddenly meet and cannot remember. Even if there appears to be a process of recognition, it is one which depends not on characteristics of the face itself but rather on a sifting of possible names, places, incidents which might have called up the memory, until we get a name that 'fits' the image. We can no more discover who an actual person is by studying his features than we can discover whom the image is of by looking at it more closely. This may be done in the case of a caricature, but a caricature is something which reminds us of the person by emphasising certain of his characteristics. And even in such a case recognition comes as a sudden feeling of rightness rather than a mounting certainty as evidence accumulates, which is the typical process of identifying the species of a natural object.

The source of some of the difficulties about the imagination which have perplexed philosophers is lack of attention to intentionality. "It is impossible to study the mental image separately. There isn't a world of images *and* a world of objects. . . . The two worlds, the imaginary and the real, are made up of the same objects" (*Ire*, 34). Sartre intends this affirmation to be taken seriously; he does not want to talk of an 'imaginary world' of unreal objects. "Someone may be tempted to oppose to my view the case where I evoke an image of an object which has no real existence outside of myself. But it is precisely the case that the chimera does not exist 'as an image'. It exists neither in that way nor in any other" (*Ire*, 17). For to exist 'as an image' is not to exist at all. The only cases where it is at all plausible to talk of an 'imaginary object' are those where the thing in question is really in one sense 'public', where it has a name and a definition. A chimera does not exist, but a picture of one can be recognised because there are public criteria for calling it a picture of a chimera. In this sense the chimera is external, the intentional object of the image or picture. An original image, the product of someone with a 'good imagination', has to be brought to public notice, to be communicated, and the communication consists in telling what it is an image of, not in trying to describe the actual character of the image.

One way to get clearer about the nature of images, Sartre suggests, is to examine other intentional objects. I may wish to bring to mind the face of my friend Peter. If I fail to do this, I may make use of a photograph or caricature to assist me. "Mental representation, photograph, caricature: these three different realities appear, in my example, as three stages of the same process. From the beginning to the end the aim remained the same; I wanted to make Peter's face present although he was not here. However, it is only the mental representation which is called the image. Is this correct? . . . I have used three processes to give myself Peter's face. In each case there is an 'intention' and this intention points to the same object. This object is not the representation, nor the photo, nor the caricature; it is my friend Peter. Besides, in each case I aim at the object in the same way; it is on the level of perception that I want Peter's face to appear, I want to 'make it present'. And, because I cannot perceive it directly, I make use of a certain material which serves as an *analogon*, as an equivalent of perception" (*Ire*, 31). In two of the cases, of course, there is a definite physical object, about which in itself things can be said. But when I am using physical objects in this way I am not concerned with them as they are in themselves; I am, as it were, looking through the photo and caricature at Peter's face. Hence remarks about their objective characteristics are out of place. But because such remarks can be made it might be thought that an analogue could also be found for the mental image. In certain cases this can be done, for instance in movements of the hands when someone is trying to imagine how to do something. The movement of the hands is not itself the mental image, but the material, as it were, which is used to bring to mind the action in question. Similarly the visual image may have as analogue the movement of the eyeballs; it has been suggested that movements of the eyeballs in sleep can give clues as to the extent and even the subject of dreams (cf. *Ire*, 98–110). But the detailed examination of what may go on in the body or brain is of less interest than the purely philosophic considerations.

If the function of images is to point or refer to objects, it might seem that they are almost the same as words; Sartre, however, wishes to avoid confusion between the two classes: "Thus, if I think about a horse and I produce, in the course of these thoughts, a mental image of a horse, this image would be [for the writers he is criticising] a sign for my thoughts. But a sign of what? Aren't words sufficient? As well say that when, looking at a flesh and blood horse, I think about it, the horse is a sign for my thoughts about it" (*Ire*, 111).[1] The function of an image is to 'put us in the presence' of the object we are thinking about; the function of words, on the other hand, is to enable us to communicate with others, and for this something independent is required, something for which there are public rules. "If then language teaches us something, it can only be by its exteriority. It is because the mechanisms by which sounds and phrases are arranged are in part independent of our minds that we can read our thoughts in them" (*Ire*, 112). Hence, contrary to what some philosophers have thought, images are not essential to mental life, for we do not

[1] In the passage that I quote here, Sartre uses the word 'sign' to describe the word: from what he says about it, however, it is clear that his use is nearer to the English 'symbol'. The reason why he has not used the latter is that he has reserved it for literary and artistic cases, as in "The playwright uses x as a symbol of the corruption of the times." Sartre says of this: "Thus the function of such a schema is in no way to aid understanding; it has a function neither of expression, nor of support, nor of exemplification. I would say, using an indispensable neologism, that the role of the schema is *presentificatory*" (*Ire*, 137).

have to 'be in the presence of' what we are thinking about. This is not to deny that for some people recourse to imagery is the easiest way to solve certain problems. But people vary very greatly in this respect, and some deny that they ever have mental images at all. Galton, in his *Inquiries into the Human Faculty*, suggests as the result of his questioning that scientists tend to have less mental imagery than humanists, but that there is no rigid distinction between the two types of mind in this matter.

Ultimately, though we can compare the imagination with other mental activities, it is irreducible to them; it is a particular power of the mind which has considerable importance for all other mental functions. Sartre calls his discussion of the analogue of the image 'The Probable' to indicate that it does not form a central part of his thesis. The discussion of intentionality and of the place of the image in mental processes is independent of the section I have just been dealing with. However, this section does serve to indicate how Sartre avoids making the image into a 'thing': "In this chapter and the following ones I use for greater convenience phrases and expressions which seem to give to the imaginary object a causal power over the mind. It should be understood that this is only a metaphor. It is easy to see what the real process is. For example, an image has no persuasive power but we persuade ourselves by the very act in which we form an image" (*Ire*, 127). This is expanded elsewhere: "It must be understood that the imagination has *also* the function of *proving*: it *represents* objects in such a way to us as to incline our judgments in the direction which we desire: the drawings of a madman do not merely *express* his terrors; they also serve to maintain them and to shut him up in them" (*StG*, 429 n.). For although the image is *of* the object, it is not that object. The image of the loved one is not as satisfactory as the real presence of the loved one, for it is much less full, less complete. "In every one whom we love, there is something which goes beyond us, an independence, an impenetrability which demands further acts of approximation. The image never has any of this impenetrability, it is never more than we know about it. No doubt I scrupulously say to myself that there is this impenetrability, this *foreign* character of the person loved. But I don't *feel* it. So that the image, whilst becoming more banal, becomes also more fitted to my desires than Annie ever was. . . . Perhaps [on her return] I may regret the complacency and simplicity of Annie's image. But that is because I have forgotten the emotional impoverishment which was an indispensable correlative of it" (*Ire*, 187).

I must omit many fascinating details of Sartre's analysis of the role of the image in mental life and his examination of the problem of dreams and its relation to the rest of the imagination. On dreaming he concludes: "A dream does not appear—contrary to what Descartes thought—as the apprehension of reality. On the contrary, it would lose all its meaning, all its nature if for an instant it was seen as real. It is above all a *story* and we take the same kind of passionate interest in it that a naïf reader takes in the reading of a novel. The dream is lived as fiction and it is only in thinking of it as fiction that is given as such that we can understand the kind of reaction which it produces in the dreamer" (*Ire*, 225). Sartre reaches this conclusion because of the radical separation he has made between images and perceptions; if the two things are of such different orders, then there is no possibility of the kind of confusion that Descartes talks of in the *First Meditation*. That there is some important difference between experiences in a dream and experiences of reality is indicated by the fact that we can confuse a dream with reality, but that we never confuse reality with a dream.[1]

Sartre draws far-reaching conclusions from his study of the imagination; in the final section he introduces an important concept which serves both to explain why human imagination functions in the way it does and also as a foundation for his next work, *L'Etre et le néant*. "What is common to the image of Peter and the image of the centaur is that they are both aspects of Nothing [*le néant*]" (*Ire*, 231). Sartre's use of this term has, more than any other single feature in his writings, been the cause of their

[1] I have discussed this question at greater length in 'Dreams', *Supplementary Proceedings of the Aristotelian Society*, 1956, 208–28.

dismissal by English-speaking philosophers. Ayer's comment in an article on Sartre is in many ways typical: "In particular, Sartre's reasoning on the subject of *le néant* seems to me exactly on a par with that of the King in *Alice through the Looking Glass.* . . . The point is that words like 'nothing' and 'nobody' are not used as the name of something insubstantial and mysterious; they are not used to *name* anything at all."[1] But it would seem that when the King takes 'nobody' to be the name of somebody he is making a joke which would be obvious even in French; if Sartre were silly enough to be taken in by such a play on words there would be no justification for taking any of his works seriously. What is needed is an attempt to give the 'cash-value' of this usage, to see what Sartre does with it and why he found it necessary to employ it. This analysis will, I hope, establish that it is an essential feature of a series of arguments and that there is nothing 'metaphysical', in the pejorative sense of the word, about it.

I have shown above how Sartre stresses the difference between an image and a perception. Hitherto I have not indicated the nature of this difference. Clearly it cannot consist in any extra feature of the image, for if it did the image would be to that extent different from the object, just as a picture does not contain an extra feature to show that it is a picture. Similarly, no special feature in a realistic novel indicates at every stage of the description of the action that this action did not really take place. In the text there is nothing to enable the reader to decide if he is faced with fact or fiction; nowadays few novels even begin with "Once upon a time . . .". There is *no* difference between the real and the fictional description. Similarly, there is *no* difference between the image and its object. Or, to put it in Sartre's way, *nothing* is the difference between them. This is more than a fanciful way of expressing something that could have been said 'aseptically', more than a reflection of a desire to shock by using a metaphysical image. It is more than this for Sartre because he is going to say that *nothing* is an essential element in the mind. Hegel, in attempt-

---

[1] *Horizon*, XII, 18. I have examined Ayer's criticism in more detail in 'Sartre and le Néant', *Philosophy*, April and July 1961, 177–87.

ing to say something rather like Sartre, in the *Phénoménologie* used the terms 'negative' and 'negating', and it might seem that such terms are more down to earth, less 'metaphysical' and hence preferable to 'nothing'. Sartre finds it impossible to use the notion of negation as the primary one, because he thinks that negation depends on a more fundamental power of the mind. Negation depends on the existence of language with its devices for expressing negation; Sartre wants to explain how it is possible for human beings even to be able to use a language in the first place. Language is possible because of the power of 'nihilation' or 'dematerialisation' (*irréaliser*), which is what makes imagination possible. Negation, the possibility of denying the existence of something, depends on the ability to imagine that something: "And if negation is the unconditional principle of all imagination, reciprocally it can never take place except by and in an act of imagination. What is denied must be imagined. In fact the object of a negation cannot be *real* because that would mean affirming what is being denied— but no more can it be *nothing* because *something* is denied. So the object of a negation must be thought of as imaginary. And this is true for the logical forms of negation (doubt, restriction, etc.), as for its active and emotional forms (defence, consciousness of impotence, of lack, etc.)" (*Ire*, 238). Hence Sartre uses the more abstract word in spite of the example of Hegel. Perhaps the best way of dealing with this usage is to accept the word 'nothing' and its relatives as a new technical term of Sartre's until the way in which it is to be employed has become clear, together with the justification for its use.

The nihilation or dematerialisation operates in two ways. First, consider the case of the image of an existent but absent object, for example a friend. "My image of him is a certain way of not touching him, of not seeing him, a way he has of *not being at* a certain distance, in such a position. . . . In this sense I can say that the image includes a certain nothingness. . . . However lively, touching or strong an image may be, it gives its object as not being [*comme n'étant pas*]. That does not prevent me from reacting to the image as if its object were present, was face to face with me.

. . . But the false and ambiguous state at which I thus arrive only puts in higher relief what has just been said: it is in vain that I seek by my behaviour towards the object to create the belief that it really exists; I can hide for a moment but not destroy the immediate consciousness of its nothingness" (*Ire*, 25–26). Nevertheless, I think of my friend as existing somewhere, as actually being in Berlin at this moment. This is what distinguishes the case from that of the centaur, which is not thought of as being anywhere, but as being purely nothingness. In so far as both are cases of the denial of the presence of the object, the 'nihilation' is the same. Not only images have this nothingness, but all 'intentional things', those which point to something beyond themselves, such as pictures, words, etc. For these are also physical objects, exist in their own right and have no inner connection with anything outside themselves. A word may be considered merely as a combination of sounds, or a picture as merely a collection of marks on paper. Even an image may be considered as whatever neural or cerebral happenings are involved in, or take place at the same time as, its occurrence. But these are not the *real* or important characters of a word as a word, etc. Considered as objects, all these things are of little interest. It is only when they are given their 'intentional value', thought of as pointing beyond themselves, that they take on their true character. Sartre describes this as "being not what they are and being what they are not". The phrase Sartre uses, "ne pas être ce qu'il est et être ce qu'il n'est pas" is a literal translation of one that Hegel uses in a similar way, "das nicht zu sein, was es ist, und das zu sein, was es nicht ist". The phrase may be cumbersome, but its meaning is clear; the important point about all intentional things is not their actual characteristics, but what they imply; in other words their central nature is not what they are, but what they point to. It is in this sense that they all contain *nothing*.

But this is an essential feature of the human mind: "I may now conclude: imagination is not an empirical power added to the mind, it is the mind itself in so far as it is free; every concrete situation of the mind in the world is pregnant with the imaginary in so far as it is always present as a way of going beyond the real. . . . The imaginary is produced out of the world by a mind which *remains in the world*, and it is because the mind is transcendentally free that man can imagine" (*Ire*, 236–7). By "free" in this passage Sartre means 'not causally determined'. This connection between imagination and freedom, *via* the notion of nothing, is central to the argument of *L'Etre et le néant*, and, of course, vital for the whole theory of mind. If the universe consisted of a rigid chain of causes and effects and nothing more, there would be no room for minds. For it is of the essence of mind that it involves questionings, doubtings, thoughts of possibility. But within universal determinism there can be no possibilities. These only enter through our thoughts about the world. Similarly with all sorts of other mental phenomena. All thought and language involve freedom in this sense. For to make a statement is not just to respond to a situation, it is to *say* something about it. It would be possible to construct a machine which responded to different colours by an appropriate sentence, e.g. it would make the sounds "This is red" when presented with a red object. We might want to call such a device a 'talking' machine, but the inverted commas would emphasise the difference between its noises and ordinary human communication. Wittgenstein remarked:

We say 'The cock calls the hens by crowing'—but doesn't a comparison with our language lie at the bottom of this? Doesn't it look quite different if we imagine the crowing to set the hens in motion by some form of physical causation?[1]

The machine would not be using a language, but merely reacting to the situation by a causal mechanism. Our language involves rules, which can be obeyed or disobeyed. A machine cannot disobey a rule; if it fails to respond correctly (in the way we expect it to) we say that it has broken down, not that it has disobeyed. Only someone who can *follow* a rule can break it. Similarly, deliberate lying is always a possibility for human beings; this is

[1] *Philosophical Investigations*, §493.

not a mere epistemological difficulty, but an important part of what being human involves.

All such experiences are experiences of *nothing* or of freedom, of not being a part of the causal chain of the world, but of standing outside it, though in contact with it. To be conscious is to be outside the stream of impressions, to be able to think of what is not present, to be free from the necessity of reacting to any particular impression that might be occurring. It is possible to 'dematerialise' or nihilate even strong impressions, such as pains, in the interest of something else. Human beings are separated from the world by *nothing*; it is this which enables them to act as they do. The connection between nothing and freedom will be discussed at greater length below, in the context of *L'Etre et le néant*; I hope enough has been said here to show that Sartre is using the term to point to an important feature of experience. I have mentioned the likenesses between Sartre and Hegel; here is a romantic expression by the latter of ideas very similar to those that have been under discussion:

Man is this night, this empty nothing, which contains everything in its undivided simplicity; a richness of an infinite number of representations, of images, of which none comes precisely to his spirit, or which are not in so far as really-present. It is this night, the interiority of nature which exists here:—the *pure personal self*. In the fantasmagorical representations it is night all around: here arises suddenly a bleeding head, there another white apparition, and they disappear just as suddenly. It is this night that is seen in looking into a man's eyes, looking into a night which becomes *terrible*; it is the night of the world which is presented to us. *The power of drawing from this night images or of letting them fall: position of autonomy, interior consciousness, action.*[1]

[1] *Werke*, xx, 180–1; tr. Knox.

III

L'Etre et le néant: Introductory

O N THE appearance of the English translation of *L'Etre et le néant*, several reviewers pointed out that it is a work of philosophy of a type no longer to be found in this country. It is long, 722 closely printed pages; it is written in a style no longer familiar to English readers, owing much to that of Hegel and Heidegger. The English reader often wishes for the clarity of a Ryle or a Russell when struggling with the more obscure passages. But the main difference between it and contemporary English philosophy is that it deals with a wide range of problems, attempting to bring them into a single system which has ethical implications. In this sense it is a work of metaphysics. I have much sympathy with anyone who hesitates to embark on reading such a work; my own philosophic education and convictions made me doubtful of the value of the effort required to come to grips with this book. But, if the initial reluctance is overcome, then much of interest and value will be found in Sartre's greatest work. By writing this book, I am obviously putting myself in the position where I must claim that objections like those above are not really valid, though this can only be done in the last resort by the detailed examination which I undertake below. But before coming to grips with the philosophy, it is advisable to look at these three main objections in more general terms.

It is clear that the book is too long by modern English standards. Sartre certainly is, and always has been, a fluent writer. The infant Sartre in *Les Mots*, filling notebooks with romances, is a prototype of the later Sartre pictured in Simone de Beauvoir's *La Force de l'âge*, sitting at a café table to write articles and novels. The picture of Dubreuilh in *Les Mandarins* is also a representation of Sartre; on a cycling holiday he calmly sits beneath a tree and continues with his manuscript whilst his companions rest or admire the view. Such facility is to be envied by less productive writers, though it has sometimes led Sartre into turgidity and, though less often, into publishing writings that were better discarded, or heavily revised before being given to the public. But such strictures do not apply to *L'Etre et le néant*. The argument is complex, but it is divided up into manageable sections; much of the bulk is due to detailed examples which are of considerable assistance to the reader; in this respect the book is not nearly as difficult as Kant's *Critique of Pure Reason*. Sartre's tendency to situate his own views at each stage by reference to the works of previous philosophers also makes for length, though for those familiar with the history of philosophy the comparisons are helpful. Undoubtedly some parts of the book are of minor importance and can be skimmed, though even in these there are some fascinating insights. Perforce I have concentrated on the more exciting passages, and on the main line of the argument; I hope that what I say will encourage readers to tackle the work itself. I can only endorse Miss Murdoch's conclusion to her review of the English translation:

It is doubtless the case that writers of brief and meticulous articles will always look askance at writers of large, unrigorous emotional volumes; but the latter, for better or worse, have the last word.[1]

It is possible to find sentences that are turgid and almost incomprehensible, though some of those quoted as examples of this fault are clearer in context. But much of the writing is clear and easily followed. Sartre can be a stylist; *Huis clos* is a play written with great distinction and economy. The passages in *La Mort dans l'âme* describing the French Army awaiting, in a state of primal innocence, the arrival of the German victors in 1940 have an almost lyrical beauty. There are difficulties in following any complex train of thought, though those encountered in this work are

[1] *New Statesman and Nation*, 25 May 1957, 676.

nothing like as great as those involved in understanding Kant's Transcendental Deduction. Part of the difficulty at the stylistic level springs, I think, from the French language itself. For the spirit of that language is not well adapted to philosophic thought. This may seem a surprising thing to say about a language and a people renowned for clarity, but it is that very clarity which is here the enemy. So often in reading French one finds that the writer has confused a clear expression of his views with having produced well-argued views. Once he has clearly stated his position there seems to the writer nothing more to be done. In the course of this work I shall indicate some places where Sartre has fallen into this trap. But he is aware of the difficulties of using French as a philosophical language and has to battle with it to express what he wants to say. This is obvious in small details, e.g. his bracketing of the *de* in *conscience de soi* to destroy what might be a misleading possessive. It can also be seen in the whole Germanic tenor of his language. This is an attempt both to make his readers come to grips with his views and to make the French language into an adequate philosophical instrument. For many of the subtleties of expression available in English or in German do not exist in French.

The third charge against *L'Etre et le néant*, that it is a work of metaphysics, is itself so vague, at least as the term is currently used in this country, that there is little point in examining it here. In so far as it implies that the work is woolly, the answer lies in detailed study. This will reveal that much of *L'Etre et le néant* is startlingly concrete, and many passages would not be out of place in the *Concept of Mind*. But these passages are employed in the construction of something of wider import than Professor Ryle attempts. It is worth noting, however, that Sartre frequently denies any metaphysical intent. This denial is not, of course, a defence against the English charge; Sartre is thinking of the sense of the word normal on the Continent. He several times contrasts the *description* of the world, which he calls 'ontology', with the attempt to *explain* the world, metaphysics. The former is both possible and desirable, the latter impossible. "That is why, in virtue of the absolute contingency of that which exists, I am certain that any metaphysic ought to end in 'That is (or exists)', that is to say by direct intuition of contingency" (*EN*, 359). Throughout his work Sartre remains true to the conception that philosophy must start from the fact of the existence of our world, and all explanation must remain inside the world.

Although *L'Etre et le néant* does not explicitly discuss moral questions, the problem of morality underlies much of its thought. I said in Chapter I that, at the time of writing *La Nausée*, Sartre was unable to describe a form of life which would fit the insights he had by then acquired; he still had not reached conclusions on these topics by the time he had finished this book, of which the final words are "All these questions . . . can only be answered on an ethical plane. I shall devote my next work to them" (*EN*, 722). Sartre has not *explicitly* produced this work, for reasons that I shall discuss below.[1] Nevertheless, the long discussions of 'bad faith' and of 'situation', together with the emphasis on 'freedom' and 'action', show that Sartre was trying to formulate a foundation for his future morality. The book was completed during the period of the 'phony war', 1939–40. Simone de Beauvoir reports that on one of Sartre's leaves, in February 1940, she was struck by the change in moral and political attitude, which was manifest in his consideration of the notions of situation, bad faith and authenticity. She reports: "He did not know then—he couldn't know in advance and didn't want to prejudge any issues—in what exactly his political engagement would consist; but he was convinced that he had duties towards the younger generation."[2] What is interesting about this statement is that it appears that Sartre had already made the leap direct from the analysis of the individual situation to a political solution of the problem, by-passing conventional areas of morality. His later concern with politics and his preoccupation with Marxism is thus not solely the result of the defeat of 1940 and his subsequent association with the Resistance movement, but depended on more fundamental features of his thought. It is important to note here that the later political

[1] See Chs. IX and X.   [2] *La Force de l'age*, 442.

thought, at least up to the writing of *Critique de la raison dialectique* in 1960, is a development of the thought of *L'Etre et le néant*, not a denial of it.

What is *L'Etre et le néant* about? It might best be considered as an attack on the traditional philosophical views of the nature of the mind and its relation to the external world, a Continental version of the *Concept of Mind*, though one bringing more and heavier artillery to bear on the Cartesian tradition. For though it may be claimed that "The chief and persistent influence on British philosophical thought about the human mind has been Descartes",[1] his influence in France is far more obvious and central than it is in England. Any French philosopher seems to be compelled to start his reflections by coming to grips with Cartesianism; there is no figure in English philosophy who plays the same central role in both the teaching of, and the thought about, philosophy as Descartes does in France. There are two factors to account for this; first, it is undoubtedly true that Descartes is the greatest philosophical figure that France has produced; on this there would be general agreement, and none on an equivalent English philosopher. Second, because of the position the French have felt themselves to occupy in European culture and the belief that this culture is largely dependent on the Cartesian tradition, any educated Frenchman will have come into contact with the writings or thoughts of Descartes explicitly. No Frenchman would miss the references to the Cogito in *La Nausée*, many educated Englishmen would. Hence *L'Etre et le néant* is much more concerned with the Cartesian view as actually stated by Descartes than is the *Concept of Mind*, with its bald characterisation of that view as the "dogma of the ghost in the machine". Ryle uses a logical rapier to deflate theories, but the rapier itself is an extension of common sense. For his book "does not give new information about minds. We possess already a wealth of information about minds, information which is neither derived from, nor upset by, the arguments of philosophers."[2] Sartre uses

[1] Bernard Williams, *Encounter*, 86, Nov. 1960, 38.
[2] *The Concept of Mind*, 7.

blunter, more devastating weapons. If Ryle's aim is to "determine the logical geography of concepts",[1] to leave everything as it was but to map it correctly, Sartre's aim is to flatten in the interest of building a new edifice. To drop the metaphor, Sartre expects his philosophy to change men's views of themselves and of the world around them, to have effects on their lives, not just on their talk about their lives. It is in this sense that he is in the European metaphysical tradition, whereas the majority of contemporary English philosophers are not. For when we are told, as is nowadays fashionable, that metaphysics is like poetry, there is an echo behind this remark of Bentham's "Pushpin is as good as poetry"—the object is not to enhance the value of poetry but to depreciate metaphysics; to see the world in a new light is a pleasant way of amusing yourself, but it doesn't make any real difference to anything.

For what Sartre has to say has effects not only in the traditional sphere of ethics but also in the field of psychoanalysis. Though it stems in the main from the work of Heidegger, the growing school of 'Existential Psychoanalysis' also acknowledges an indebtedness to Sartre; one of the chapters of *L'Etre et le néant* is entitled 'La psychanalyse existentielle'. I shall deal with this topic later, but here it is worth pointing out that what is said there can be seen as having direct relevance to the problems of treating mentally ill patients; Sartre's criticisms of Freud are not purely academic, but also practically oriented. This is at least partly because he has seen that the claim that there exists an unconscious mind raises ethical as well as purely epistemological difficulties.

But, when all this has been said, there still does remain a difficulty for those trained in, or even influenced by, the current English tradition in reading a work whose title contains the word 'being' and whose sub-title is 'Essai d'ontologie phénoménologique'. For the very idea of an examination of being seems meaningless; to the question "What is there?" the only answer, and it is not a helpful one, is "Everything"; no *general* characterisation seems possible. Even though Sartre distinguishes between his approach and metaphysics, characterising the latter as a kind of

[1] ibid., 8.

attempt at a super-science that would 'account' in some not very clear sense for there being a world at all, his division of being into two kinds, *l'en-soi* and *le pour-soi*, together with the question he asks in his introduction: "Why do they both belong to *being* in general? What is the meaning of being in so far as it includes these two radically distinct regions of being?" seem to indicate that what follows can only be muddled and obscure. Many Continental writers have indeed taken Sartre's ontology as if it were something of the same kind as traditional ontology; there are plenty of articles entitled 'Sartre's ontology'. My claim that Sartre is often close to the empiricist tradition would seem to be refuted by this discussion of being. Two points can be made about this. First, it is natural that Sartre should write in the philosophical language in which he was educated; further, given the lack of philosophic communication across the Channel, it is unlikely that he would be aware of developments in this country. Second, until the cash value of his terms has been discovered by actual analysis of their use, it should not be assumed that it is the same as that of the traditional concept of being. Part of the trouble has arisen from failure to notice the qualifying "phénoménologique" which is attached to "ontologie" in the sub-title of the work. Sartre says in his conclusion that to ask questions about the 'nature' of being in a metaphysical sense, as also to ask in a general way "Why is there being?" is useless, for all 'whys' are, in fact, posterior to being and presuppose it. "Being is, without reason, without cause and without necessity; the very definition of being shows its original contingency. [In another sense] I have already given my reply, for the question is asked not on a metaphysical level but on the ontological: 'there is' being because the *pour-soi* is such that there is being" (*EN*, 713). This last phrase could be put in the form "there is being because there is consciousness of being" without radically distorting Sartre's thought.

I must admit, at this point, to a particular dislike of the pair of Hegelian terms used by Sartre, which can only be translated into English as 'in-itself' and 'for-itself'. I have been very tempted to translate them by 'things' and 'consciousness' respectively.

This would have the advantage of enabling me to translate Sartre's words and to comment on them in reasonable English, but it would have the disadvantage of differing from other writers on, and translators of, Sartre. Hitherto I have avoided the difficulty by using the French originals, which do not sound so barbarous to English ears. Henceforth I must, with reluctance, talk of the in-itself and the for-itself.

If Sartre's remarks about being are considered superficially, he would appear to be committed to some 'ontological' doctrine, to be talking about being in a general way. Wittgenstein described the kind of trap that Sartre might appear to have fallen into as follows:

The evolution of the higher animals and of man, and the awakening of consciousness at a particular level. The picture is something like this: Though the ether is filled with vibrations the world is dark. But one day man opens his seeing eye, and there is light. What this language primarily describes is a picture. What is to be done with the picture, how it is to be used, is still obscure. Quite clearly, however, it must be explored if we want to understand the sense of what we are saying. But the picture seems to spare us this work: it already points to a particular use. This is how it takes us in.[1]

Many of those who have written favourably on Sartre, as well as his attackers, appear to have been taken in by such a picture. They have assumed that Sartre is talking in the way Wittgenstein describes. I wish to maintain that Sartre has not fallen into this trap, and that the major part of L'Etre et le néant is concerned with the use to be made of this picture. The claim that being is divided into the in-itself and the for-itself is only a way of saying that the world seems to contain both things and minds, and that things are subject to causal laws, whereas minds are not always so subject. To say this is not to fall into a Cartesian dualism, or rather it is possible to avoid such a dualism. For the error of Descartes was to assign things and minds to radically different categories, to describe them as different *substances*. Once they have been placed in such different boxes it becomes impossible to account for any

[1] *Philosophical Investigations*, 184.

communication between them. Indeed, the main problem for Descartes was to deal with the union of mind and body; in a letter on the subject to Princess Elizabeth[1] he seems to be driven into admitting that he cannot really adequately account on his own principles for the sort of union we seem to experience. By calling them different *substances* he has made them parts of separate *modes of being* between which there can be no communication. The point of Sartre's difficult introductory section seems to lie in an emphasis on the oneness of being; he argues that both bodies and minds, the in-itself and the for-itself, exist in precisely the same sense. And 'existence' here means what it does in normal speech; Sartre equally wishes to avoid the danger of being called an idealist. He insists that there is a world of objects which exist independently of consciousness. Even to say this is already to lay oneself open to a philosophic risk, because it seems to bring the for-itself into the centre of the picture. The world cannot be described as it is in itself, for it is human beings who do the describing. The danger of talking of the in-itself is that it might be thought that a neutral description of the world was possible. The attempt to avoid these dangers gives a gnomic, Parmenidean, character to many of Sartre's statements about the in-itself.

For much of what Sartre says about it seems very similar to what Parmenides said about the real nature of the universe. It is, and within it there is only being; nothingness has no place. "The in-itself has no secrets: it is *massive*. . . . It is entirely positive. It knows no otherness: it never affirms itself as *other* than any other being; it can have no relation with any other. It is itself indefinitely and it exhausts itself in so being" (*EN*, 33–34). But Parmenides was attempting to describe what the universe was really like, in contrast to the way in which it appeared to men; Sartre is doing something very different in the passage I have just quoted. He is trying to express the fact (or what he is arguing is a fact) that the world, except in the case of human minds, is the sphere in which causal laws operate. That it has no secrets does not mean that these causal laws are all known to us—it is obvious that many are

[1] 31 May 1643.

not—but that these unknown laws are not *hidden*. Who or what could do the hiding? The laws can be discovered by the appropriate techniques. But these very techniques of physical science leave no room for gaps, no place for chance; scientists may admit lacunae in their knowledge of nature, but not lacunae in nature itself. The world is what it is. "Being in itself cannot 'be potentially' nor 'have powers'. In itself it is what it is in the absolute fullness of its identity. The cloud is not 'potential rain', it is, in itself, a certain quantity of water vapour which, for a given temperature and pressure, is strictly what it is. The in-itself is actuality . . . the possible comes into the world by the existence of human beings. These clouds cannot change into rain except in so far as I go beyond them to think of rain, just as the crescent moon only lacks a portion of its disc if I go beyond it to think of the full moon" (*EN*, 142). Human beings, because they have bodies, are part of the world in this physical sense; hence they would also seem to be unfree, subject to the laws of causality. Sartre's attempt to reconcile human freedom and a universal causal order is discussed below, in the chapter on the human body. All I have tried to do here is to show the sense of Sartre's statements about the in-itself, and to argue that they are not so peculiar as they seem at first sight. There are obvious difficulties from a scientific point of view in accepting some of what he says about the causal order; he does not mention the problems of indeterminacy in modern physics. This is because he is not interested in the world except in so far as it is a stage for the activities of human beings. If he can succeed in reconciling human freedom with this rigid causal system, then *a fortiori* it will have been reconciled with an indeterministic account.

It is impossible to give an equally brief account of the for-itself, for that is the real subject of the whole of *L'Etre et le néant*, but some of the remarks in the introduction require mention. Sartre reinforces his stress on intentionality: "Every consciousness, as Husserl has shown, is consciousness *of* something. . . . A table is not *in* consciousness, even as a representation. A table is *in* space, beside the window, etc." (*EN*, 17). To think or talk of a table is to refer to an existing object. He introduces a new notion, that of the "pre-reflective cogito", as a development of intentionality. The claim that he makes is that every instance of being conscious is also one of being in some sense self-conscious. Sartre's explanation of this is as follows: "If I count the cigarettes in this case, I have the impression of discovering an objective property of this group of cigarettes: *there are twelve of them*. This property appears to me as one existing in the world. It is possible that I am not aware of myself as counting them. I don't 'know myself counting'. The proof of this is that children can make a spontaneous addition without being able afterwards to *explain* how they set about it; Piaget's tests which show this are an excellent refutation of Alain's formula: To know is to know that one knows. However, at the moment when the cigarettes are revealed as a dozen, I have a non-thetic consciousness of my activity of adding. If I am questioned, if someone asks me "What are you doing?" I would immediately reply "I am counting", and this reply does not only include the momentary consciousness that I can get by reflection but also those consciousnesses which have passed without being reflected on, those which are for ever *unreflected* in my immediate past. Thus reflection has no primacy over the consciousness reflected on; the former does not reveal the latter to itself. On the contrary, it is the non-reflective consciousness which makes reflection possible; there is a pre-reflective Cogito which is the condition of the Cartesian [or reflective] Cogito" (*EN*, 19–20). He continues: "This self-consciousness should not be considered as a new consciousness, *but as the only mode of existence which is possible for a consciousness of something*." It is from this point onwards that Sartre writes the *de* in *conscience de soi* in brackets, to "indicate that it only stands for a grammatical rule". All that is meant by the term "non-thetic" in this passage is that the consciousness that I have of the activity does not involve my explicitly formulating to myself what I am doing. Nevertheless I am conscious of it in the sense that I can immediately reply to a question about it without having to stop to think about it, or to look back over my past activity. Only in so far as I can, given the question, state what I am doing, can I be said to be conscious of it. In the ordinary sense of 'unconscious', I am said to be unconscious of those activities about which I cannot answer this type of question; "What are you tapping your fingers on the desk for?" "I didn't realise I was."

What Sartre is saying in this passage is also expressed by Stuart Hampshire in that very Sartrean book, *Thought and Action*, though Hampshire's formulation is more linguistic than Sartre's:

It is a condition of referring to anything, which is in turn a condition both of meaningful discourse and of meaningful action, that I should be able to point (in some way) away from myself. This makes it necessary that the gesture of pointing to myself, to 'here' must show in its physical pattern that it is reflexive, in the sense that it turns back to its point of issue. I may be uncertain in discriminating objects that stand at the far end of the indicating gesture. But I cannot fail to indicate a being that points when I turn the gesture back on itself. This is the sense of the Cogito, the literal sense, which, because it is the presupposition of the use of language, cannot be clearly expressed in language.[1]

Sartre differs from Hampshire in claiming that what is under discussion is the pre-reflective Cogito, not the Cogito of Descartes. Both agree that in some sense I must be able to state that it is 'I' who am acting or thinking. It is not clear how this is to be understood. We can imagine a computer which gave correct verbal answers when asked what it was doing. It could be programmed to say such things as "I am multiplying such and such numbers together." And for certain purposes it might be useful to have this information in verbal form. But this would not make us want to say that the machine was *conscious* of what it was doing, no matter how elaborate the pattern of verbal responses was. This is not simply because the machine had been programmed to respond in this way; there is a sense in which a training in language can be seen as a kind of programming to respond in the correct fashion to questions. One important reason for the refusal to describe the machine as conscious would be that its 'consciousness' would be limited to what it was *doing*; it could not claim to, nor be said to,

[1] *Thought and Action*, 82.

feel any emotion. Indeed, if it did so claim, we would fail to understand it. More important would be the fact that this response would be an immediate one, concerned only with the actual activity; the machine could not give a general reply, such as "I am calculating, namely multiplying" without additional programming. Finally, the machine could not be said to be conscious of a world of objects outside itself and in some sense opposed to it. All these notions are involved in that of self-consciousness; it is not an accidental fact that 'I' can be said to perceive external objects, feel sensation or emotions, do or intend to do things. Russell somewhere suggests that the Cogito should run "There are thoughts, therefore there is a thinker". But it is not a trivial grammatical fact that the omission of the personal pronoun sounds peculiar. Rather it is the essence of all these things that they should be referred to a subject, even to an incarnate subject, though Sartre himself only develops the latter aspect later on.

If we try to think of self-consciousness as radically different from consciousness, as an operation or perception performed on some "conscious material", we soon fall into an infinite regress of consciousness of being conscious of being conscious of . . . like Spinoza's *Idea ideae ideae*. The picture at once conjured up is that of the senses as private television sets transmitting their pictures of a (problematic) external world to the screens in front of which the self is placed. When we become conscious of what is going on in perceiving the world, then it would appear that there must be a further 'self' which is looking at the whole scene. Consciousness of perceiving this table is not something in addition to perceiving the table; it is that very perception, albeit regarded in a slightly different manner. To be looking at the table in a proper sense is to be able to say that one is looking at it; this is a different state of affairs from having one's eyes on the table 'without seeing it', and this is what Sartre is claiming by his talk of the pre-reflective Cogito. This may be made clearer if we look at another of his examples: "Pleasure cannot be distinguished—even logically —from consciousness of pleasure. Consciousness (of) pleasure makes up the pleasure, as the very manner of its existence, as the matter of which it is made and not as a form which is imposed after the event [*après coup*] on a hedonist matter. There is no more a consciousness *first* which *afterwards* receives the state of pleasure like water to which colouring is added, than there is first a pleasure (unconscious or psychological) which afterwards receives the quality of consciousness, as if it were illuminated" (*EN*, 21). The two things are one and the same, both in the case of pleasure and in the case of perception.

It is important to distinguish between the pre-reflective Cogito which Sartre is discussing and genuine reflection, which is a very different kind of mental operation. This can be seen from the following example: there are some emotions which cannot be considered coolly. Once I start to reflect on my anger it is no longer genuine present anger, it is the anger of a moment ago, and by that very fact no longer of the same quality. To realise that one is angry with somebody else is no longer to see him merely as hateful, but already to realise that this apparent objective quality is dependent on subjective feelings. In this sense, "reflection poisons emotion" by radically altering its character. This is because to reflect on anger or on any other violent emotion is to take up towards it the same position as another person might take. In reflection I consider my anger as I would consider your anger. No reflection, however, need be involved in an emotion or mental state. To express one's anger does not require reflection, for it does not involve contemplating or analysing the state. If a man were to consider his anger coolly, then to that extent he would no longer be really angry. Sartre also puts this in terms of intentionality by saying that there is only room in the mind for one intention at one time; there cannot both be anger at Peter's foolishness, something which is directed to an external object, *and* consciousness of that anger, something directed on an internal object. The same applies to the perceptual case; it is impossible both to look at the table and to introspect or reflect on the act of looking. To carry out the latter activity, attention must be turned away from the table itself. But in order to say that one is looking at the table there is no need to think about the act of looking; perceptual consciousness of the table is all that is required.

Previous writers, Sartre thinks, have confused the two Cogitos: "But it must be remembered that all the writers who have described the Cogito have dealt with it as a reflective operation, that is to say as an operation of the second degree. Such a Cogito is performed by a consciousness *directed upon consciousness*, a consciousness which takes consciousness as an object" (*TE*, 44). All that is claimed for the pre-reflective Cogito is that it is not, like Descartes' Cogito, a means of discovering the essence of the soul, but merely a means of referring to certain facts about the mental life of human beings. In one sense it certainly tells us about the nature of the mind, but not in any metaphysical manner; rather it reminds us of certain necessary features that must be possessed by anything that is to be called a 'consciousness' or 'mind'. Sartre does not proceed by explicitly referring to features of our language, but the outcome of his discussion is not so very different from that achieved by linguistic analysis. The term 'for-itself' is justified as a description of mind or consciousness because of the possibility of performing activities described under the heading of pre-reflective Cogito, of being aware of what one is doing. Where no such awareness can occur, it is the realm of the in-itself. The two terms can thus be seen as comparatively neutral description, not parts of a metaphysical system.

IV

Nothingness

IN THE introduction to *L'Etre et le néant*, Sartre has indicated "the two realms of being"; the next stage is to show what it means to say that there are two such realms, and how they are related. In an important sense the whole of the rest of the book is an attempt to deal with this one great question by splitting it up into a variety of small questions. The basic perspective of the discussion is provided throughout by the distinction between the in-itself and the for-itself, and, conversely, the meaning of this distinction is revealed by the conclusions Sartre reaches. As in his discussion of the imagination, *le néant*, nothingness, is an important link or element; Sartre suggests that the first place in which to look for the connection between the in-itself and the for-itself is the imagination, just as Descartes did (*EN*, 37). In Chapter II I have tried to show that this use of nothing is not "metaphysical" in a pejorative sense. Sartre himself obviously wished to guard against this charge in *L'Etre et le néant*, in particular by distinguishing his view from that of Heidegger. The latter appears to have reified nothing in the famous phrase "das Nichts nichtet", nothing nihilates. This appears to talk of nothing as if it were something that could act. In a passage clearly aimed at Heidegger (*EN*, 58), Sartre says "le Néant ne se néantise pas, le Néant *'est néantisé'* ". The barbarous French can only be translated by barbarous English; I suggest "Nothing does not nihilate itself, nothing *'is nihilated'* ". Nothing does not exist and hence cannot be talked of in active terms.

Sartre tries to bring out his meaning by giving examples of human experiences which are of nothingness, which form the justification of the use of negative terms in ordinary speech: "There exist an infinite quantity of realities which are not solely objects of judgment [mere linguistic forms], but which are experienced, fought against, dreaded, etc., by human beings and which contain negation in their very structure, as a necessary condition of their existence." These are genuine, not empty, negations because they depend on an experience of nothing. Because of the nature of language, it is possible to formulate textbook examples of negation which are not the result of any experience. For example, a man looking for a friend in a café might say, after looking round the customers, "Peter is not here". He could also have said, equally truthfully, "Wellington is not here, Paul Valéry is not here" (*EN*, 45). The failure to find the expected friend among the customers is a particular experience of disappointment; there is no *failure* to find the Duke of Wellington there. The linguistic device of negation depends on the possibility of such experiences. It might be said that to have an expectation is to realise that it may not be fulfilled. When we talk of a dog 'expecting' to find the buried bone in the place in which it hid it and from which we know it has been removed, or of his 'disappointment' or 'puzzlement' at its absence, the inverted commas seem a natural warning against thinking that the dog is feeling just as we would feel in such a situation. All we are really entitled to say is that the dog dug a hole in a certain place and behaved in certain ways when it had gone down a certain distance—what set the processes in motion is totally unknown to us and probably quite unlike anything that we would call a 'thought of the bone being at a certain depth'. For Sartre this difference between man and animal does not depend only on the fact that men can express such feelings in language; rather it is because men are capable of being separated from the world in this kind of manner that they are capable of having a language. The nature of the for-itself is such that it brings nothingness and hence negation and all that follows from it into the world. "Thus I have reached the first goal of my inquiry: man is the being through whom nothing comes into the world. But this answer immediately gives rise to another: What *is* man in order that he should bring nothing into the world?" (*EN*, 60).

The answer that Sartre gives is that in order to do this man must be free. If *L'Etre et le néant* has as its theme human consciousness, then throughout the book freedom is the hall-mark of that consciousness; the rest of the work can be seen as concerned with the way in which this freedom or liberty is compromised, ignored, concealed by various types of behaviour. It is hardly going too far to say that Sartre's entire *oeuvre* is a discussion of different aspects of freedom, epistemological, moral and political. Here again there is a close similarity between him and Hegel; there may be wide differences between what the two philosophers say about freedom, but for each it plays the same central role of the concept around which are grouped all their important insights. The separation between man and the world, his being always at a distance from it, which I have discussed in connection with the imagination, is here widened to become a general account of what distinguishes human existence from all other kinds of existence, the very essence of the for-itself. "What I call freedom is thus impossible to distinguish from the *being* of 'human reality'. Man is not *first* a being and free *afterwards*; there is no difference between the being of man and his *'being-free'*" (*EN*, 61). Many of Sartre's more controversial positions, such as his rejection of Freudian psychoanalysis, are further specifications of this statement.

Even at the epistemological level Sartre denies the existence of 'mental causation'. He argues that if the image of a dead or absent friend were to be produced by a strict causality, if some object belonging to him *caused* his image to appear in the mind, there would be no way in which it could be distinguished from a genuine perception. If something *ensured* that an image of the person associated with it came to mind, then the image would be a part of the same scene as that in which the object existed, would have the same degree of reality as the object itself (*EN*, 64). As many philosophers have pointed out, what distinguishes perception from imagination is that in imagination what appears to the mind is in some sense under the mind's own control, and the real is what resists the mind, cannot be dismissed from it. An association can only be a reason or motive for the appearance of a particular image, and "motivation is not causation". Sartre insists on this because he wants to maintain that human beings must be either wholly free or wholly determined; there is for him no possibility of a hybrid state. He thinks that once one 'fragment' of determinism is admitted into the mind, it will, as it were, corrupt the whole. Such a claim appears paradoxical, and Sartre has to use a great deal of space in reconciling it with normal experience and ways of talking. The dangers that he has to face are firstly that of contradicting phenomena that are well known and second that of merely redefining the word 'freedom' in such a way that it is no longer useful. There are many passages where he seems to be committing this latter error, where Sartrean freedom of the mind appears to deserve the name as little as Rousseau's criminal who is "forced to be free" deserves to be considered so. I think Sartre is well aware of the dangers and tries to avoid them; the extent to which he succeeds can only be judged at a later stage of the argument. Here I can only point out that there are qualifications to come.

For Sartre man not only is free but can become conscious of his freedom: "It is by anguish that man becomes conscious of his freedom, or, in other words, anguish is the manner of existence of freedom as consciousness of existing" (*EN*, 66). In this work I have followed several other writers and translators of Sartre in rendering *angoisse*, the German *Angst*, by *anguish*. *Dread* might seem to be a better term, but is perhaps too 'intentional', too easily implies 'dread of something'. It is fairly clear that Sartre means a generalised unease not directed to any definite object. Like the nausea of *La Nausée*, anguish has come to symbolise the typically existentialist attitude to the world. Again, I would like to repeat that the striking character of Sartre's term should not lead us to give it too important a place in everyday experience; there is no need to feel it, for it is not necessary that we should be conscious of our freedom. Anguish for Sartre is like fear in that it is unpleasant, unlike it in that it is not directed to a particular danger that might be anticipated. He gives the example of a man walking along a cliff path, who might be afraid of stepping on a loose stone or a slippery surface, or of a rock falling from above. These are real dangers and precautions can be taken against them. But the man might stand on the edge of the path and look down and whilst doing this be overcome with a feeling that there is nothing to stop him throwing himself over. He might even feel 'drawn down' by the precipice. His decision not to jump will be of no help in getting rid of the anguish that this thought gives rise to, for he will at once realise that no decision in such circumstances can guarantee that he will not change his mind a few moments later. Freedom is such that no present decision can bind a man in the future. We all know the resolve to get up early tomorrow, and know that however firm it may be on going to bed nothing can ensure that it will be put into effect when the times comes to leave the warm bed for the cold outside. The importance attached to promises in our dealings with others arises from the fact that they are devices to neutralise as far as possible this perpetual risk of a change of mind, a new decision which cancels a past one. For Sartre it is the *contemplation* of this perpetual possibility which is the source of anguish, the realisation that nothing stands in the way of stepping off the cliff. It is in this sense 'anguish in the presence of nothing', which does not mean that 'nothing', a special kind of object, is what causes the feeling, but rather that there is no object of which we are afraid when we feel it. Hence anguish is not a common experience; it only arises when freedom is, so to speak, idling, when it is not being employed in the normal round of activities. In the majority of cases when a decision is made it is put into effect; only in rare ones is the possibility of a change of mind brought home in this haunting way.

However, even without the feeling of anguish, the realisation of one's freedom can be painful. Hence there are those who seek to deny its existence. The bourgeois of Bouville in *La Nausée*, Lucien in 'L'Enfance d'un chef', wanted to claim that they were what they were in the same way that a physical object is what it is, or that they had duties which compelled them to act in certain ways as a body is thought to be compelled by the laws of nature. "Thus we flee anguish by trying to look at ourselves *from outside* as *another person* or as a *thing*" (*EN*, 81). This defence mechanism is "bad faith" (*mauvaise foi*), a "lie in the soul". The comparison between lying and bad faith is to be taken seriously, for in order to lie the truth must be known—a lie is deliberate. Freudians would argue that there is the possibility of unconscious deception. Sartre will not admit this: "Thus psychoanalysis substitutes for the idea of bad faith the idea of a lie without a liar, it claims to understand that it is possible that I do not lie to myself, but *am lied to*, because it puts me in relation to myself in the situation of another *vis-à-vis* me, it replaces the duality of the deceiver and deceived, essential condition of lying, by that of the 'id' and the 'ego' " (*EN*, 90). There are enormous difficulties in these notions and the correlative one of the censor, e.g. how is it that the censor allows lawful impulses to pass whilst repressing unlawful ones without being aware of them? Further, there is the question of the resistance that the analyst meets when he is getting near to a hidden complex. For Sartre the analytic procedure implies not the discovery of the contents of an unconscious concealed behind an iron curtain, but rather the pointing out of features of the patient's conduct which he is expected to recognise as his own, though hitherto he has ignored them or concealed them from himself. It is the uncovering of the meaning or motivation of the neurotic action, not of its cause. It is only because motivation is at issue that we can come to understand the neurosis, make sense of it, for the connection between the neurosis and the behaviour it provokes is always made obvious by the completed analysis. Again it is for this reason that self-analysis is often said to be impossible or very difficult. If the unconscious was separate from the rest of the mind, something for which the self was not responsible, then there ought to be no difficulty for the owner in unravelling its secrets, just as there is no special difficulty for the doctor in diagnosing his own disease. It is only because there is a *motive* for hiding what has been going on that the problem arises. Sartre quotes one analyst: "Every time I have pushed my investigation far enough, I have found that the core of the psychosis was conscious" (*EN*, 93).[1] Sartre deals with these topics in greater detail in his discussion of 'existential psychoanalysis' in the final section of the book. Here his only concern is to point out that it is at least possible to see many of the things which have been described as 'unconscious' in a different light, and indeed that they must be so seen if his theory of freedom is to be maintained. The claim that actions are the result of unconscious determination may be a device of bad faith.

Bad faith is a complex phenomenon or set of phenomena, of which the common feature is an attempt to conceal from oneself, as well as from others, some fact of which the person is really aware. Sartre takes homosexuality as an example. The man who says "I am a homosexual", meaning thereby that he is so by nature and that there is nothing he can do about it, any more than a table can help being a table, or a Negro being black, is in bad faith. He is said to be in bad faith because there is always the possibility of his adopting another mode of relationship to other people, even though it may be very difficult to do so. Freedom to change is implicit in the human condition, and so men cannot be treated in the same way as things. On the other hand, a man may fall into bad faith by denying that he is a homosexual whilst admitting that he has done certain actions. He is refusing to admit the public interpretation of his behaviour by stressing the fact that he is not bound to continue with the course of action he has adopted in the past. In a sense this is true, but in certain cases we can say that it is very unlikely. These two different ways of talking about oneself are thus both in bad faith, both ways of escaping from the self as it actually is. The first denies responsibility by transferring it to a 'nature' given by heredity or environment; the second denies it by maintaining that his past actions are no longer 'his'. The first Sartre exemplifies by the defence given

[1] Sartre is quoting from Stekel; but more examination is needed of the phrase 'far enough' here.

by some Nazis at War Crime Trials, "I was only a simple soldier, I obeyed my superiors' commands"; the second by the habitual drunkard who swears after each bout to give up drink (and means it at the time). The Nazi ignores that it is impossible to be *merely* a soldier, the drunkard that the genuineness of his oath depends not on the intentions whilst making it, but on the future course of his behaviour.

But to criticise bad faith in these terms is not to imply that sincerity is a remedy. It is possible to be sincere about one's past life, because what was done in the past, particularly in the distant past, can be regarded as the actions of another person. The converted drunkard on the Salvation Army platform can be sincere about his unregenerate life because it is no longer *his* life that he is talking about. "The essential structure of sincerity does not differ from that of bad faith, since the sincere man considers himself to be what he is *in order not to be such*. This explains the well-known fact that one can fall into bad faith by the very effort to be sincere" (*EN*, 105). By being sincere we attempt to disarm the very impulse which is admitted, for a person who admits a low impulse is less low *in so far* as he admits it. Popularly, sincerity is thought to be manifested in admitting bad qualities rather than good ones. But human nature is ambiguous, and neither admission nor denial is the complete truth. Only after death can a man really be said to have been anything. This is the sense of such sayings as Malraux's "Death changes life into destiny" and Solon's "Call no man happy till he is dead". In Sartre's formula, whilst living "I am what I am not and am not what I am". Human beings cannot "coincide" with themselves in the way in which a table is a table and nothing more. A man may be a bachelor and a university lecturer, sad, happy, etc., but these are only contingent and temporary features. The fact that human beings live in a temporal dimension and so are always changing is neglected by those in bad faith, Sartre claims. An example of this is the waiter who attempts to *be* an object: "Let us consider this waiter. His movement is quick and forward, a little too precise, a little too rapid, he leans forward a little too earnestly . . . he gives himself the rapidity and pitiless speed of a thing. He is playing ... at *being* a café waiter. ... [From the inside] what he is trying to realise is the being-in-itself of a waiter, as if it were not precisely in his power to reject the duties and rights of this condition, as if it were not his free choice to get up each morning at five o'clock or to stay in bed, even though it meant getting fired. As if from the fact that he plays this role it does not follow that he also transcends it, he is something *beyond* it. However, it is undoubtedly true that he *is* in one sense a waiter—otherwise he could just as well call himself a diplomat or journalist. But if he is such, it is not in the sense of the in-itself. He is a waiter in the sense of *being what he is not*" (*EN*, 98–100). This passage should be read in full, as an example of the two poles of existence, the facticity of being a waiter and the transcendence of being more than merely a waiter. The analysis of bad faith thus gives the cash value of the phrase "being what one is not and not being what one is"; it proves that it is not merely an example of the systematic misuse of the verb 'to be' mentioned by Ayer.

The revelation of bad faith, though not under that name, is a fairly common literary device; Sartre, of course, has often employed it. Perhaps the clearest example is in the story 'L'Enfance d'un chef' I have already mentioned. Here I will quote the conclusion of this story as a brilliant fictional example of bad faith in action. "He had sincerely made an inventory of what he was. But if I am only what I am, then I'm no better than that urchin over there. The first maxim Lucien gave himself was, Don't try to introspect, there is no greater danger. He raised his hand to his forehead gently, with infinite precautions, as if he held a lighted candle. Then he thought for a moment, and the words came of their own accord. He muttered '*I have rights*'. Rights, something of the same kind as triangles and circles; the latter were so perfect that no specimen existed. Thousands of figures could be drawn with a compass without achieving a single circle. Generations of workers could, in the same way, scrupulously obey Lucien's orders without ever exhausting his right to command. Rights were beyond existence, like mathematical objects and religious dogmas. He had long thought that he existed by chance, derivatively; but this was because he hadn't thought about it enough. Long before his birth, his place in the sun had been marked out. Even before his father's marriage, he had been waited for, he had come into the world to occupy that place. 'I exist,' he thought, 'because I have the right to exist.' Somewhere in France there was a young girl, a girl from the provinces with eyes like flowers, who was keeping herself chaste for him; perhaps she tried sometimes to imagine her future master, that terrible and gentle man, but she couldn't; she was a virgin and recognised in the most secret places of her body his sole right to possess her; he would marry her, she would be *his* wife, the tenderest of his rights. When she undressed at nights, with graceful movements, it would be like a sacrifice. He would take her into his arms with the approbation of the world, he would say to her 'You are mine'. She would give him what she had the right to give only to him, and the act of love would be a delightful census of his property. His tenderest right, his most intimate right: the right to be respected for his flesh, obeyed even in bed. 'I'll marry young,' he thought. He also decided to have many children; then he thought of his father's work; he wanted to continue it and wondered if M. Fleurier would die soon. A clock struck noon; Lucien got up. His metamorphosis was over. An hour ago, an adolescent full of uncertainties entered the café; it was a *man* who left it, a boss among the French" (*Le Mur*, 244–5).

The story as a whole gives the context and explanation of Lucien's attempt to escape from the doubts and uncertainties of the human condition. But for Sartre this desire to escape is not pathological but natural. For we are by nature "unhappy consciousnesses, without any possibility of escaping from our unhappy state" (*EN* 134). Though it is natural, Sartre obviously regards this desire as reprehensible; description has already become judgment with the term 'bad faith'. But because he regards the world and all that is in it as contingent, the assertion that God exists only as another means of escape from the human condition, it might seem that he has no valid ground for condemning Lucien, or the waiter who plays at being a waiter. It might even be argued in the case of the latter that it is the only way open to the man of making his life tolerable. Sartre never gives explicit reasons for his condemnations; he assumes that the reader will agree with him or, in the case of his stories, forces that agreement by the whole tenor of his description. I think that he assumes certain ethical values even at this stage of his argument, and so finds it impossible to describe human beings in neutral terms. Just as he claims that "If every metaphysic assumes a theory of knowledge, so every theory of knowledge assumes a metaphysic" (EN, 16), it might be said that every description assumes a moral standpoint, even if this is not made explicit. Because human beings are of this ambiguous nature, it is wrong to deny it, to pretend to be something else. Sartre's ethical views might be said to begin and end in the motto "know thyself". To begin with it because unless we are self-aware to some degree there is no possibility of any genuinely human action; to end with it because once the situation is seen clearly there is no more to be said *on the ethical level*. I will discuss this point at greater length in Chapters IX and X, but it is, I think, clear that Sartre's point of view is one that many would find acceptable; we do value self-knowledge. Hence any analysis of a failure in self-knowledge is bound to be a criticism.

This is brought out in Sartre's long description of suffering (EN, 135–6), the theme of which is that we never suffer as much as we feel we ought to. "That which we call 'beautiful' or 'good' or 'true' suffering, and which moves us, is the suffering that we see on the faces of other people, better still in portraits, in the face of a statue or on a tragic mask. That is suffering which has *being*. . . . The suffering that *I* feel, on the contrary, is never adequate. . . . I can never be surprised by it, for it only exists to the degree that I feel it . . . Every groan, every expression of one who suffers aims to carve an effigy of suffering in itself. But this effigy will never exist except in the eyes of others, for others." Although it is true that we often behave in such a way as to impress our suffering on ourselves and on other people, it might seem that Sartre is exaggerating here. For there are, we want to say, times when we are overcome with grief. But in general these times are of short duration. After that brief period, we do harbour and tend our suffering. This happens when we have begun to reflect on it; another instance of "reflection poisoning emotion". But this poisoning is due to the fact that we are always something more than sufferers; it is impossible to coincide with our suffering just as it is impossible to coincide with any thing. "Concretely, every *for-itself* is lack of a certain coincidence with itself. This means that it is haunted by the presence of that with which it ought to coincide in order to be *itself*" (*EN*, 145). If it were possible for man to *be* something, then this lack would no longer be felt; there would be no possibility of bad faith.

The source of these problems is, as I have hinted above, the fact that human beings are temporal, exist in time in a way in which other things do not. Sartre is not raising the general problem of the nature of time, but stressing its importance for human beings. It is time as it is experienced which is important, as psychologists have sometimes seen better than philosophers. One of them writes:

Man the person lives with his past, the present and the neighbouring future all clearly relevant in explaining his thought and action: and the near future is influential to a degree nowhere else remotely approached among the species of the living.[1]

Indeed, it is only for human beings that time can be said to exist at all; an object, for instance, has no past. It might be thought that the history of a thing provided it with a past; in Sartre's example, there is a difference between a new nail and one that has been bent and later straightened again, for the latter will bend at the first blow of the hammer. This has been described as the action of the past of the nail on its present. But this kind of talk is confused. What causes the nail to bend where it has bent before is not the past happening, but its present molecular structure. This may be

[1] H. Stack Sullivan, *The Interpersonal Theory of Psychiatry*, 369.

explicable by what has happened, just as some things which happen to human beings now may be explained by what happened to them in the past, for example this present disease may be the result of changes in the body produced by past happenings. But in general when a human being thinks of the past it is the past which he now experiences which is central. "It is in this sense that we can accept Hegel's remark: '*Wesen ist was gewesen ist*' [essence is what has been]. My essence is in the past, it is the law of its being" (*EN*, 164). The past which bears on the individual is mainly the past which he is still aware of, which makes him think of himself as being a certain kind of person. In this sense what is done now or in the future can change the past, not by altering anything in it, but by giving it a different value. Indeed, many present decisions cannot be judged until time has elapsed; to merit any description it is necessary to have carried out appropriate actions over a period of time. Sartre takes the example of the religious feelings of a boy of 15. It is impossible to say at the time whether they are genuine or mere symptoms of a normal adolescent upheaval. From a future point of view it may be possible to decide this question. If the boy later became a priest they might well be said to have been genuine; if he soon after became an atheist and remained so they would not have been. Objections may be brought about the particular form of Sartre's example, but I think the point is a fair one. A better instance might be that I used above; the drunkard's resolve to reform will have been genuine if he never after touches alcohol.

For reasons which will become clearer below, Sartre believes that it is always possible to make a radical change, to alter one's past, though in many cases this may be unlikely. Acquired habits may haunt the present, but they do not dominate it. Thus it is only after death that it is possible to say precisely what a man was: "At the moment of death we *are*, that is to say we are without defence against the judgment of others; it can be decided what we really were, we have no chance of escaping from a summing up such as an all-knowing intelligence might make." But until death, possibilities are open and the account of an individual's past will vary with the time at which it is given. At death the past, and indeed the whole being of a man, becomes public property. In the words of Garcin in *Huis clos*, the dead have "fallen into the public world". But there are limits to this reassessment, for certain parts of the past are, in this sense, unalterable, belong not just to a man's essence but to his *substance*. Hence it follows that "at each instant *I am not* a diplomat or a sailor, that I am a professor . . . the past [in this sense] is that which I am, without being able to live it. The past is substance" (*EN*, 163). This section of the past, that about which nothing can be done, is like human *facticity*. By this term Sartre means the set of facts that are true of the individual as a body, e.g. born at a certain time, of certain parents and having such and such physical characteristics. At this stage, Sartre is more concerned with the past as experienced than the past as substance, as facticity.

Similarly, the present as experienced by men is not a dimension-less instant, nor that strange notion of psychologists, the "specious present". Sartre claims that both these ideas arise from the *reification* of the for-itself. "In this sense, it would be absurd to say that it is nine o'clock for the for-itself; but the for-itself can be present to a hand pointing to nine o'clock. What is falsely called the Present is the being to whom the present is present" (*EN*, 168). At a particular moment many things are happening in different parts of the world. But they are not part of the present, because they are not all *present* to an individual. (This is a typical example of a Sartrean play upon words.) For one man, some of them may be in the future, if they are involved in his projects. But only things actually present to (in the presence of) an individual constitute a Present. Hence this is not a part of time, in the public sense, at all. For what is being done at a particular moment, for example typing this particular character, only has significance in the context of what has just been typed and what is going to be typed after it. And all of this word or sentence only has meaning in the context of the intention of writing the whole book. In this example the uselessness of the notion of the 'specious present' can be seen, for even if it were the case that the whole sentence was 'present' in some way to the writer as he typed one character, no one would want to claim that the whole book was present in the same way. But in order to understand the single action fully the whole context is required. The psychologists have confused the fact that what is to be done or said is implicit in what is done at an instant with the idea that this whole is present in a temporal sense. What is implicit need not exist.

Hence the present and the future are non-existences in the same way that the for-itself is a non-existence, a being with nothing at its heart. In this they are different from the past, which, as we have seen, is partially substantial. The future has reality only as a part of somebody's project or intention. "But I do not obey the 'clear representation' of the future gesture nor the 'firm intention' to accomplish it. Representations and volitions are idols invented by the psychologists. It is the future gesture which, without being explicitly considered, comes back over the positions I adopt to illuminate, to link and to modify them. . . . There is not a moment of my consciousness which is not similarly defined by an internal relation to the future; whether I write, smoke, drink, or rest, the sense of my consciousness is always at a distance, over there, outside" (EN, 169–70). Because the sense of actions is always future, there is a possibility of failure. "Hence that anguish which I have described above and which comes from the fact that I am not sufficiently that future which I have to be and which gives meaning to my present: thus I am a being whose meaning is always problematic" (EN, 174). Further, only in so far as a being has a future can it even be said to *have* a past in the conscious sense. It is interesting that the Existential Psychiatrists have found that some mental troubles arise from what can only be called a failure of temporality:

The problem is not at all that these patients happened to have endured impoverished pasts; it is rather that they cannot or do not commit themselves to the present and future. Their past does not come alive because nothing matters enough to them in the future. Some hope and commitment to work toward changing something in the immediate future, be it overcoming anxiety or other painful symptoms or integrating one's self for further creativity, is necessary before any un-covering of the past will have any reality.[1]

Just as there is no past for physical objects, so there is no future or present for them. *We* can talk of what is going to happen in the physical world, e.g. that the bomb is about to explode, but all that is happening is that the fuse is burning at a certain point. That there is a continuous connection between this point and the explosive is something that we have discovered. And the fact that this stage of the process is 'present' only means it is in the presence of us. Part of the difficulty in talking of this arises from the problem of describing things as they are in themselves that I mentioned above. Sartre concludes that the "problem" of tem-porality is a pseudo-problem, resulting from trying to talk about human beings and objects in the same terms. "But the truth is that there is no problem. If we thought that we had encountered one, it was due to the fact that, in spite of our efforts to think of the for-itself as it is, we have been unable to avoid confusing it with the in-itself. For if we start with the in-itself, then the appari-tion of change is bound to be a problem; if the in-itself is what it is, how can it no longer be it? But if, on the contrary, we start with an adequate understanding of the for-itself, it is no longer change that needs to be explained, it is rather permanence, if such a thing exists" (*EN*, 193–4).

Sartre goes further and says that temporality is a necessary feature of human existence, that a being who does not "coincide with" himself is bound to exist in time. "Present, past and future *at the same time*, spreading itself in these three dimensions, the for-itself is temporal from the single fact that it nihilates itself" (*EN*, 188). If a human being could coincide with himself, could *be* a waiter in the same way in which a stone *is* a stone, then he could never escape from that condition, any more than a stone could escape from being a stone. The waiter would no longer *be* a human being. The situation he was in would be very like that which occurs in certain serious cases of catatonic schizophrenia:

[1] *Existence* (ed. May, Angel and Ellenberger), 70.

The basic trait and essence of the tragedy of the insane is that, as already indicated, there is no temporal standard at all, and the entire psychic condition might just as well be considered as eternal, that therefore fundamentally meaningful communication is excluded in every way and every free decision is paralyzed *a priori*.[1]

The final form of bad faith or of confusion about being that Sartre attacks is the desire to be both conscious and at the same time to exist in the way in which an object exists, to reach "the impossible synthesis of the for-itself and the in-itself: [to become a being which] would be its own foundation not as nothingness but as being and [which] would retain in itself the transparency necessary for consciousness at the same time as the coincidence with itself of the in-itself" (*EN*, 133). Such a being would be God; hence there can be no God. Too much emphasis can be placed on Sartre's atheism. No doubt in his public statements about the subject he has adopted a polemical attitude; he is reported to have announced to a group of newspaper men awaiting his plane that "God is dead". He has been accused of talking as if the worst of God's offences was that He did not exist, of conducting a campaign against God. I am concerned with his philosophy primarily, and I think it is clear that on the view of consciousness that he is putting forward it does not make sense to talk of a Being who has the set of attributes which are usually attributed to God within the Christian world. To use moral or scientific arguments against the existence of God is to put oneself on the same ground as the believer. No doubt there are those who have examined these arguments and, as a result of finding them wanting, have come to the conclusion that there is no God. But to conduct the investigation in this way is to ignore the main difficulty which, I think, Sartre sees, namely what God's existence would be like. There are problems of existence where the question of the nature of the existence of the object is not at all in doubt, the case of a normal physical object. For example, there are no philosophical problems about the existence of the Loch Ness monster; all that is needed is the weighing of evidence which is of the same kind as that for the

[1] ibid., 311, footnote.

existence of any other object. But God is not like this. Leibniz saw the problem when he said that it was necessary to show that God was possible before proceeding to a proof of His existence.[1] Sartre finds Him impossible because inconceivable, though this does not prevent him from seeing that the notion is one which naturally *haunts* mankind. "Human reality is naturally suffering, because it is perpetually haunted by that totality which it is without being able to be it, for it cannot attain the in-itself without losing itself as for-itself. It is thus by nature an unhappy consciousness, without any possibility of escaping from this unhappiness" (*EN*, 134). It should be noted that in *L'Etre et le néant* it is not the possible *existence* of God which haunts mankind, it is the desire to *be* or to become God, the synthesis of the two types of being, the in-itself-for-itself. But because this notion is contradictory, the desire is a form of bad faith.

The final chapter of the section on the for-itself is entitled 'Transcendence', but Sartre's use of the word has no metaphysical overtones. He is concerned with the way in which the for-itself is related to the world, or rather creates a *world*. The theme of the chapter is that "the world is human" (*EN*, 270). By this he means that the organisation of objects into a whole which can be called the world is the work of human beings; things are not spatially related, it is we who relate them in this way. Sartre is not adopting a Kantian position here; he does not mean that we impose various categories on "things-in-themselves" which are devoid of any such characters, in the way that Kant argued we did. Sartre rather means the same things about aspects of the world such as quantity and quality, spatiality and causality, as he has already said about possibility.[2] He is like Kant in that he is trying to trace out a path between idealism and realism. Idealism is unsatisfactory because there is being in-itself, a world existing outside of us. For it would only make sense to talk of the for-itself as negative if there were something outside it for it to negate. "The character of non-extension of the for-itself is in no way a

---

[1] *Monadology*, sect. 45.
[2] Cf. My remarks in Ch. III, above, pp. 47–8.

mysterious positive virtue of spirituality hiding under a negative title: it is a relation which is ek-static by nature, for it is by and in the extension of the transcendent in-itself that the for-itself realises its own lack of extension. The for-itself could not first be unextended afterwards to enter into relation with an extended thing, for, however we consider it, the concept of unextendedness could not have meaning in itself, it is nothing but the negation of extension" (*EN*, 228). Realism, on the other hand, fails because it ignores, like materialism, the negative and temporal character of the for-itself (*EN*, 253). Sartre is sure that his own view ignores the traps into which these common philosophical positions fall.

V

The Existence of Other People

FROM 'being for-itself' Sartre turns to 'being for-others', *le pour-autrui*, by which he means to indicate the social facts of existence. The first section deals with the existence of other people; here the very title points to a different approach from that normal in contemporary English discussions of an analogous problem. For here the problems raised by solipsism are put in terms of the existence of 'other minds'. It is assumed that for this purpose, at least, there is no need to doubt the existence of other physical *bodies*; the difficulty is to know (or to know how we know) that these bodies are animated by minds like our own. The task of the philosopher is, as it were, to elucidate the way in which it is possible to penetrate the veil of bodily behaviour and get to the mind within. The main question is the kind of evidence that there would have to be for the existence of a mind when all that can be observed is motions of matter. But closer inspection of the type of English arguments I am referring to would show that they are really more concerned with what knowledge of another mind would be, than with genuine doubts about its existence. Hence the discussions seem legalistic rather than scientific, concentrating on 'evidence', 'credentials' or 'proof'. The following quotation is from one of the better-known English contributions to the problem of 'Other Minds':

Up to now, in challenging me with the question 'How do you know?' you are not taken to have *queried my credentials as stated*, though you have asked what they were: nor have you *disputed my facts*, though you have asked me to detail them. It is this further sort of challenge that may now be made, a challenge as to the *reliability* of our alleged 'credentials' and our alleged 'facts'.[1]

The philosopher seems to be arguing his case in a court of law, to be rebutting the sceptic's claim. It is for this reason that the word 'evidence' is such a stumbling-block in epistemological discussions. The picture of the knower as a lawyer or detective laboriously assembling clues arises irresistibly, and every time we claim to 'know' something, we feel that we must, if we are to be philosophically respectable, be ready to defend this claim against a sceptical attack. In doing this, or in using the correlative slogan "If I know, then I can't be wrong", we have already given the advantage to the sceptic; the knower must always be on the defensive.

This attitude to knowledge is part of that compartmentalisation of philosophy which many would see as a conspicuous feature of the subject in recent years, and which is another manifestation of the belief that serious contributions to the subject will only come from "brief meticulous articles". A writer in this tradition will find it natural to treat the problems of epistemology in complete isolation from those of ethics. The same man who expresses doubts as to the legitimacy of the transition from evidence of 'mind-like' behaviour to the existence of a mind would quite happily assume in a discussion of ethics that the existence of other people was unproblematic. For Sartre, as indeed for other writers of an 'existentialist' type, no such rigid separation of the different parts of philosophy is possible. An example of this is the way in which Sartre includes the category of 'instrumentality' (*ustensilité*) at the same level as those of quantity, quality and potentiality. "And this instrumentality is not posterior to or subordinate to the structures previously discussed; in one sense it presupposes them, in another it is presupposed by them. An object is not an object first of all and an instrument afterwards, it is an *object-instrument*" (*EN*, 250). Some objects appear to us in this way; indeed, in the majority of cases we identify an object by its use or

---

[1] J. L. Austin in A. G. N. Flew (ed.), *Logic and Language, 2nd Series*, 132; italics in original.

function in a social context, we don't first see a mere physical object and then decide what it is for. Hence many of the discussions of how we come to know about things in the external world are, for Sartre, misplaced or founded on a misunderstanding. At a deeper level, the denial of the existence of a "problem of knowledge" lies in Sartre's description of the for-itself as 'nihilation'. Unless there were a world of transcendent objects to be nihilated there would be no conscious minds to know them. Hence Sartre's discussion of the problem of knowledge is mainly taken up with showing that the traditional theories do not apply, either because the problem does not arise in the form in which it is normally stated, or, if it does arise, then the traditional theories can be seen to be inadequate to solve it.

This is particularly clear in his treatment of the existence of others, which may be taken as a pattern for a whole series of arguments on related topics. Sartre's starting-point is the various arguments that have been put forward for solipsism, the theory that nothing besides one's self exists. But the examination of these arguments is made only in order to show what a theory must do to 'refute' solipsism. "In fact, if solipsism is to be rejected, this can only be because it is impossible, or, if it is preferred, because no one is really a solipsist" (*EN*, 307). A *theory* as to the existence of others will not do, for this will still leave the matter in the realm of the dubitable; it would always be possible to imagine getting better, or perhaps negative, evidence. It makes perfect sense to imagine situations where there could be more or less evidence of the existence of a *particular* person, e.g. the person who disarranges the papers on this desk, or who stole a book from the shelves. Such a suggestion is in principle no different from that of the existence of a hidden *object*, e.g. a deposit of iron-ore which affects the compasses in this area. The methods of confirming the two hypotheses are the same, the assembling of evidence, the setting of traps, etc., in the first case, collecting evidence and carrying out drilling operations in the second. But Sartre claims that it is precisely because we are already *certain* of the existence of other people that such a particular investigation makes sense. If it is a question of getting to know that there is a 'mind' behind the mask, the problem is very different. The hypotheses just mentioned were reasonable because in each case there was the possibility of direct, non-evidential, knowledge of the thing that was proposed to account for the changes that had been observed. We know what it would be like to find someone disorganising the papers on the desk, or to find iron-ore in the core from the drill. "If the other person is in principle and in his 'for-itself' outside my experience, the probability of his existence as *another self* could never be increased or weakened, it could neither grow nor decrease, nor even be measured; it loses its very nature of probability and becomes a fictional conjecture" (*EN*, 307). In fact, unless we were *certain* that there were other beings like ourselves, there would not even be a *possibility* of discovering that there were. This means that any "proof" must give us something other than the other person as an *object*.

Such a proof cannot be genuine, any more than the Cogito is a proof of my existence. For it doesn't make sense to doubt that I exist, and no one, not even Descartes, has ever genuinely doubted that he existed. Even if the Cogito were a proof, there then would arise the question of the validity of its argument or the truth of its premisses; there would still be room for doubt. But just as the Cogito is not a proof, but rather an unpacking of the notion of the self, so what is needed for other people is a similar unpacking. This will show that just as I have always, in some way, practised the Cogito, for "in fact, I have always known that I exist", so "I have always known that other people exist, that I have always had a total though implicit *understanding* of their existence, that this 'pre-ontological' understanding comprises a surer and deeper knowledge of the nature of other people and their relation to my being than all the theories that have been constructed about it" (*EN*, 308). The existence of this unreflective knowledge of others is shown by certain fundamental attitudes that can be taken towards oneself, e.g. shame: "I am ashamed of myself *as I appear* to another" (*EN*, 276). Sartre does not mean that one can only be ashamed in the presence of another person, but that unless the possibility of behaviour being observed by another person existed, then the emotion of shame would not exist. There are a number of similar attitudes towards the self which depend on such a possibility of being observed, though particular manifestations do not depend on actual observation; they merely presuppose it. Sartre gives a long example, which I will paraphrase (*EN*, 317–18): I am looking through a keyhole at what is happening in the room beyond. At that moment I am only conscious of the scene and of the keyhole as an obstacle and an instrument. My 'self' does not enter into my consciousness. Suddenly I hear footsteps in the corridor. I feel that I am being looked at; immediately I become conscious of myself. I am caught in the act, become 'somebody who looks through keyholes' and am ashamed of being such a person. My being, in a popular phrase, is 'transfixed by the other's gaze'. Thus it is my self-consciousness which constitutes the knowledge of the existence of other people. Indeed, for this to occur it is not even necessary that someone should actually be looking at me: "My certainty of the existence of other people is independent of these experiences, and it is it [the certainty] which renders them possible" (*EN*, 340).

The original relation with other people is thus 'the look' (*le regard*). This is not the eyes of the other person, but something different: "If I apprehend a look, I no longer see the eyes. . . . The other's look hides his eyes, it seems to go *in front of them*" (*EN*, 316). The best example of this is the battle of looks of two people passing in an empty street; each tries to 'stare the other down'. The victor in this encounter can look at the other without himself being looked at. This image of Hegel's life and death struggle between master and slave is an attempt to make the other into an object whilst remaining a subject oneself. But consciousness of another's gaze may take place without contact of looks, for instance when I become aware of another looking at the scene which I am contemplating. In such a case my world, the arrangement of objects with me as a centre, is broken up or stolen from me. In Sartre's striking image, the other's appearance on the scene acts as a "waste-pipe" (*EN*, 313) through which *my* world, this scene as my own property, is drained away. These phenomena are not *evidence* for the existence of at least one other person, rather the phenomena are the experience or certainty of the existence of *others*. Each of us realises that at most instants of life there is the possibility of 'being looked at', and this realisation *is* 'knowledge of other people's existence'.

It is not just a matter of the possibility of being seen at every moment; in some sense I am always watched. "Perpetually, wherever I may be, *they* are looking at me [*on me regarde*]" (*EN*, 342). Each person thus exists not only for himself, but also for others. Sartre compares this realisation with Adam and Eve's discovery that they were naked (*EN*, 349); it is a "fall" in the sense that each has "fallen" into the middle of a *world*, cannot think only of himself as he appears to himself, but must always remember how he appears to other people, to "them". The feeling of guilt towards God is only a generalisation of this feeling into one of being actually seen at every moment. More important for Sartre's purposes is, however, the fact that being looked at reveals existence as a *body*, a being having an outside as well as an inside. When caught at the keyhole it is the body which is seen, but the body as it is *for other people*, not as it is for the subject. Sartre regards this distinction as of great importance for dealing with the problem of sensation. He operates with a fourfold set of distinctions; my body as it is for me, my body as it is for others, the other's body, and the body as a physical object. All of these must be kept distinct; failure to do so has been the source of a great deal of philosophical confusion. The body as a physical object is a sophisticated notion, based on *scientific* investigations: "It would be an enormous error to believe that the body of the other which is originally revealed to us is the body [studied] by anatomo-physiology" (*EN*, 415). He quotes the way in which a child or an animal is puzzled by a corpse as an example of the difference. It is always another *person* who is revealed by the sight of a body, or, in other words, we never see just a *part* of another's body behaving, but always somebody doing something, even though his intention may be obscure. When we do catch a glimpse of a part of the body without being able to see the rest of it, for instance we see a hand moving over the wall in search of the light switch, the rest of the body being concealed by the door, the effect is strange and sinister. In this example I have already set the hand in a context; it should be imagined as seen with no idea of the action it is performing, so that it can be looked at simply as a thing. We are seldom in a position to do this, so that it may come as a real shock when we actually *look* at the hands of a friend as things; they may then appear as ugly or obscene. For Sartre the obscene is the body not acting, contemplated as flesh and nothing more (*EN*, 470–2).

Thus Sartre's discussion of the existence of others leads into that of the relation between mind and body, or perhaps, as I have not exactly followed the order of his exposition, is the same argument. Just as we have always known that there are other people, so we have always understood the intentional nature of their movements, in the sense that we see the movement as having an intention, even though we may be unaware of what the intention precisely is. For Sartre, as for Wittgenstein, "The body is the best picture of the soul."[1] Sartre does not make much use of the words 'soul' and 'mind' in his discussions, for he regards them as misleading; he explicitly condemns the whole notion of 'mind' (*esprit*) as being used as a name for a kind of box into which are put things which cannot be dealt with (*EN*, 377). The point of using the term 'for-itself' or 'consciousness' is partly to avoid the dualism which almost inevitably arises from carrying on the discussion in terms of 'body' and 'mind'; the natural tendency is to look on the latter as something which is not bodily. Such a way of talking is not simply an error of philosophers influenced by Descartes; it can be seen in the reaction of non-philosophers first coming across such a book as Ryle's *Concept of Mind*. Many feel that something is being taken away, that Ryle is denying the existence of one of the familiar features of the world. (Sometimes Ryle himself seems to take the same view, in spite of his explicit

[1] *Philosophical Investigations*, 178; cf. *EN*, 372 ". . . the body *is* the soul in so far as the for-itself is its own individuation."

disclaimers.) For the errors that Ryle is combating are more deeply seated, both in ordinary thought and in ordinary language, than he allows. Hence the frequent accusations of reductionism. The reasons that lead people to think of Ryle's (or Sartre's, for in this respect they substantially agree) programme as reductionist are twofold; first the ordinary mind-body distinction, and second a misunderstanding of 'behaviour'. There is a tendency to take behaviour as consisting of separate bodily movements, e.g. a clenching of the fists, a flushing of the face, the uttering of certain words are considered to be signs which refer to something hidden, the anger itself. Hence when a philosopher claims that these movements "do not *express* anger, they *are* the anger" (*EN*, 413), people feel that something has been left out of the account. In reality it is they who are mistaken, for they have assumed it is possible to perceive a mere movement of a human body. In rare instances, as I have suggested, this is possible. But normally we never see "a clenched fist"; we see "a man who, in a certain situation, clenches his fist" (*EN*, 413). In fact, it is the complete set of actions which is the anger; we may very well be aware that someone is angry without being able to say what precise signs of that anger we have noticed. We always perceive the human body as a whole.

These confusions arise from a failure to take account of Sartre's fourfold distinction. Mere bodily movements are of no interest when other people are under consideration, though they may be of concern to the anatomist. To the typist at work, the actual movements of the fingers are of no more importance than the motions of the mechanism which causes the keys to hit the paper; in both cases it is the intention which is paramount. Similarly, "From nothing in the field of sight does it follow that it is seen from the eye."[1] All we are conscious of is a world of objects 'out there'. In fact, it is clear that those who have talked of the problem of 'Other Minds' have agreed with Descartes that "The soul [or mind] is more easily known than the body", in the sense than they have thought of their individual minds as

[1] Wittgenstein, *Tractatus Logico-philosophicus*, no. 5. 633, cf. *EN*, 397–8.

easily known, others' as known only by means of their bodies. When the problem becomes that of *the* relation between the mind and body, the 'body' considered is that of physiology, an assemblage of nerves, bones and muscles, acted upon by physical forces such as light-waves and so on from the outside and (perhaps) by acts of will from within. Knowledge of the external world is thus mediated by the sense-organs, giving rise to the "problem of perception". But, as has often been pointed out, our knowledge of the structure of the body is itself dependent on perception. "My perception of the other's sense-organs is the foundation for an explanation of sensations and in particular of *my* sensations; but, reciprocally, my sensations so conceived constitute the sole *reality* of my perceptions of the other's sense-organs. . . . In *appearance* the structure of the classical theory of sensation is exactly that of the argument of the liar. . . ." (*EN*, 378).

It is only possible to escape from this situation by taking seriously the distinction between my body as it appears to me and my body as it is conceived by science, or between my own and another's body. For the agent, his body is not generally a *thing*, a physical object existing in the world. The problems come from the attempt to "unite my consciousness not to *my* body but to that of *other people*" (*EN*, 365). Even when the agent discovers his body as a thing, when it is observed in a shameful act, it is still the body as an expression of intention that is discovered, not *the* human body as it is studied by the physiologists. Hence it is necessary to take the body as it appears to the agent in order to deal with the problem of the relation to the world which is perception. The first question is the meaning of the word 'world' in this context. I have already pointed out that Sartre says "the world is human",[1] but there the discussion was in terms of the *public* world, which owed its organisation to the fact that men were conscious of it. But in such a public world it is impossible to understand the relation of consciousness to body, for there it is still *the* body which is considered. For an individual, the world is *his* world, seen from a particular point of view. This is not a

[1] See above, p. 71.

contingent fact, but a necessary part of human existence: "To exist is for human beings to *exist-in-a-place*" (*EN*, 371).[1]

Sartre's argument runs as follows: "*For me*, this glass is to the left of the carafe and slightly behind it; *for Peter*, it is to the right and a little in front. It is not even conceivable that the world could be looked at in such a way that the glass could be seen *at the same time* to the right and left of the carafe, in front of it and behind it. This . . . is because the fusion of right and left, of front and rear, would lead to the total disappearance of '*thises*' in original indistinction. Similarly, if the foot of the table hides the pattern of the carpet from me, this is not the result of the finitude or of the imperfection of my senses, but because a carpet which was not either hidden by the table, or under it or above it, or at the side of it, could not possibly have any relation to it, and would no longer belong to the 'world' in which the table *existed*" (*EN*, 368–9). That things lie behind or beside other things, that a small nearer object will conceal totally a large distant one, are essential characteristics of *perceiving* a world at all. In a confused way people sometimes talk as if they could imagine a different situation, connected perhaps with 'disembodied existence', in which all objects were perceived 'as they are'. (Actually, what most people call to mind when they claim to be imagining this is seeing the world from a particular viewpoint, but one which is not part of a body. This would be a conceivable state of affairs perhaps, for the laws of perspective would still exist for the disembodied perceiver.) But what it would be to "perceive all objects as they are" is quite incomprehensible when examined closely. Each object would have to be seen out of relation to every other. Normally, from whatever point of view I look at this chair, something is hidden by it, including parts of the chair itself. Even if God could perform such a feat, what He did could not be described as 'perceiving a world', for neither would the separate things con-stitute a 'world', nor could such an intuition be called 'perception'.

---

[1] I have translated Sartre's *être-là*, which he intends as the French translation of Heidegger's *Dasein*, by 'exist-in-a-place'. This seems more satisfactory, though perhaps less accurate, than 'to-be-there'.

It may be that in dreams we sometimes seem to be doing some-thing that might be described in this way, but then it is already doubtful whether dreams reveal a 'world' to us and whether our relation to the dream can be described as 'perceiving' it. *Perception* can only exist from a particular point of view; so far from such phenomena as perspective being limitations on our senses, they are an essential part of having a perceptual relation to a world.[1]

Nevertheless, it has been argued both by philosophers and psychologists that certain illusions make it essential to talk of the 'sensations' by which we learn about the world; there are the well-known examples of relativity of sensation, for instance that tepid water feels cold to a warm hand. "But this fact that is pompously called 'the law of the relativity of sensation' has nothing whatsoever to do with sensations. It is a quality of the object that is revealed to me. Simply, a comparison of this objective quality of the water with an equally objective piece of information—that given by a thermometer—gives rise to a contradiction. This contradiction enables me to choose freely the real objective fact. I will call the objective fact that I have not chosen 'subjective' " (*EN*, 375). It might be objected that though this solution may deal with such instances as the contradiction between a judgment of the temperature and the reading given by a thermometer, it does not cope with Berkeley's example of the *same water* appearing hot and cold to a pair of hands at different temperatures. For here we are faced with two contradictory pieces of information at the same level; there seems no reason to choose one rather than the other, whereas there are complex reasons for choosing the evidence of the thermometer when it conflicts with feeling. But, in order to talk in terms of sensations in this situation, there must already be some accepted beliefs about reality and the non-contradictory nature of the world.[2] It is only *because* we believe certain things that we can talk of our senses

[1] On this point, cf. H. H. Price, in *Contemporary British Philosophy, 3rd Series* (Allen & Unwin, 1956), 389–400, and *EN*, 380–1.

[2] "To establish the existence of sensations, one must start from a kind of realism." *EN*, 377.

'deceiving us'. But if we then go on to talk as if all knowledge of the world was mediated by sensations or by sense-data, we are faced with the problem of *constructing* a real world from these peculiar materials, as well as with the difficulty of the nature of the sensations themselves. For these latter are "hybrid notion(s) between the objective and the subjective, conceived from the standpoint of the object and subsequently applied to the subject, a bastard existence which cannot be called factual or theoretical; sensation is the pure day dream of the psychologist which must be rejected by any serious theory about the relation between consciousness and the world" (*EN*, 378).

For we are conscious of a world made up of *objects*, and it is this that we call 'reality'. The unreal character of a dream arises from the fact that we are not set in such a world, that the 'things' in the dream do not have the same characteristics of solidity and perspective as do objects in the real world. It is not because dreams are incoherent that we know that they are dreams, but because the things in them have none of the density of real objects; we cannot go on finding out more about them.[1] The imaginary character of dreams, as mentioned in Chapter II, is already implicit in the language used to describe them. Dreams are not instances of the perception of an unreal world. If in ordinary life we perceive objects, then in dreams we might be said to "quasi-perceive" them (compare Sartre's "quasi-observation"). It is argued, however, that in dreams we are faced with sensations which are the same as the sensations we get in perception, except for the fact that they do not arise from objects in the world. The point of looking at dreams in the way sketched above is that it removes this temptation. The model of the self as a little man inside the body looking at the world through the cameras and microphones of the senses will not do. We don't perceive objects by means of the senses if this implies that we might have perceived them by other means. Rather, for Sartre, sight is one of the ways in which we are *in* the world. The "sense of vision" and perceived

[1] cf. *L'Imaginaire*, 225, and my 'Dreams', *Supplementary Proceedings of the Aristotelian Society*, 1956, 208–28.

objects are two sides of the same coin. "Thus blindness, colour-blindness or short sight originally represent *the way in which there is* a world for me, that is to say they define my visual sense" (*EN*, 383). The image of a 'real world' with which we come into contact with a moderate degree of efficiency through the senses arises from a confusion, that of failing to distinguish the body as an object of scientific study from the body as it is 'lived'.

For this discussion of the senses is not irrelevant to the problem raised above, that of the nature of the body. A 'world' for us must be organised round a point of reference, seen in perspective, etc. Normally we can look at that from which we have a point of view, for instance we can, instead of looking out *of* the window, step back and contemplate the window itself. I can even remove my glasses and look at them. But the body is the "point of view on which I can no longer take a point of view" (*EN*, 394), the centre of all perspectives. But, and this is an important fact about human existence, the centre of all our perspectives is not a bare point, it is a body. To relate this centre to the body as it is experienced Sartre connects perception and action. Contemplation would not give us a world of objects, but a set of qualities; the watchers in Plato's cave took shadows for realities because they could not go up to them, try to move them and so on. A being confined to one spot would be unable to distinguish between a real thing and, for example, a reflection of it. It is by action that we discover the "coefficient of adversity of things" (*EN*, 389), their resistance, their 'thinginess'. Perspective is not simply a matter of an object appearing smaller farther away or of one object concealing another, it is also the fact that it is necessary to travel a certain distance in order to reach the object, overcome certain obstacles to get there, and so on. "Perception . . . is only revealed in and by projected actions" (*EN*, 386).[1] Sartre thinks that the basic error of those who talk of the 'construction of the world' from sense-data or sensations is that they ignore the fact that we act *in* the world, investigate it and use things as instruments. Here the

---

[1] Sartre's discussion of this point should be compared with S. Hampshire, *Thought and Action*, 45–57.

category of instrumentality is of great importance; to recognise a thing is, in many cases, to recognise what it is for, its use. But action and instrumentality must not be interpreted in terms of others' bodies. "Here again there is a clear risk of committing the same error which was condemned in the case of the senses, that is to say of interpreting *my* action as *it is for me* in terms of the action of another' (*EN*, 384). This is because we tend to think of another's body as the instrument by which he achieves his purposes, just as we could, by threats or promises, achieve our purposes through the instrumentality of his body. Hence the temptation to think in a dualistic fashion of the body as the instrument of the soul. But *my* body is not a collection of instruments which I may use or refrain from using, it is the centre of instrumentality, the instrument which I am, the one that I cannot use by means of another instrument. The argument is exactly parallel with that which leads Sartre to talk of the body as the point of view on which it is impossible to take a point of view.

In dealing with the world, in living and acting in it, we are not conscious of our bodies on an unreflective level, just as we are not normally conscious of the eyes in looking, though, of course, something may make us conscious of them. "It is better to say, using the verb 'to exist' transitively, that it [consciousness] *exists the body*. Thus . . . the relation of consciousness to the body is an *existential* relation" (*EN*, 394. It is perhaps worth noting that this is one of the rare appearances of the word 'existential' in the text of *L'Etre et le néant*.) It is, of course, difficult to talk about this relationship without slipping into dualistic expressions; indeed, the very use of the word 'relation' tends to mislead. For I *am* my body, it is my point of insertion into the world. But I don't *live* my body, for my life consists of projects *in* the world. In this sense the body is that which we continually *go beyond*; it represents the past, facticity. (The phenomenon which seems to contradict this, namely sexual activity, is discussed below.) The term 'facticity' has already been mentioned,[1] but at this point it is necessary to look at it more fully. For there do seem to be many

[1] See above, p. 67.

instances in which the body seems to need distinguishing from the self, cases where it is a hindrance to our projects, whether through disease and injury, or lack of original endowment. For example that fact that I am short-sighted *prevents* me from taking up certain professions, the cut on my finger *hinders* me from typing as rapidly as usual. In an extreme case, what has happened in the past may be a permanent restriction, for instance the amputation of a limb. But here again the trap of judging one's own body by those of others must be resisted. That I lack something which another possesses cannot be realised from within, but only by a comparison of what I can do with what he can. "Even this infirmity from which I suffer, from the very fact that I am alive, I have assumed; overcome it by my own projects, made of it the necessary obstacle for my existence, and I cannot be infirm without choosing myself as infirm, that is to say choosing the manner in which I exist my infirmity (as 'intolerable', 'humiliating', 'to be hidden', 'to be revealed to all', 'object of pride', 'justification of my failures', etc. etc.)" (*EN*, 393). Of course, it is a contingent fact that each should have the body he has, was born at such a time to precisely these parents and so on, but everyone must have a body, two parents, a time of birth, nationality, etc. The body, in so far as it represents the situation in which each finds himself, *is* this contingency. "My body is the contingent form which the necessity of my contingent existence takes." Sartre means by this that to exist in this world is to have a set of all possible characteristics which can belong to bodies, though which set is a matter of chance. Further, each body is affected by what has been done to and by it in the past, and some of these results are irreversible. Thus *facticity*, the facts of bodily existence, is the way of living in the world, in some sense *is* the body itself.

For Sartre, this facticity does not destroy freedom; whatever an individual body may be, the attitude taken toward it and the projects formed are not determined by it, though the range of possibilities may well be. Sartre even goes so far as to argue that facticity renders freedom possible. The argument he puts forward is that finitude is a condition for *choice*; an infinite being could not be said to have to exercise choice, for he could be everything at the same time. In fact, a being that *could be* everything would have actually to be so; possibility and hence choice exists only for the finite. The meaning of 'could be' applied to an infinite being is problematic. Hence limitations are a necessity for choice and freedom. This is an extension of an argument often used in connection with the laws of nature; these are said not to be restrictions because without some regularities in nature it would be impossible to operate on the world at all. Further, when the difficulties of operating under conditions of free-fall are realised, it can be seen that gravity is helpful as well as a mere hindrance. Sartre seems to be going beyond this position in an implausible way in saying that *nothing* in the material world, the body included, restricts freedom. (Here I am only dealing with facticity; different kinds of obstacles to freedom will be discussed below in Chapter VII.) He argues that a human body must have certain characteristics; we can so easily imagine not having any particular one of these, because we see others who possess different ones, that we fail to notice that we could not exist without any of them. It is perhaps absurd, as Sartre says, that an individual should have this particular set of characteristics, in the sense that no ultimate reason can be given for his possession of them, but it would be impossible for him not to have any, or even to lack any single one. And the possession of these characteristics is a condition of action and hence of freedom. Again, an individual may think that he is less free than another because he has a disability the other lacks. But for Sartre the point is that freedom represents the range of an individual's possibilities, a concrete, not an abstract, set.

It is possible to take a reflective view of the body, but this is not the same as knowing the body as an object. For, as psychologists have discovered, the image that a man has of his body may be very different from his actual body. This can be seen not only in its gross manifestations, such as phantom limbs, but also in such instances as the reference of pains to sites in the body where it is wrongly believed that a particular organ is situated. The reflective view of the body Sartre calls the "psychic body". A man is aware of his psychic body when he attends to his body instead of what he is actually doing, for example when he concentrates on a pain. The continuous manifestation of the psychic body is *nausea*. This notion plays a different role in the context of *L'Etre et le néant* than it did in *La Nausée*, for at that stage of his thought he did not distinguish between that which manifested existence as such and that which manifested the psychic body. But after the distinctions Sartre has introduced about the body, it becomes even clearer than it was in the earlier context that there is no reason to say that Sartre finds all existence nauseating. There is no need to experience the psychic body in most cases. There are occasions, such as awakening from an afternoon nap, when we do experience something like an insipid taste of the body; here the body is at its most contingent. The final importance of the notion of *nausea* is that it does provide an explanation of all actual feelings of sickness in the face of things we find revolting. It is no explanation to say that certain things make us feel sick because they are nauseating. It has been suggested that such objects make us vomit because we imagine eating them. It is not at all clear why we should imagine this; we certainly don't imagine eating most of the objects that we come across, and even if it is argued that the things we find nauseating are chiefly those which might serve as food, and that therefore we imagine the nausea we would feel in eating them, this still does not explain why eating those things should induce nausea. However, it does seem clear that nausea is connected closely with the human body and its food. As I have said above (p. 12), the things that induce an immediate feeling of nausea in us are the most blatantly contingent evidences of bodily existence, excrements, blood, etc. It is interesting that these should tend to be regarded throughout the human race as nauseous, a feeling that is clearly not shared by animals. Thus there does seem to be some reason to accept Sartre's suggestions. I must re-emphasise here that this is not a central part of Sartre's argument, but one of those penetrating and fascinating asides which so often occur in *L'Etre et le néant*. Many of them are worth more consideration than can be given in a general account such as this one. Though it may seem strange that a discussion of the existence of other people should finish with the consideration of the individual's own body, I hope it is clear that Sartre has followed a line of argument which is natural; it might be summarised: I discover the existence of other people, or rather am certain of the existence of others; for a variety of reasons this leads me to confuse the nature of my relation to my own body, which I misconstrue on the analogy of my experience of the other's body.

VI

Relations with Other People

CONSCIOUSNESS of the body as a body is nausea, the "taste of myself" (*EN*, 410); this is the way in which we can experience our bodies. At the same level we can experience another's body as flesh. As I have emphasised above, we rarely look on another person as a mere thing or object, we normally see him in action, involved in a series of projects and manifesting his freedom, in which case his body has an instrumental or transparent character, we see him *through* his body. In sexual desire, however, what is of central importance seems to be the body as flesh. Such an experience may be commoner than that of nausea, but it is of the same order in that it tends to concentrate on what is normally transcended. I have already remarked that philosophers have tended to ignore the body, and that most bodily of all our activities, the sexual; in *L'Etre et le néant* Sartre sees concrete relations between embodied individuals as basic to the understanding of what it is to be a person. Hence this section of the argument is a filling out of the abstract discussion of our knowledge of the existence of others. The phenomenon of the 'look' was not a *proof* of others' existence, it was a *manifestation* of it. More complex relations are similarly manifestations of the basic knowledge that they do exist as other people.

Sexual desire and flesh seem intimately connected: "It is not an accident that desire while aiming at the body as a whole gets into contact with it mainly by means of the least differentiated masses of flesh, the ones least provided with nerves, the least capable of spontaneous movement, by means of the breasts, buttocks, thighs and stomach; these are a kind of image of pure facticity. It is for the same reason that the real caress is the contact of two bodies in their most fleshy parts, contact between bellies and breasts; a caressing hand is already too delicate, too much like a perfect instrument" (*EN*, 466). However, it is not just flesh that interests us, even in sexual desire, it is flesh as manifesting another person. For this reason concrete relations with other people are complex, involving both bodily and emotional features. Because it is a relationship with another *person* that is involved, sexual desire cannot be treated merely as a feature of the body, a contingent property of human beings. But many writers have talked as if it were a biological accident, having no significance except as a source of moral problems. The very habit of talking of sex as an 'instinct' shows this, though it also marks a failure to give adequate philosophical consideration to the problem. There is a relatively clear application of the notion of instinct to animal behaviour, in contrast to that which is learned. Birds build their nests by instinct, in other words a bird reared in isolation is capable of constructing a nest if provided with the right stimulus. It is not so obvious that there are any such 'instincts' in human beings except those manifested by new-born babies. But what perhaps was in the minds of those who talked of sexual desire in this way was that it was something that the bodily constitution forced on the mind, a 'passion' in the Aristotelian sense. It is possible to overcome sexual desire, but not to prevent its occurrence.

Such an attitude to sex, that it is a mere biological fact, like hunger or thirst, is for Sartre a misunderstanding. Hunger is a desire for food which arises from certain biochemical states of the body, and in normal cases it disappears with satisfaction, or, to put it in another way, food is the intentional object of hunger. It is not nearly so obvious what the intentional object of sexual desire is. To say 'sexual intercourse' is obviously inadequate, first because most sexual desire is directed towards a particular person and hence satisfaction would not be obtained by intercourse with anyone; hunger, on the other hand, can generally be satisfied by any of a wide variety of foodstuffs. Second, there can occur what can only be described as sexual desire in children too young for satisfaction by intercourse; even if there is an unwillingness to accept all Freud has to say about infantile sexuality, this seems to be a fact. Further, to look upon sexual desire as on the same level as other desires will not do for most people. "For everyone knows that there is a great gulf between sexual desire and the other appetites. We all know the famous saying 'Make love to a pretty woman when you want to just as you would drink a glass of cold water when thirsty.' Such a view is unsatisfactory and even shocking" (*EN*, 456–7). This is not because it is untrue to say that the sexual act does satisfy (in the sense of remove) the desire; it clearly does. But we should feel that anyone who looked on sexual activity solely as a means of getting rid of a desire that was troubling him had misunderstood or undervalued sex. It might be argued that this was because sexual desire was just a more complex kind of bodily desire, one that normally could be satisfied only with a particular person, in the same sort of way that hunger can only be really satisfied with food that is genuinely nourishing, though the immediate pangs may be stilled by anything that will fill the stomach. Sexual desire is more complex than hunger, but its complexity lies along another dimension. Its very quality as desire is different from that of other desires. Hunger is distracting, but this distraction can be kept in the background and ignored so long as it is not too great. "The expressions which are used to refer to [sexual] desire mark its particular nature. It is said *to take you, to overwhelm you, to paralyse you*. Is it possible to imagine these words being applied to hunger? What would an 'overwhelming' hunger be like?" (*EN*, 457). A starving man might experience an overwhelming hunger, but starvation is a rare experience. But almost all instances of sexual desire have this quality, for desire "compromises me, I am an accomplice of my desire" (ibid.).

Sexual desire is a form of "incarnation", in the literal sense that a person under its influence is "trapped in his flesh", experiences his body *as a body*, as composed of fleshly parts in a way which is not true of other physical desires. Similarly the aim of sexual activity is to make the other person feel her flesh as the agent feels his, to make her become a body. Hence the importance of the caress which is aimed at the most fleshy parts of the body. For a caress is not a way of finding out about someone else's body, nor a preparation for *using* it; it should be noted that we also caress certain physical objects, rich materials, etc. In such cases we are not regarding the objects as instruments, but as matter, 'in their flesh' as it were. The difference between these cases and the sexual is that in the latter it is hoped that the result of the caress will be to arouse or strengthen sexual desire in the other person, to increase his or her incarnation. Thus it is an attempt to act on another's freedom which is involved, and it is this which makes sex so different from all other desires. For they are only involved with inanimate objects. But to be aware of the existence of another person is to be aware of his freedom. Hence sexual activity is on a different level; it involves a relation between free agents though for various reasons the people involved may attempt to deny this. Sartre treats of the subject in terms of two circles, desire-sadism and love-masochism, both of which arise because of the ambiguous nature of sex itself.

"Nevertheless, desire itself is pledged to failure" (*EN*, 466).[1] For sexual satisfaction destroys desire by satisfying it and hence puts an end to the mutual incarnation. Freedom is restored and bodies again become agents rather than things. The relationship of desire is thus unstable. An attempt to overcome this instability, to trap the freedom of the other more permanently in her flesh, is *sadism*. "In fact as soon as I try to take possession of the body of the person whom I have brought to incarnate herself by my own incarnation, I destroy the reciprocal incarnation, I transcend my own body and turn towards sadism" (*EN*, 474–5). In other words, I tend to use my own body in the normal semi-instrumental way whilst expecting hers to remain flesh. But sadism contains its own failure, for it is impossible, according to Sartre, actually to *compel* someone to do something. However much physical pres-

---

[1] The phrase "voué à l'échec" is not easy to translate; Miss Barnes has "doomed" for "voué", but I think that "pledged" better brings out the idea that desire carries the seeds of its own destruction in its very nature.

sure, including torture, is used, it is always open to the other person to hold out a little longer; to give in is a decision; everyone is free, even on the rack. In a sense, what Sartre claims is true, the individual is free to decide what degree of pain he will accept as "intolerable"; there are plenty of instances in history of men who have held out under extreme tortures, and this was not because they were less sensitive to physical pain than others who gave in. This means, Sartre says, that the sadist will realise his failure when the tortured individual looks at him.[1] "Then he discovers that he cannot act on the freedom of another person, even by compelling him to humiliate himself and to beg for mercy, for it is precisely in and through the absolute freedom of the other that there comes into existence a world where there is a sadist and his instruments of torture and a hundred pretexts to humiliate and deny oneself" (*EN*, 476). Sartre's analysis of sadism goes astray by stressing the activities of a torturer extracting information. No doubt the activities of the Gestapo were in his mind when writing the passage. But this emphasis has distorted the line of his own argument. If we take the works of the Marquis de Sade as representing sadism, then it would seem that the sadist inflicts pain in order to arouse his own desire by emphasising the flesh of the other person. This desire is then sometimes satisfied on the victim. Such a process is more like that of mutual incarnation that Sartre has described under the name of desire than the clinical proceedings of a Gestapo headquarters. Indeed, a certain amount of physical violence to the other person is common as part of sexual activity; this led Freud to say that there was an element of sadism in most people. The trouble here is that the words sadism and masochism have come to be used in loose senses, so that any infliction of pain on another person is qualified as sadistic. But to assume that all torturers, even when they enjoy what they are doing to their victims, are simply obtaining sexual pleasure is to go beyond the evidence. There is a pleasure to be obtained, for some people, in humiliating others, and reducing them to the level of mere flesh may be the most effective way of achieving this. But it need not be

[1] There was a striking scene on this theme in the film *Roma, città aperta*.

sexual pleasure in the full sense of the word. Correspondingly, much of what passes for sexual activity between individuals may be rather the manifestation of power and so on. Sartre over-simplifies in the text of *L'Etre et le néant*, but seems well aware of the problems in his description of the so-called 'sexual' relations of the characters of *Huis clos*. Here again part of the trouble springs from an oversimplified view of sexual desire itself; even if Sartre does not deal with the problem adequately, he does make us aware of the complexities.

Love and masochism are likewise to be seen as attempts to act on the freedom of another person, though love is more complex than desire. The lover does not want to be loved by someone lacking freedom, he "wants to possess a free person as a free person." . . . "But, on the other hand, he cannot be satisfied with that important variety of freedom which is free and voluntary engagement. . . . Who would be satisfied with the words: 'I love you because I have freely committed myself to love you and I don't want to break my word; I love you in order to be faithful to myself?' Thus the lover demands an oath and is annoyed by the oath. He wants to be loved freely but demands that this freedom should no longer be free" (*EN*, 434). The lover wants to be loved absolutely, hence the attempts to view the love as in some way *necessary*, e.g. "We were made for each other" and other such popular phrases. However, love again carries its own destruction with it. To love is to want to be loved, and thus to want the other person to want to be loved. Sartre considers this an infinite regress, and uses it to explain the "perpetual dissatisfaction of the lover" (*EN*, 445). It is true that it is difficult to see what the lover's object actually is. Normally this problem is masked by a set of social conventions, which define some activity or state as the natural goal of love; for our present society this goal is marriage. For Sartre this would be a transformation of love into something different, for love as such has nothing to do with society. Indeed, the presence of a third person (or persons) destroys the 'absolute' character of love. The look here again acts as a waste-pipe to drain away the lovers' mutual world. Hence the desire of lovers for secrecy and also the "perpetual shame (or pride—which comes to the same thing here) of the lover" (*EN*, 445).

Masochism, the attempt to escape from the inevitable failure of love, is an attempt to become an object for the loved person, to emphasise dependence and hence to compel a reaction. This again leads to failure, for the very fact of *making* oneself into a ridiculous or obscene object is itself an activity; the agent humiliates *himself*. We are back in the realm of freedom. "Masochism is thus in principle a failure. There is nothing surprising in this when we think that masochism is a 'vice' and that vice is, in principle, love of failure" (*EN*, 447). But Sartre's analysis of human relations seems to lead to the conclusion that they are all 'pledged to failure', and thus all vices. And this depressing view springs from the very mode of knowledge of other people, the look. For the look, if not actively hostile, is profoundly alien; in the Hegelian sense, it 'alienates' one's being. As Sartre says at the beginning of his study of concrete relations with other people: "The descriptions which follow must be envisaged under the heading of *conflict*. Conflict is the original meaning of being-for-others" (*EN*, 431). This sentiment is re-echoed by some of the concluding words of the section: "The essence of relations between consciousnesses is not *Mitsein* [being together], it is conflict" (*EN*, 502). The only feeling of togetherness that Sartre can visualise at this stage is the "us-feeling, the experience of the galley-slaves when a high-born lady looks at them, or, in contemporary terms, the class-consciousness of the proletariat in the face of a member of the bourgeosie". And these are feelings rather than genuine relations. He admits the possibility of an experience of "we", but in most cases it is the mistaken experience of a single person.

Sartre does, however, hold out a ray of hope in an otherwise depressing chapter; in a footnote he says: "These considerations do not exclude the possibility of a morality of deliverance and salvation. But this can only be achieved at the end of a radical conversion which I cannot discuss here" (*EN*, 484). Though he nowhere gives details of the nature of this radical conversion, it is clear both from his personal relations with Simone de Beauvoir and from his later commitment to certain forms of political action that Sartre does believe in the possibility of genuine human relations. "Hell is other people." Garcin's cry at the end of *Huis clos*, is not Sartre's last word on the subject. Indeed, it is clear from the context of the play that all three characters are in hell precisely because they are prevented by their own choices from establishing any proper relations with those around them. Their hell consists in the fact that they must continue the circles of love-masochism or desire-sadism without the possibility of escape by radical conversion. But Sartre clearly regards this as a fault and a failure to do what is possible for living human beings. In this sense he is not pessimistic; as so often with Sartre it is necessary to distinguish between painting a gloomy picture and being pessimistic. I think he is right in stressing basic hostility as an important feature of human relations. Though this is often latent, it can be seen, as suggested above, in two people meeting by chance. Such hostility is often masked in everyday life because we already have some relations with many of the people we meet, and many of those unknown to us are thought of merely as means towards our own ends; the shop assistant is only an instrument to get us what we want, and in most cases is not even considered as a person. An interesting example of this basic hostility towards the 'other' is the device of projecting it on to a class or race, the Negroes or Jews, who become the 'incarnate others' (scapegoat) for a group or nation, acting as a kind of lightning conductor to dispose of feelings of hostility which might upset other social relations. Such a projected hostility may be of great value in keeping a group united, as can be seen in war-time. It may well be, as Sartre suggests in *Critique de la raison dialectique*, that economic scarcity is an important element in fostering this feeling, but this is clearly not the whole story. For at a deeper level there is also a feeling of hostility to those 'near and dear to us'; it should not be forgotten that most murders are of close relations. It is not merely that love can easily become hatred, rather that most love also contains an element of hatred as a result of its very nature. There is a profound level at which each consciousness may be said to pursue, in some sense, the death of the other. To deny this view of Hegel and Sartre is to fall into a facile optimism, and hence to fail to realise the difficulty of genuine human relations. Such difficulty must be seen before there is any possibility of constructing a satisfactory moral system.

VII

Language

Wir sehen hiermit wieder die Sprache als das Dasein des Geistes.
(Hegel)

I HAVE included a separate chapter on language even though
Sartre nowhere discusses its problems in isolation from other
philosophic questions; I have done this for two reasons, first
because I think he has some interesting things to say, and second
because there is a tendency to imagine that the 'existentialists' are
blind to the important linguistic issues so much discussed in this
country at the present time. Hence the subject-matter of this
chapter is more technical, more concerned with details of current
philosophic discussions, than are the others in the book, though
I believe it can be understood in isolation from such discussions.
The chapter is also more difficult than the others, and this is unavoidable from the nature of the subject-matter; to think clearly
about language requires concentration and argument on matters
we do not normally think about. Philosophers in England tend
to be considered, and even to consider themselves, as "linguistic
philosophers", albeit without any clear agreement on the meaning
of the phrase. Elsewhere philosophers tend to see this concentration on language as resulting from an erroneous conception of
philosophy. As so often in such cases, there are things to be said
on both sides; here I am concerned to show that there is less
difference between the views of Sartre and those of some English
philosophers than might appear at first glance. There is an important difference of attitude between the two sides, however;
this can be characterised roughly by saying that an English philosopher nowadays tends to begin by assuming that the problem he

is faced with can be tackled by looking at language, whereas Sartre is unlikely to examine language except when it has actually given trouble. Nevertheless, he has said quite a lot about the topic; the principal discussions of it in *L'Etre et le néant* occur in the sections on 'Concrete relations with other people' and on the 'Situation' (*EN*, 440–2, and 592–606). There are also some important remarks in the volumes of *Situations*, particularly in the long essay on the work of Parain entitled 'Aller et retour' (*S.I*, 189–244).

The difference in attitude that I have just referred to springs from two causes. First, Sartre is writing for a less specialised audience than are most English philosophers. There has been a tendency among the latter to write for other philosophers, not for the lay public; there are complex reasons for this, of which one is the example of G. E. Moore, whose point of departure was generally the odd things said by other philosophers. Second, and more important, is the fact that Sartre has been always a considerable user of language, a playwright and a novelist as well as a philosopher. Hence he is constantly aware that communication is not only the transmission of clear and distinct ideas from one intellect to another, but can involve the use of language at many different levels, from that of the discussion of a technical point in philosophy to the ritual formulae imparting no information and affecting no attitudes which constitute so much of the conversation of everyday life. In the latter case, a thought-out reply would almost amount to a breakdown in 'communication'. For Sartre, in fact, the remedy for the difficulties which arise from language lies not in their abstract discussion, but in the use of language itself; tools are best improved by refinements introduced by the users, not by arm-chair critics. We do communicate with some degree of success; by continuing to try we shall succeed better, even though the enterprise is not an easy one. "Our first task as writers is thus to re-establish language in its dignity. After all we think with words. . . . And then I mistrust things which can't be communicated, for they are the sources of violence. When it seems impossible to us to share those certainties we possess, the only thing left is to fight, to burn or to hang. No, we are worth no more than our lives and it is by our lives that we must be judged; our thought is worth no more than our language and it must be judged by the way it makes use of that language" (*S. II*, 305). This should not be taken as implying that Sartre has fallen into the trap of thinking of language as an instrument that we happen to use for various purposes. He makes it clear that for him it is no more an instrument than the body is an instrument. But just as we can make our bodies better able to do certain things by practice, so we can do the same with language. But there are numerous different things we can do to improve the body, not one grand method producing a perfect one. Similarly, the improvement of language is a piecemeal affair, depending on the problem that faces us. "It [language] can lie, fool, alter, universalise at the wrong time; the questions which it raises are technical, political, aesthetic, moral. . . . But there is no metaphysical problem of language" (*S.I*, 241).

There is no one problem, still less a single solution. A perfect language cannot exist. Sartre encountered the idea of a perfect language in the work of Brice Parain, who visualised a perfect language as one in which philosophic problems cannot arise, though he considered the matter rather differently from Wittgenstein at the period of the *Tractatus Logico-philosophicus*, whose meaning was summarised by the author as: "What can be said at all can be said clearly; and whereof one cannot speak thereof one must be silent." Nevertheless there is a parallel between what Parain said and the early doctrines of Wittgenstein. For Parain, philosophy exists because there is "play in the gearing" of language (*du jeu dans l'engrenage*). Sartre recounts it: "When Parain learnt that 'the strictest social orders taught history, philosophy, literature', he must have felt to some degree the same shock that the Pythagoreans did before the incommensurability of the sides of a right-angled triangle. If a society philosophises, it is because there is 'play in the gearing' that there is a place for the dream of an individual, for each person's fantasy, for questions and for failure to understand. Finally, it shows that there is no really rigorous social order. For Parain believes that philosophy and literature are the absurd dreams of an imperfect language" (*S.I*, 211). Parain's solution was, like Wittgenstein's, the restriction of language to a single function, although he chose a different one. Wittgenstein concluded that the language of science was the only legitimate one: "The right method of philosophy would be this. To say nothing except what can be said, i.e. the propositions of natural science. . . ."[1] Parain's suggestion was more in tune with the language invented by George Orwell in *1984*, 'Newspeak', though he welcomed what Orwell had pictured as a nightmare. A language for the giving of orders would have no room for play in the gearing. "Parain threw himself heartily into his other dream, that of an authoritarian community of work, where language is expressly reduced to its subaltern role of an intermediary between desire and action, between the bosses and their men, where everybody understands because everybody obeys, where the suppression of social barriers leads to the suppression of play in the transmission" (*S.I*, 207). There is an obvious difference in the nature of the remedies; Wittgenstein at the time of the *Tractatus* saw only the troubles which arose from the fact that it was possible to philosophise, and these were of an intellectual nature. Parain was thinking of philosophy as one symptom of "the sickness of a time [which] is cured by an alteration in the mode of life of human beings",[2] and hence as needing a more radical solution.

It is very tempting to think that a language which serves only for the transmission of orders would be perfect, in the sense that no problems of a philosophical character could arise in it. An example of such a language is provided by Wittgenstein:

The language is meant to serve for communication between a builder A and an assistant B. A is building with building-stones: there are blocks, pillars, slabs and beams. B has to pass the stones, and that in the order in which A needs them. For this purpose they use a language consisting of the words 'block', 'pillar', 'slab', 'beam'. A calls them

[1] *Tractatus Logico-philosophicus*, no. 6. 53.
[2] Wittgenstein, *Remarks on the Foundations of Mathematics* (Blackwell, 1956), 57.

out:—B brings the stone which he has learnt to bring at such-and-such a call,—Conceive this as a complete primitive language.[1]

It might be thought that there was no room for play here, that no ambiguities or other linguistic difficulties could arise. But what would happen if A called out 'Block' and B brings a 'pillar'? We could say "No, I said 'Block'". There is no such recourse open to A. In fact, this is not a language at all, what is involved is mere response to signals. A dog could be trained to react in the way that B does. However many orders were added to the 'vocabulary' of A, even though B always 'obeyed' them, it would still not be a language in the normal sense of the word.[2] It is not a language because there is no similarity between the response of A and B. If B makes the noise written 'slab' he has said nothing, because no use has been given to such a signal. In an ordinary language, the words used by one person can (logically) also be used by another. If B called in English to A "Bring me a slab", it might be that he had no right to issue such an order, but we could understand and comment on his attempt. Though the social situation might prohibit B from issuing an order, language would not. In Wittgenstein's example there is no such reciprocity. A language, as distinct from a code of signals, is a set of signs or symbols which can be used by everyone.

More important from Sartre's point of view is the fact that Parain in attempting to reform language in this direction is making an "attempt to destroy words by means of words" (S.I, 209). Sartre compares it with the surrealist attempt to destroy painting by means of paintings. In other words, such a projected reform is something that we can understand because we are language users already. We may think, because we can remember periods on the barrack square, that we can imagine what it would be like to exist in a society where the only communication was by orders. In fact, we cannot do this; we are really thinking of an isolated part of our social life which depends for its existence on

---

[1] *Philosophical Investigations*, § 2.

[2] On this point, cf. R. Rhees, 'Wittgenstein's Builders', *Proceedings of the Aristotelian Society*, 1959–60, 171–86.

the rest of that life. The difficulty is like that which comes from Wittgenstein's instruction "Conceive this as a complete primitive language." In fact the danger in talking of "language-games" in the way which is popular now in philosophical circles is that it leads people to think that bits of language can be separated off and used in isolation.[1] Although language does not form an organised whole, it does not follow that small fragments can function on their own as languages. For instance, giving orders is a part of what we can do with our language, but it could not form the whole of a language. Even to describe such a situation adequately the rest of language is required, and the suggestion that it is possible is a philosophical suggestion, just as the activity of demonstrating to someone who has tried to say something non-scientific that "he has given no meaning to certain signs in his propositions"[2] is philosophical. In fact, there is no general remedy for "play in the gearing" of language, there are only particular remedies for particular difficulties. Further, new problems will always arise after the old ones have been solved.

When I said that Sartre has a different attitude to language from that of contemporary British philosophers, I did not mean to imply that he actually regarded it as less important than they do. Indeed, it might be claimed that he is less interested in purely philosophical issues that arise in its boundaries because he regards it as more important as a human activity than do many who talk about 'linguistic philosophy'. He finds less need to discuss it in isolation because he sets language in relation to the rest of human activities, even makes it more central. "The problem of language is exactly parallel to the problem of the body and the descriptions which apply in the one case also apply in the other" (EN, 442). "I am language, for language is nothing else than existence in the presence of other people" (S.I, 237). Consequently Sartre regards many of its problems as due to that same ambiguity he has already discussed in relation to the body. Confusions in this sphere arise

---

[1] I don't think Wittgenstein often, if ever, fell into this trap; many of his less critical followers do.

[2] *Tractatus Logico-philosophicus*, no. 6.53.

from neglecting the difference between the body as it appears to the self and the body as it appears to other people. Language is different when we think of it from the point of view of the speaker or writer from when we look at it from the point of view of the hearer or reader. In speaking or writing, language is very like the body in action. "The speaker is *situated* in language, clothed in words; they are the prolongations of his senses, his claws, his antennae, his spectacles; he operates them from inside, he feels them as he does his body, he is surrounded by a verbal body of which he is hardly conscious and which extends over his world" (*S.II*, 65). "We are in language in the same way as we are in our bodies; we *are aware* of it spontaneously in transcending it towards other ends, as we are aware of our hands and feet" (*S.II*, 71). We are at home in our native language as we are at home in our bodies. This is not to deny that we may be uncertain about some parts of our own language, that occasionally we have to think what we are going to say, call to mind rules of grammar. The position is like that of unfamiliar types of action; we have to concentrate on how to move our arms and legs in learning a new game or dance. Similarly, in speaking a foreign language we are continually conscious of rules, have to call to mind that certain conjunctions take certain tenses, that adjectives must agree with their nouns and so on. Here we do appear to be manipulating an instrument because we first have to think what to say and then to translate it into the other language; it is only when there is no need for this kind of process that we really know the foreign tongue—it is then no longer 'foreign' to us, we are 'at home' in it. In normal communication we are unaware of language as a separate thing, just as in most actions we are unaware of our bodies; it would be as odd to talk of doing something 'by means of the body' as it would be to talk of communicating 'by means of language'. (This is not to deny that there are special cases in which both forms could be used.) But Sartre has said enough to justify his statement that language is no more an instrument than the body is.

Of course, there *are* linguistic rules, and these can be discovered

by grammarians, taught to children and foreigners and so on.
"Thus, language, a free project *for me* has specific laws for *other
people*" (*EN*, 600).[1] The rules are only noticed by people standing
outside the actual communication; indeed, awareness of the rules
and meanings of words may well not be enough to enable one
to understand a conversation: "If we were to listen to a recording
without commentary of an ordinary conversation in a family of
Provins or of Angoulême, we would understand nothing; for it
would have no context, that is to say it would lack the common
memories and the common perceptions, the situation of the couple
and their plans, in short the world that each of the speakers knows
appears to the other. It is the same with reading; people of the
same period and of the same society, who have experienced
the same events, have the same taste in their mouths, they have the
same complicity with each other and between them there lie the
same corpses" (*S.II*, 117). Faced with a conversation such as
Sartre envisages, we would be conscious of the language, of the
words used; we would be trying to understand what is said. But
in normal communication none of this occurs, the language used
is 'transparent'. "Thus it often happens that we find ourselves
knowing something which we have learnt by means of words
without being able to remember a single one of the words which
conveyed it to us" (*S.II*, 70). This may lead to mistakes; the
medium, though it seems transparent, can also distort. Nevertheless, language does appear transparent in many cases.

Thus in most of everyday life we live as if language did not
exist independently of us. Of course it does; we are born into a
world where it has rules which we did not make and which a
single individual cannot alter; every word used has a definite
meaning which can be found in the dictionary. For Sartre this

[1] The word I have translated "language" in this quotation is "le langage".
Sartre appears to be using this as a term of greater generality than "la langue",
for example in a passage on p. 595, where he sets up the hierarchy "le dialecte,
la langue, le langage". I think Sartre is here modifying de Saussure's division
between "le langage", human language in general, "la langue" the systematised
language of a people or group, and "la parole" the speech or language of an
individual.

constitutes an important aspect of our 'situation', our existence in a world already filled with "objective meanings which are given to me as not having been put there by me. . . . If one thinks, for example, of the innumerable meanings independent of *my* choice which I discover if I live in a town: streets, houses, shops, trams and buses, directions, warning sounds, radio music, etc." (*EN*, 592). Indeed, to live in a community is to know how all these things are organised, to know how to speak the language and what customs to follow. "Belonging to the *human race* is defined in fact by the use of certain general elementary techniques; to know how to walk, to know how to take hold, to judge the relief and relative size of perceived objects, to know how to talk, to know how to distinguish, in general, the true from the false" (*EN*, 594). To talk in terms of 'knowing how' refers to the use of a technique which exists independently of the individual, which has been established by *other people*. As I have already said, this technique is not *felt* as something alien; it does not appear to constrain our freedom. For Sartre it is important to show not only that there is no feeling of constraint, but also that there is no genuine constraint in following rules which the individual did not make. For everyone is always in a situation, but must remain free. I shall be discussing Sartre's general treatment of the problem of the 'situation' in the next chapter, where it will become clear that what he has to say about language is closely related to the general solution he propounds.

When we think of language as something given, the two things that most strike us are the rules of grammar and the meanings of words, the units of discourse and the rules for putting them together. But discourse consists not of words but of statements, commands, prayers and so on; these are expressed in sentences and "the sentence is not *composed* (*made up*) of words" (*EN*, 597). For words are "only the traces of the passage of sentences, just as highways are only the traces of the passage of pilgrims or of caravans" (*EN*, 598). In the beginning there was no road between two places, people just walked as they wanted to between them. Because a number of them chose the same (or approximately the same) route, there eventually came to be a well-worn track. Once that existed, it was the obvious route to choose. Whether it is possible to imagine a similar process as providing for the origins of language is not here in question; the point that Sartre is making is that words only really 'exist' when they are functioning in sentences: "It is only in the sentence that the word gets its real function of designation; outside it, it is just a propositional function, if it is not simply a rubric formed to group together absolutely separate meanings" (*EN*, 597). The illusion that words have a 'life of their own', a genuinely independent existence, arises from looking at language as something fixed and dead. When it is found that a word has changed its meaning in the course of time this is not normally the result of someone (or of many people) *deliberately* using it in a different way. For the user, the sentence which contained the different use seemed to express his meaning exactly *without* doing anything different to what was done by other people around him; he was not thinking of doing violence to the language. Only for the philologist looking back over a series of such events is there such a thing as a change of meaning; it is his activity which gives rise to the illusion that there *is* something that can be called the 'meaning' of a word.

For one of the troubles which arise from believing in the existence of 'meanings' of words is that it seems to make speaking or communicating into stringing together words to 'express thoughts'. Sartre is convinced that discourse is not a translation of anything lying behind it. His talk of language as a technique should not be taken to imply that words or sentences are used to do something. There are, of course, cases where a sentence is used, e.g. to show ability to speak a language, to impress by skill in handling learned words, but these are not instances of *saying* anything. For normally to utter a sentence is to say something, and this activity is different both from responding to a situation and from assembling words. The central problem of language is not meaning but assertion; any view which regards speaking as consisting of stringing together words in accordance with rules will fail to do justice to this fact. There are an indefinite number of appropriate statements that could be made about any situation; the one that is actually uttered depends on considerations which are both extra-linguistic and outside the situation itself. The rules of language do not determine any actual utterance by themselves or in conjunction with the situation. In this, speaking a language is unlike playing a game, in which the point is to do something in accordance with particular rules. The point of speaking is something which lies outside the rules of language.[1] For this reason Sartre talks of a statement as a *project*:"The statement is a project which can only be understood on the basis of the nihilation of something given (that which is to be *talked about*) on the basis of a proposed end (what *is said*, which itself presupposes other ends in relation to which it is only a means)" (*EN*, 598). To extend the example I have used earlier (pp. 37–8), a machine which responded to colours presented to it by producing a form of words which described the colour (enabled us to tell which it was), would not be saying anything, not be making a statement. This would be because it would have no purpose in 'saying' what it did. It is also true that it would be unable to 'nihilate' the situation, for there would be a causal chain leading from the presented colour to the word produced, it would not be a free agent, but here the further fact that it would gain nothing by producing the words is central. For a human being always has something to gain even from the most banal statements of everyday life. And in the case of most discourse there is not only a point to the actual statement, but this point is itself part of a wider 'project'. To put this in a different way, to the question "Why did you say that?" there is always an answer which is not just in terms of the existing state of affairs. To "Why did you say that it was raining?" we would normally expect something more than the reply "Because it *is* raining." It is not enough to utter true statements, there must also be a point in uttering them, and this point is bound up with the whole life of the person talking. For example, most of the statements we make about the weather are not for the purpose of

[1] On this point cf. G. C. J. Midgley, 'Linguistic Rules', *Proceedings of the Aristotelian Society* 1958–9, 271–90, and particularly 277.

conveying information about it to other people; nevertheless, they are not entirely pointless. In the joke, the escaped lunatic who remembered only that sane people always made true statements did not remain at liberty for very long.

From the collection of statements actually made by a group of people, linguists can extract a set of rules. "But these schemata which apply, for example, like the laws of a dialect, are in themselves abstract. Far from it being the case that they regulate the constitution of the sentence and are the mould into which it is poured, they only exist in and by that sentence. In this sense the sentence appears as the free invention of its rules" (*EN*, 600). We don't speak in accordance with rules, but that we speak in the way we do enables rules to be abstracted from our speech. It is worth adding that as far as one's native language is concerned, few rules were ever formally learned; learning to talk is mainly a matter of listening to others talking and copying them. There is a further important difference between learning to talk and learning to do most other things. For example, learning to swim is learning a particular technique for attaining a limited number of ends—such as crossing stretches of water—and that it facilitates this is the reason for learning the technique. But there isn't an end or even a set of ends for the sake of which we learn to talk. We don't learn to talk *for* any reason. Indeed, the having of reasons is largely subsequent to being able to talk. Hence if talking is to be called a technique at all, it is in a radically different sense from what is normally called a technique. The ability to make appropriate sounds or to apply rules may be thought of as a technique, but a child is only said to be able to talk when it can say things, when it "chooses something to say beyond [*au delà de*] syntax and morpheme" (*EN*, 602).

But, and Sartre does not deny this, unless what we say does fit in with the current rules, we shall not be understood. Hence it is the common language that we speak, not a personal one. Use may be made of a certain number of idiosyncrasies in speaking or writing, but if there are too many of them, there will be a failure of communication. This does not mean that freedom is limited by having to use the public language. For it is only if there is such a thing as a public language that the possibility of saying anything at all arises; its existence is a *condition* of this aspect of our freedom. Because what we say is not the result of the rules of that language, it appears to us as something which is operated quite freely, just as what we do is not given by our bodies, though the ways in which we can move are, in fact, restricted by the arrangements of bones and muscles. There is a feeling of restriction when expressing oneself in a foreign language, for here what we want to say is normally formulated in our native language and then translated into the other; we may find that we don't know the right words, or enough of them. It is in respect of our English vocabulary that the words of German available appear limited in number. Of course, our English vocabulary is, in an objective sense, likewise limited, but it does not *appear* as limited, for there is nothing 'lying behind' it that we want to express. To learn a new word is to be able to express oneself better, but this does not mean that there was previously something in the mind that could not be expressed for the want of a word. How could it have been known what it was? "No doubt a contemporary of Duns Scotus was ignorant of the use of the motor-car or aeroplane; but he only appears as ignorant from our own point of view, for we look upon him as deprived of something from the point of view of a world where the car and aeroplane exist. As he had no relation of any sort with these objects and the techniques involved in them, there is for him something like an absolute nothingness, unthinkable and undecipherable" (*EN*, 604). In an important sense language is given (appears to us) as *complete*; we are not, and could not be, aware of any gaps in it, except in the trivial sense of not knowing the name for a particular object. It is for this reason that Sartre talks of it as a "world", something without any gaps. It is gap-free in the same way that the field of perception is always full, without any gaps. For what can't be seen in the visual field is concealed by some other object which is itself a part of that field; there is no possibility of a gap in which nothing is seen.

For Sartre, as for the 'linguistic philosopher', the investigation of language is not something that requires to be done by detailed scientific enquiries. This is not to deny that legitimate investigations are undertaken by grammarians and philologists, but merely to claim that their conclusions are irrelevant to the problems that interest a philosopher. For the latter, Sartre's remark about feudalism is intended to apply to all such contexts: "It is not necessary to generalise from numerous detailed examples to establish the feudal technique; this technique exists necessarily and completely in each individual piece of behaviour and can be brought to light in each case" (*EN*, 606). Sartre might refer to this procedure as an "intuition of essences", but the method is basically that of any philosopher who attempts to establish his point by means of examples which illustrate it rather than by a statistical survey of evidence.

VIII

Freedom

I HAVE repeatedly emphasised how Sartre stresses man's freedom, and how his claim that man is free is involved in other of his doctrines. But these earlier mentions of freedom have been partial, in terms of some particular aspect of human existence, and in this respect do not constitute a solution to the complex problem of human freedom. Even though it has been established that human consciousness is outside the causal chain of the world of things, it by no means follows that man can act or refrain from acting in a moral sense. Part at least of the problem of freedom lies in the fact that there is a lack of clarity about the very claim that man is free. Hence the object of this chapter is to consider the matter from a different angle. Sartre is quoted as having said "If man is not free, then his liberation would not make sense."[1] By this slightly paradoxical remark he means that only in so far as human beings are 'at a distance' from the world is it possible to set out to liberate them from the chains that they have forged for themselves; if those chains were part of the nature of the universe, if men were part of the causal network, then no such project would be meaningful.

A comparison with Freud is here helpful. He, like Sartre, wishes to liberate mankind, though from a burden which is conceived in different terms. For Freud, the burden is that of the past, which weighs on all men, not only on the obviously neurotic. His efforts are directed to the uncovering and hence the sterilisation of those traumatic experiences of our childhood and youth which, from their hiding-place in the unconscious, return to plague us, and

[1] Quoted by Jeanson, *Le Problème moral etc.* 309–10.

which cause us to react in stereotyped ways laid down long ago to situations which require handling from an adult point of view. Although we are all to some extent haunted in this way, Freud is convinced that the degree of haunting can be reduced, that there is an ideal of rational action, behaviour objectively fitted to the situation, which can be approximated to by men. Psychoanalysis is a method for increasing our rational activity. Hence it may be said, contrary to what many followers and critics of Freud have claimed, that there is a rational ideal implicit in his work, and that it is this ideal which makes sense of that work. For unless it is possible to attain rationality in some degree, then there is no way of criticising or trying to cure a particular neurosis, no standard by which the cure may be judged. One philosopher has summed the matter up: "His [Freud's] whole method of treatment rests on an assertion that men can face and cope with their situation rationally, if only they are given the opportunity."[1] In this context coping with a situation rationally is very like being free in that situation; Freud's aim could also be expressed as 'freeing the individual from his complexes'.

Unfortunately the nature of the unconscious as conceived by Freud ensures that this rationality or freedom can never be total. A neurotic may be 'cured' in the sense that he is no longer affected by the obviously troublesome complexes, but it would seem that an interminable analysis would be required to ensure the removal of *all* complexes.[2] It is impossible, even if it were desirable, to remove the unconscious completely; hence it is always there, like a reservoir of infection awaiting the opportunity to fasten again on the victim. We are perpetually under this threat and so are only accidentally free. Even though an individual is satisfied that his last act was done freely, he can never be sure that his next one will be. But if freedom or rationality is made a matter of chance, it is really denied. The argument here is the same as that

---

[1] A. MacIntyre, *The Unconscious* (Routledge, 1958), 93.

[2] "Freud insisted that analysis was 'really interminable' no matter how regularly in practise analyses do come to an end." P. Rieff, *Freud, the Mind of a Moralist*, 333n.

often applied against those who would solve the problem of free will by invoking the principle of indeterminacy in physics. If it is only an accident that ensures that what is done now is not done as a result of the past, then it matters little that there was no determination.

Sartre naturally criticises Freud in so far as he implies that there are limits to man's freedom, though this criticism does not imply lack of respect for the achievement of the founder of psychoanalysis. Indeed, the fourth and final part of *L'Etre et le néant* may be seen as a long dialogue with Freud. The latter tries to explain why men are not always free; Sartre, as a result of the position he has already taken up, has to explain why it is that men deny that they are free in situations in which he claims that they are. In a world where men are all too ready, partly as a result of Freud's work, to plead that their actions were not their own responsibility, this is a difficult task. It is partly for this reason that Sartre is driven to exaggerate his position, to make everyone responsible for everything; he quotes with approval Jules Romain's phrase, "In war, there are no innocent victims", adding, to make the responsibility clearer, "You get the war you deserve" (*EN*, 641). If responsibility runs, as Sartre asserts, from the smallest incident in personal life to the widest happenings in the world, it is not surprising that "for the greatest part of the time we escape from the anguish into bad faith" (*EN*, 642). Clearly the word 'responsibility' is not being used in its normal sense; some of the victims of the last war did not 'deserve' their fate in any way. Nevertheless there can be a general feeling of guilt 'in the face of the world', and it is to this that Sartre is referring. (This point is discussed further below, p. 128 f.) I must again stress that Sartre still regards the issues here raised as non-moral, even though they may appear to be moral. At this stage Sartre thinks of a morality as something which provides a set of criteria or reasons for assessing choices and actions. Bad faith is not condemned *morally*, but rather because the effect of bad faith is to prevent the individual from choosing at all. Bad faith plays the same kind of role as does Freud's unconscious, in that it is something to be removed before there is any possibility of a genuine choice. There are grounds for saying that psycho-analysis is a pre-moral discipline; it renders morality possible without determining the nature of morality. An individual free from complexes and unconscious determination is in a position to choose, but what he should choose is not given by the system. Similarly, the final section of *L'Etre et le néant* removes, or is intended to remove, obstacles that men may put in the way of their own freedom, leaving open the question of what they should do with this freedom.

As I have mentioned, the thesis that Sartre is defending is that freedom is one and indivisible and is possessed by all men. Such a claim sounds paradoxical, a fact of which Sartre is well aware; it also would seem to involve some change in the ordinary meaning of the word 'freedom'. This point does not explicitly cause Sartre any difficulty; he seems to be aware that he is *extending* the mean-ing, but not that such a procedure needs to be justified closely. As so often, it is advisable to see what he does with the notion and then to decide whether the procedure is legitimate. To talk of a man (or all men) as free is, Sartre says, dangerous, for it leads us to think of men as possessing a *property* of freedom (*EN*, 513–14). But freedom is no more a property in the normal sense than nothing is a thing; to talk of someone as free is only to say that nothing determines his actions. And this for Sartre is only an extension of the notion that there is 'nothing' at the heart of human existence. If we are to make use of the notion of an 'action', determinism must be eschewed, as in the case of 'assertion' and the other things already discussed. But in order to see what is involved in the claim about freedom, it is necessary to look at what have traditionally been regarded as the major obstacles to freedom; these can be divided into two main classes. First, those which involve what were traditionally called the 'passions', emotions and desires or other internal pulls and pushes; and second, the outside world, what Sartre has called the individual's 'situation'.

Put very crudely the traditional view about the passions can be stated as follows: there are various motives[1] which incline men to act in various ways (reason may or may not be included among them), and, after some process of selection amongst them, one finally gives rise to an action. The trouble with such a way of looking at the mind (or the man) is that it makes it into an object which is swayed by arbitrary forces; one thinks of Descartes' pineal gland pushed now one way, now the other, by different streams of animal spirits. In Sartre's words, to talk of the mind in such a way comes down to "treating motives [*les mobiles et les motifs*] as if they were things" (*EN*, 515). In the case of emotions this way of thinking of them makes them into 'psychic forces', the mental analogue of physical forces. The whole argument of Sartre's early *Esquisse d'une théorie des émotions* was directed to showing that emotions are not arbitrary psychic happenings but rather particular ways of dealing with the world, though less satisfactory ones than ordinary rational procedures. The violent emotions are 'magical' attempts to attain a goal when rational means have failed. For example, a man faced with a great danger and having no escape open to him may faint in order to "make the danger vanish". Milder emotions may cause us to project qualities on to the world instead of admitting that they are due to our attitudes; a man may say "I am angry *because* he is hateful" when

[1] Throughout this section Sartre makes use of the distinction in French between *motif* and *mobile*, which is hard to render exactly into English. *Mobile* means the same as the English *motive* used to refer to something internal to the agent, as in the following passage: "And, at the same time, I can have motives (*mobiles*): feeling of pity for certain classes of oppressed people, shame at being on the 'right side of the barricades' as Gide says, or again an inferiority complex, a desire to scandalize my neighbours etc." (*EN*, 523). As Miss Barnes rightly says (435), "For *motif* there is no true equivalent". She translates it by "cause". This will not do, as may be seen from the earlier part of the above quotation: "For example, I can join the Socialist Party because I believe that it serves the interest of justice and humanity, or because I believe that it will become the principal historic force in the years following my joining; these are *motifs*." I think we too would talk of these as *motives* in English, though "reasons" would also do. When the detective asks "Who had a motive?" he is asking both for those who disliked the victim and for those who had something to gain by the murder. I have rendered both *motif* and *mobile* by the English *motive*; the context will generally show which French term was used.

the true state of affairs would be represented by "I find him hateful *because* I am angry" (*Esquisse*, 49).

Sartre wishes to argue that in all cases of emotion we have *chosen* to react in these ways; we have not been compelled, though, of course, he agrees that if a man has always reacted in a certain way the habits he has set up are hard to change. But they are hard to change, not impossible to change. 'Chosen' seems an odd description, and the full justification of its use will only be seen after I have discussed 'fundamental choice' below. The claim is that what is apprehended as, e.g., frightening depends on a set of attitudes and these are, in the last resort, under our control. For fear is always intentional, fear *of* something, and hence cannot be explained merely by the release of additional adrenalin into the blood-stream. There must always be a reason or motive for this release, and the bare external stimulus is not enough. The frightening object has got to be apprehended as actually threatening, and this involves an assessment of the total situation. A tiger encountered in the wild is frightening, one seen in the zoo behind bars is not. The fear is not the result of a bare stimulus but of a set of attitudes. Further, the reaction to the whole situation may be rational or irrational. (This is not to deny that there may exist situations in which no rational behaviour is possible, e.g. the imminent explosion of an atomic bomb a hundred yards away.) But this reaction is not forced on us either by the situation or by the state of the body. There are no passions which exist in their own right and which serve as motives for our actions.

As regards motives in the second sense (*motifs*), the situation is different, for they are objective facts, those things in the external world which we cite as reasons for our actions. But nothing in the external world constitutes in itself a reason: "In a word, the world only advises us if we ask it questions, and we cannot ask it questions except on the basis of a pre-determined aim. Far from the motive determining the action, it only comes to light in and through the project of an action" (*EN*, 524). In both cases, then, our motivation depends on our aims and not the other way about; we do not first select a motive and on that basis an aim.

Our intentions are the vital factor in both kinds of motives, and it is in the light of these intentions that the world, or our own constitutions, appear to have qualities which push in a particular direction. There is naturally a constant interplay between the two sorts of motives; a *mobile* may be only a particular way of grasping a *motif*. Deliberation, a weighing up of different motives, does not exist; what appears to be deliberation is "always fixed". "When I deliberate, the chips are down [*Quand je délibère, les jeux sont faits*]" (*EN*, 527). Again, "When the will intervenes, the decision is taken and its only real function is that of making the announcement." The ordinary picture of deliberation will not do, for there are no pre-existing objective things among which we choose; in selecting something to count as a motive, we have already decided what to do. There is no real room for deliberation. A development of an earlier example will make Sartre's meaning clearer. A walker's tiredness manifests itself as much in the way in which he looks at the road ahead of him as in his bodily feelings; the thought that it is 'too far to go without a rest' is his tiredness. And if he 'decides' to stop immediately, it is not a decision in the normal sense, formed by weighing the physical tiredness against the desirability of going farther before stopping, but a particular way of experiencing the tiredness. It is considered as 'too great to be overcome'. Another man, who has a different attitude to his body and to the world, may well carry on. (I am assuming that the walker is not so physically tired that his body is incapable of moving another step, and would like to add that this is a rare state. Even though a person may claim that he cannot go on, a greater inducement may well enable him to.) The walker may feel that he has thought the matter out, but he has not really done so.

Ultimately, motives, intentions and actions are not three separate things, but form an "indissoluble unity" (*EN*, 527). It is the possibility that language gives of separating the three that leads us to think that there is a process of deliberation. "It is no more possible to separate the intention from the action than thought from the language that expresses it and, as it often happens that our speech reveals our thought to us, so our actions reveal our intentions, that is to say they allow us to separate intentions, to schematise them, to make them into objects instead of limiting us to living them" (*EN*, 564). In this sense, Sartre approves of the programme of behaviourism (*EN*, 556). The unity of these things is dependent on what Sartre calls the "fundamental project" or "original choice" of a person. This, in so far as Sartre would allow the term, constitutes the 'essence' of the person; it is fundamental in the sense that it does not concern his "relations with such and such a particular object in the world" but rather his "being-in-the-world in its entirety" (*EN*, 559). By talking of a single fundamental project or original choice, Sartre wishes to stress that a person is a unity, possessing a certain "style" or manner of living which can be detected in every one of his actions, even the most trivial; everything that a man does is revealing (*EN*, 656). This original choice can be discovered by a type of investigation which Sartre calls "Existential psychoanalysis"; this is 'existential' because it deals with the way that the person has of living his life, 'psychoanalysis' because of its similarities with the procedures of Freud. He has given detailed examples of this technique in his books *Baudelaire* and *Saint Genet*, in his study of Tintoretto[1], and in his scattered remarks on Flaubert in *Critique de la raison dialectique*.[2] The essential difference between Freud and Sartre here is that the latter does not think of the analysis as being curative, as getting rid of the cause of the trouble, but rather as revealing a man's original choice so that he is in a position to change it. There has grown up in Switzerland and America a school of 'existential analysts' who combine the curative aims of Freud with techniques which grow out of existentialism, though the similarity with Sartre depends more upon the influence of Heidegger on him and them than upon any reliance on *L'Etre et le néant*. Nevertheless some of the members of the school do refer to and praise that work. This difference between Sartre and orthodox analysis is best shown by noting

[1] *Temps modernes* XIII (1957), 761–800. Reprinted in *Situations IV*.
[2] Sartre has recently said that he is writing a book on Flaubert.

that the original choice is a single act which is responsible for the whole style of life of the person, as can be seen in this remark: "Here we touch the original choice which Baudelaire made of himself, this absolute commitment by which each of us decides in a particular situation what he will be and what he is" (B, 20). This choice is often made during childhood or youth; Baudelaire is represented as having made it at the time of his mother's re-marriage when he was seven years old. Similarly Genet's choice of himself as a thief took place during his childhood, but presumably he has since made another as a result of that long coming to terms with himself which is analysed, albeit confusedly, in *Saint Genet*. Sartre's emphasis on the importance of this basic choice enables him to say that we are responsible for our lives; he asks of Baude-laire "And if he deserved his life? If, contrary to what is normally thought, men only get the lives they deserve?" (B, 18).

If all motives and intentions refer back to the fundamental pro-ject it would seem that little remains of the freedom Sartre has been emphasising, particularly if the time of the choice is child-hood; it is hard to see how an infant can be aware of what he is doing, and, if he is not, then it is odd to call him responsible. The original choice would thus appear to be only an eccentric name for the Freudian complex. The fundamental project or original choice might just as well be relegated to the unconscious. Sartre will not allow the existence of a genuine unconscious, however, for a really unconscious idea could never be recognised as 'belong-ing to' its owner. Even in the course of psychoanalysis the patient is brought to *admit* his unconscious intentions or motives. The therapeutic technique is radically different from that of an ordinary doctor. He tells the patient that he has a certain disease, and the latter believes him because of the doctor's superior knowledge. If the patient wishes to confirm the validity of the diagnosis, he has to proceed in the same way as the doctor did. But for the patient to be cured there is no need for him to know anything about his disease. The analyst not only has to tell the patient what his trouble is, but also get him to recognise or admit it. If patients could be cured merely by telling them their troubles, then the curative process would be much simpler, and self-analysis would be perfectly possible. But because recognition, and recognition against resistance, is involved, a long process of analysis is needed. For Sartre the important point about this procedure is that it involves the admission that the patient is in some sense conscious of the trouble; it is not just the result of a past happening (*EN*, 661–2 and 537).

An inferiority complex is the way a person has of living his life, of experiencing his relation to others (*EN*, 537). The actions that lead us to judge he has such a complex are not caused by it, but rather are *manifestations* of it. For an action can only be understood as having a particular aim and as being a part of a series of wider or more general aims. The question "Why did he do that?" may refer to a bodily movement whose part in an action was not clear, or to an action whose part in the whole scheme of life was not obvious. To think of the general aim or intention as the *cause* of the action is to be confused, for it is only in so far as the intention is still adhered to that the action is performed; the particular action is a reaffirmation of the intention, a manifestation of it. A man cannot bind himself by a decision, though he may reaffirm it by his actions. It is in this sense that the original choice is free; it does not cause the future behaviour. If we consider only a particular choice, e.g. that of being a student and working for a degree, this analysis is plausible. The student still has the opportunity, at each stage of the course, of revising his original decision, of deciding that the degree is not worth the effort, or, more commonly, of acting as if this were his new choice. What seems less plausible is Sartre's claim that by some sort of regressive analysis it is possible to get back to a single original choice or fundamental project. It even seems questionable whether one can talk of such a thing as a 'choice' at all. There is no doubt that this is what he does mean: "Thus the fundamental act of freedom is discovered; and it is this which gives its meaning to any particular action which I may consider. This constantly renewed act is indistinguishable from my being; it is choice of myself in the world and at the same time discovery of the world" (*EN*, 539).

It is arguable that to talk of anybody as a *person* is to assert that he is a unity of some sort. I am not referring to his 'character', because this term is misleading; it is generally conceived in terms of a small number of possible variations on certain themes. It is hard to think of a person's character except in terms of what can be put in a testimonial. The unity which Sartre is considering is at a deeper level than that of the superficial judgments of everyday life. A very odd situation would exist if a person's actions and intentions did not, as a whole, fit together. It is worth remembering that the claim of psychoanalysis was that in some sense even actions that apparently did not fit in could be seen to do so as a result of deeper investigation; Sartre is making a similar claim. Ultimately the test of his view will be the actual analyses: "The criterion of its success will be the number of facts which the hypothesis explains and unifies . . ." (*EN*, 663). The attempts he has made in the works mentioned above seem to go some way to establishing his claim, though unfortunately it would take too much room to reproduce them here; as in orthodox psychoanalysis it is very detailed work that is required. Sartre is not thinking of an abstract method of classification of character-types under a limited number of headings, but of something which is unique to each individual, and which that individual would admit was a true account. The aim of existential psychoanalysis is to give an account of the very being of the individual, and this can only be done by an exhaustive examination. The reason why most of his examples have been writers is that in these cases their publications provide sufficient material on which to work, or, as in the case of Tintoretto, his style of life is manifested in his paintings and in the stories of his contemporaries about him.

I must stress again that this fundamental project is something which exists only as manifested in particular actions and that each act is a renewed choice of the project. This is not to deny that it can be changed, for "radical conversion" is always possible, though rare. (Sartre talks in terms of a *radical* conversion because he regards most conversions as taking place at a superficial level.) He describes radical conversion in these terms: "These extraordinary and marvellous instants, where the previous project disappears into the past in the light of a new project which rises on its ruins and which is as yet only a sketch, where humiliation, anguish, joy and hope are blended, where we let go in order to seize and seize in order to let go . . ." (*EN*, 555). It is only a sketch because until it is completed by actions it does not fully exist. Sartre instances Raskolnikoff's decision to denounce himself, but a better example might be St Augustine's conversion. When such a conversion is genuine it involves a new way of looking at the world, a new set of intentions and values, and hence it cannot be explained in the light of previous behaviour. To *become* a Christian (or perhaps a Marxist) is to see the whole of one's life up to that instant as in some way wrong, based on false premises. Hence such conversions "have often appeared to furnish the clearest and most moving image of our freedom. But they are only one manifestation among others" (*EN*, 555). For if a person is free in changing his project, then he must also be free in maintaining it. Freedom is indivisible. There are neither privileged instants nor privileged actions; if a man is free when he enters the Church or the Party, then he is free all the time he remains in either.

But if this choice is fundamental, then there can be no reasons for it, for "in fact it is this which creates originally all the reasons and all the motives that can lead to particular actions, it is this which gives the world its meanings, its instrumental complexes and its coefficients of adversity" (*EN*, 543). It is only in terms of what he is that a man has reasons or motives, and what he is is not something given but chosen. But, as I asked on p. 122 above, in what sense can this be a choice and what are the alternatives? There is no possibility of not having made such a choice, for to exist is to exist with a fundamental project. There is no other way for a being with nothing at its core to exist. Normally we think of a choice as something which is made between alternatives presented to us in some way, and for which there is a method of selection. For even the toss of a coin is a *method* of choosing where others give no guidance. Normally the method is that of consulting our interests, intentions and so on. Where these no longer apply, there is the limit of choice, at least in the normal meaning of the word. Further, there would appear to be a difference between those who have undergone radical conversion and the rest; for the former there would seem to have been a moment at least when the choice was in some form present to their mind. For most of us, this choice was something which just happened. Though it may be permissible to push the origin of complexes back to the days of early childhood, or even to the trauma of birth itself, it would be odd to talk of a 'choice' at these times. Sartre's argument could be summarised in the following way. First, man is free, otherwise there would be no possibility of a radical conversion (this, of course in addition to the other arguments for freedom that he has put forward). Second, there is a uniform style in all an individual's actions (discoverable by existential psychoanalysis). Third, in a radical conversion he can choose a new style, a new fundamental project. Therefore he must be free in maintaining that fundamental project which he now has or is. Freedom implies responsibility, therefore he is responsible. Therefore he can be said to have chosen.

It is in connection with Sartre's discussion of radical conversion that the charge of anti-rationalism is often made, for, as I have shown, there are no reasons or motives for a fundamental project. From Sartre's point of view there could not be any such; the choice of a project is at the same time a choice of what is to count as a reason. Most philosophers would agree that the chain of reasons must stop somewhere, and where it stops choice cannot be rational. But this does not mean that it must be irrational, but only non-rational or perhaps pre-rational. If a man is continually asked "Why?" there must come a time when all he can reply is "I just want to, or like to, that's all there is to it." It is at this point that we might be tempted to talk in terms of motives or causes for the choice. Can a fundamental project have motives? In the sense of *motifs* clearly not, for it is only in the context of a project that they would be, or be seen as, motives. The case of *mobiles* is more difficult, for we tend to think of certain choices as 'within the range of possibilities' for a certain person; for example there may be one man whose conversion to Catholicism is seen as possible, though unlikely, though for another this may seem quite impossible. But, Sartre would argue, this is already to refer to their fundamental choices. Seen from the outside, these might well appear as 'character', the lines along which a man would naturally move. However, his mind isn't compelled to move in those directions; having made the choice, this is the direction in which he wants to move. Here there is only an appearance of circularity. From within Sartre's system there is none, and this is the point of view from which to examine the question. Ultimately any philosophical system must be judged from the inside at least to some extent. Sartre remarks that he was taught the refutation of Marxism as a philosophic doctrine, but those who instructed him in these philosophic moves left it quite unclear why anybody should ever become a Marxist (*CRD*, 22–23). For the reasons which those outside the system give to refute it may not be reasons for those inside. It is no good telling a rigid determinist that there is an experience of freedom; for him that experience is an illusion. Similarly, having made a new original choice, it may well appear to the maker to be the only possible one; to the new Catholic convert, the reasons he used to accept against God's existence are no longer reasons. Indeed, it is only when a change of this sort occurs that it is possible to talk of a radical conversion. Nevertheless, Sartre does not believe that nothing can be done to change people's projects; there is that 'purifying reflection' mentioned in the last section of *L'Etre et le néant*. By this I think Sartre is referring to existential psycho-analysis used as a method of uncovering one's own original choice and hence as a preliminary to changing it. This is not a rational procedure, any more than convincing somebody that this is a good work of art is a rational procedure; neither, however, is it irrational.

I think it is fair to say that Sartre is pushing the meaning of the word 'choice' to its very limit in this argument, but if it is realised that this is what he is doing, then some of the objection to his talking in terms of an original choice will be dissipated. Every action is not only a manifestation of this choice, but a reaffirmation of it. In acting, a man chooses himself. It is at this point that the meaning of the popular existentialist catch-phrase "Existence is prior to essence" can be seen. But, for Sartre, essence is only the original choice. Men do not only choose themselves in acting, they have to do so; in a sense rather different from Rousseau's, they are *forced to be free*. Every living being has to choose, and even suicide is a choice (*EN*, 559, 565). Hence there arises at a deeper level that anguish which is experience of our freedom. The examples of anguish that have been discussed above are as it were images of real anguish. This comes from the fact that choice is "fragile" (*EN*, 543), that there is no guarantee that it will be maintained, that choice is "unjustifiable" (*EN*, 542) or "absurd" (*EN*, 558–9), that there are no reasons outside the choice by which it can be justified. "But, as I remarked at the beginning of this work, for the greater part of the time, we take refuge from anguish in bad faith" (*EN*, 642). Sartre is not here advocating a morbid attitude; those who think of the attitude as morbid are precisely the 'salauds' attacked in *La Nausée* and elsewhere. The anguish he refers to is the recognition of the nature of original choice which, because it is by its very nature unjustifiable, is bound to bring doubts about its rightness to those who are aware of its nature. A man who is serenely confident of himself and who has never had any self-questionings is lacking in an important respect. A feeling of anguish is, in this sense, the only way of taking ourselves seriously as human beings. It is interesting to compare Sartrean anguish with what the Existential Analysts call 'ontological guilt': "*Second*, ontological guilt does not come from cultural prohibitions, or from the introjection of cultural mores; it is rooted in the fact of self-awareness. Ontological guilt does not consist of I-am-guilty-because-I-violate-parental-prohibitions, but arises from the fact that I can see myself as the one who can choose or fail to choose. Every developed human being would have this ontological guilt, though its *content* would vary from culture to culture and would largely be given by the culture. *Third*, ontological guilt must not be confused with morbid or neurotic guilt.

If it is unaccepted or repressed, it may turn into neurotic guilt. . . . If the person can become aware of it and accept it, it is not morbid or neurotic. *Fourth*, ontological guilt does not lead to symptom formation, but has constructive effects in the personality. Specifically it can, and should, lead to humility . . ., to sharpened sensitivity in relationships with fellow men, and increased creativity in the use of one's own potentialities."[1] The admission and recognition of this anguish is an essential preliminary to morality.

In the passage quoted above Sartre talked of the project as "choice of myself in the world and at the same time discovery of the world".[2] But the individual did not make the world, neither is it entirely under his control what the world makes of him. He exists for other people, as ugly, unreliable, clever, a Jew and so on. He is situated in the world; there is both freedom and facticity. Finally, there is the fact of death, which appears to "take away all meaning from life" (*EN*, 623), for if the individual is likely to die at any moment, there can be no point in any project. I have indicated the type of solution that Sartre gives to this problem in the last chapter; here I will develop it further, first by giving a long quotation. "Thus it must be said that the facticity of my place is only revealed to me in and through the free choice which I make of an end. Freedom is indispensable to the discovery of my facticity. I apprehend this facticity from all factors in the future which I 'project', and it is on the basis of this chosen future that my facticity appears with its character of impotence, of contingency, of feebleness, of absurdity. It is in relation to my dream of seeing New York that it is absurd and painful that I live at Mont-de-Marsan. But reciprocally, facticity is the only reality which freedom can discover, the only thing which it can nihilate by proposing an aim, the only thing on the basis of which it makes sense to propose an end. For if the aim can throw light on the situation, it is because it is a projected modification *of* this situation. . . . Thus *freedom is apprehension of my facticity*. It would be ridiculous to try and define the *quid* of this facticity 'before' freedom turns its light on it to

[1] *Existence*, 55.   [2] See above, p. 123.

grasp it as a determinate lack. My place, before freedom has circumscribed my being in a place as a certain kind of lack, 'is not' properly speaking, anything at all " (EN, 574–5). To use the example Sartre constantly employs, the mountain exists, but it is only in so far as someone contemplates an ascent that it is hard to climb. A landscape looks quite different to different people, e.g. to a farmer, a speculative builder, a painter or a military commander. Choice and situation are two sides of the same coin.

There are, however, those things which Sartre calls "unrealisables", among them the qualities that others see in us. "For myself, I am no more a professor or a waiter than I am beautiful or ugly, Jew or Aryan, witty, vulgar or distinguished" (EN, 610). These are terms that others apply to us. It is certainly true that anybody hearing his 'character' described feels somehow that the terms don't touch him. He is said to be lazy, but laziness is not something that he feels; he can admit that he stays in bed late, puts off answering letters, etc., but there are always reasons for behaving like this—there is nothing important to be done, letters not answered immediately often don't need answering. And in any case, if he wanted to, he could easily act differently. Being ugly or a Jew is in a different category, for these cannot be changed, whereas traits of character can be. (The problem of Jewishness is one which preoccupies Sartre; he constantly refers to it and to anti-semitism in his writings and in 1954 devoted a book to it, entitled *Réflexions sur la question juive*.) Jewishness might be said to constitute a crucial issue for the theory; if it can be reconciled with freedom, then the theory is safe from any attack. In one sense, Sartre argues that the case is not absolutely different from the one just mentioned; being a Jew is something abstract: "A Jew is not *first of all* a Jew and *as a result* of it proud or ashamed; it is his pride or his indifference or his shame which reveal his Jewishness, and this being a Jew is nothing other than the free way of assuming it" (EN, 612).

But in spite of this, he *is* a Jew, this is something given by his birth and no alteration in himself, no radical conversion, will make any difference to the facts. He may accept it with pride, accentuate his Jewishness, but this is very different from our relation to the mountain which becomes hard to climb because of our intention to climb it. We can ignore the mountain, so that it hardly exists for us; in society as it exists, and still more society at the time when Sartre was writing, there is no such escape for the Jew. Thus Sartre's counsel to the Jew, "Accept your Jewish nature with pride" would seem to be more analogous to a piece of Couéism: "Repeat every day 'I'm proud to be a Jew' and then you won't mind about being one." This attitude is shown in an extreme form by his remarks on colour: "Now there is no way of escape, no possibility of deceit, no 'crossing the line' which he can imagine; a Jew, a white among the whites, can deny that he is a Jew, declare that he is only a man among men. The Negro cannot deny that he is one nor demand for himself this abstract colourless humanity; he is black. Thus he is compelled to be authentic; insulted, enslaved, he stands up, he picks up the word 'Negro' that has been thrown at him like a stone, in the face of the white man he claims with pride to be black" (*S.III*, 237). This can be only described as romantic nonsense; Sartre is perilously near to talking in terms of 'accepting the universe' as the true meaning of freedom. He tries to guard against this interpretation: "For to be free is not to choose the particular historic world into which one is born—that would be meaningless—but to choose oneself in the world, whatever it may be" (*EN*, 604).

Part of the trouble here is that the precise difficulty with which we are faced is not clear; it is important to see exactly what Sartre means. The temptation is to say that the Jew is less free in that he is a Jew. Politically speaking, and particularly in France under the German occupation, this was true. Jews were barred from certain places, they were especially liable to arrest and ill-treatment; even in a more liberal society there may still exist barriers which Jews cannot cross. But here we are in the realms of political liberty, where comparisons make sense. It appears legitimate to say that we are more free in this country in 1964 than we were in 1944; at that time numerous things were forbidden which can now be done at will. But at the level at which Sartre is talking no such comparison is possible. It seems possible, because the Jew can imagine himself not having been born a Jew. But what is he imagining? That *he* was another person? It is hard to make concrete sense of this; it remains on an abstract level. If the Jew were another person, he would still be in a situation in which the opportunities might be different, but in which there would be no more of them. "Every man realises but one situation, *his own*" (*EN*, 635). And if he thinks he can imagine another, he is mistaken. Hence there are no 'degrees of freedom': "When I say that the slave is as free in his chains as his master, I am not talking of a freedom which is indeterminate. The slave in chains is free *to break them*; that means that the very meaning of his chains appears in the light of the end which he has to choose; remain a slave or risk worse to escape from servitude. Doubtless the slave could not get the riches and standard of living of his master, but these also could not possibly be the object of his *projects*. He could only dream of these treasures. His *facticity* is such that the world appears to him with another face, and he has to pose and resolve other problems; in particular he must choose himself fundamentally on the level of *slavery*, and, by that, give a meaning to that obscure constraint. If, for example, he chooses to revolt, his slavery, far from being *first of all* an obstacle to that revolt, only gains its sense and its coefficient of adversity by it. Precisely because the life of a slave who revolts and dies in the course of the revolt is a free life, precisely because the situation illumined by a free project is full and concrete, precisely because the urgent and chief problem of that life is 'Shall I attain my goal?'—precisely for all these reasons, the situation of a slave cannot be *compared* with that of his master" (*EN*, 634–5).

Sartre is saying that every man lives in a full and concrete world, every man is faced with the same question of whether he will attain his goal, whatever it may be, and thus every man is as free as every other, even though his starting-point, his problems and his goal may be different. It is only because we think that we can compare our situation with that of another person that we have the illusion of being less free than he is. Indeed, it only makes sense to talk of a situation or of facticity on the basis of freedom. A man who was the product of his situation would not really be *situated* at all. It is true, Sartre says, that we talk of the situation of a town or of a house, but this is only because we are thinking of it as a place where someone lives; we are implicitly referring to human intentions and choices. The situation of an individual is his finitude, the starting-point, and the only possible one, for any free action. Thus man is the *"being who is always beyond his being-there"* (*par delà son être-là, EN*, 634). Even that most arbitrary of all aspects of life, birth itself, is something which the individual chooses, in the sense that this does not limit his metaphysical freedom. Everyone who exists has to have been born, and this implies born of particular parents at a particular time and place. Birth is not a limitation, but, like the other aspects of the situation, a condition of freedom. The anguish discussed above can be seen as the reaction to the fact that the individual is thrown into the world and yet has to assume responsibility for being there. It is no defence to say that his situation was 'given', for there could not be a situation which was not given. But in order to make his life an authentic one, he must see that however it is lived it has been chosen. Bad faith is the denial of this fact. Sartre's argument here is complex, and seems to involve, as I have already suggested, changing the meaning of the key terms involved. He would claim that this change of meaning brought out the only useful sense that can be given to them. I think that there is something to be said on both sides here; Sartre is making a point which needs making, though it may well be that it ought not to be expressed in terms of 'freedom'. The difficulty is to know what other word could be used to express what he wants to say. Hence we must accept provisionally the claim that the individual is free in spite of being situated, or perhaps because he is situated.

The one apparent exception to this is death, which can occur at any time. At death, the individual's life can be summed up, fixed and described; there are no more possibilities. So much is true for the Christian as well, for the basis of the Last Judgment is life as it has actually been lived, not as it would have been if it had gone on for another year, or even another minute. But if we accept this view, it would seem that life becomes meaningless, for death has no relation to the plans and intentions of life. Indeed, if God selects the moment of death, then the individual is not really free, for it is He who decides the meaning of life by selecting this moment rather than any other (*EN*, 622–3). But death is not a *part* of the individual's life, of his situation, except in very special circumstances, such as a death sentence that he knows will be carried out. Even here there are possibilities, the destruction of the prison by a war or an earthquake, a change of government. The prisoner can still hope. It may be necessary to realise that one is mortal, but this is not the same as realising that one is going to die at a particular moment named in advance. Fortunately such situations are rare. Sartre pours scorn on Heidegger's suggestion that death is the only event where no man can substitute for another. In this sense, no one can do anything for another; no one can love this woman for me; someone else may love her better, or equally, but that will not be my love (*EN*, 618). Death is not something which individuates more than other activities. Death is, in fact, outside of our life, a genuine "unrealisable": "We can thus neither think of death nor wait for it nor arm ourselves against it. But our projects are also, in so far as they are projects—not as the result of our blindness, as the Christian says, but in principle—independent of it" (*EN*, 632–3). He adds that there is no point in classifying the moral values of different attitudes to death, since we all die in any case. But from the fact that we all die nothing of importance follows, though from the fact that we are mortal, have not an infinite time at our disposal, there do follow certain counsels that hardly need mentioning. There is nothing morbid about Sartre's attitude to death.

It may even be that mortality is a condition of human freedom. This is not the same as saying that *finitude* is a condition of it, which Sartre has already said, for he distinguishes between finitude and mortality (*EN*, 631). There could be a finite but immortal being, but the nature of his life would be very different from ours. He would still have to choose between alternatives at any time, but his choice would be radically different in that for most things such a choice would merely involve the postponement of the rejected courses of action, not their total abandonment. The anguish of choice would disappear, together with any commitment to the choice. For a change of mind would always be possible, so no real sacrifice would have been made. At present, if a man chooses an important element in his life, such as a career or a wife, he is committed to it; that is what is meant by saying that he has chosen it. He can later change either of these, but only at a certain cost to himself. It is facts like these which give poignancy to our lives. Without this, though it would still be correct to talk of the being as free, it would be a very different kind of freedom from that which human beings possess, a freedom without tears. This is the theme of Simone de Beauvoir's novel *Tous les hommes sont mortels*. Ultimately the existence of such a permanently open horizon would make life not worth living, would devalue it. Man cannot avoid anguish and still live a human life.

The penultimate section of *L'Etre et le néant* concludes with the notorious sentence "Man is a useless passion" (*L'homme est une passion inutile*, EN, 708). The context unfortunately prevents the removal of the sting of this phrase by adroit linguistic analysis on the lines of "To whom or to what could man be useful?" For Sartre is talking of the vanity of the project of becoming an *en-soi-pour-soi*, an in-itself-for-itself, a being that would be both conscious and an object, the foundation of its own being, an *ens causa sui* or God. "Thus it can be said that the best statement of the fundamental project of human reality is that being which aims to become God" (*EN*, 653). But the statement in the body of the text is more closely qualified than the one which concludes the chapter; Sartre has been, I think, carried away by the desire to end on a startling note. For there is for him no desire to *be* in the abstract; all desires are for particular ends. Indeed, there would be no point in doing existential psychoanalysis if the investigation were always to conclude in the discovery of one universal project to be God. "If the *meaning* [*sens*] of desire is in the last resort the project to become God, desire is never *constituted* by this meaning . . ."

(*EN*, 654). The ideal of being an *en-soi-pour-soi* is one which haunts us; bad faith is not an arbitrary temptation. It might even be considered the driving force of all activity, like the Freudian 'id'. The impossible attempt to coincide with oneself, to stop up the gap of nothingness, would appear natural for a being who is what it is not and is not what it is. In this sense man is a futile passion, for that end can never be achieved. But the cash value of this statement in its full context is that no human being is ever going to reach a state where he is satisfied, has no further desires; particular aims may be satisfied, we shall never reach final satisfaction. Man is condemned not only to be free but also perpetually to make use of his freedom.

IX

Ethics I

THE CONCLUDING pages of *L'Etre et le néant* are entitled 'Moral Perspectives', and the final sentence runs: "All these questions, which refer to pure and not to accessory reflection, can only be answered on a moral plane. I shall devote a future work to them" (*EN*, 722). In fact, no work explicitly on morality has come from Sartre's pen, unless we take the unfortunate lecture of 1946 to be such; it was published under the title of *L'Existentialisme est un humanisme*. This appears to be one of the most widely read of Sartre's philosophical works, at least in this country, and consequently most discussions of his ethics take it as a starting-point, if not as his last word on the subject. If a writer wishes to refer to "existentialist morality" it is to the doctrine set forth there that he directs his attention. As a result, English philosophers have found little difficulty in rejecting Sartre's views and in doubting his philosophic ability. For, as he himself has admitted, the lecture was probably a "mistake".[1] It is not very hard to realise that the arguments in the lecture are comparatively superficial and often inconsistent with the views put forward in *L'Etre et le néant* itself. But consideration of the context will reveal the source of these faults. It was intended as a lecture to the general public on existentialism, not as a statement of Sartre's views. Further, he is a good lecturer, in the sense that he is often influenced by the character of his audience, which may lead him to depart from his written script to make more impact. At the time it was delivered, Sartre was at the peak of his general popularity, and the audience gathered had come to attend a

[1] Jeanson, *Le Problème moral etc.* 46.

fashionable literary event rather than a serious philosophic lecture. One commentator has expressed the character of the audience in the following way: "An indication of the level of understanding to which Sartre was addressing himself is the reported fact that the opening reference to existentialism as a humanism provoked fainting among the audience."[1] Whatever provoked this reaction, I shall not, in what follows, rely on the lecture for material for this chapter.

I have already pointed out that ethical concerns are never far from Sartre's mind; hence his failure to produce a book specifically on ethics must spring from causes other than a simple lack of interest. The purpose of this chapter and the next is to show both what Sartre has to say about the subject and to account for his not writing a book on it. One reason might be suggested, namely that he finds it impossible to write on the topic. After criticising some ethical doctrines, he remarks: "I do not present these contradictions to condemn Christian morality: I am too deeply convinced that morality *as such* is both impossible and necessary" (*StG*, 211). This is typical of many of his statements about ethics; as so often the Cartesian temper leads him to adopt what might be called a 'tragic' view of the situation, seeing it entirely in black and white instead of a series of greys. The reader of this chapter will often, I think, feel inclined to comment on the quotations that I give that things are not as bad as all that; morality may be difficult, but there is a world of difference between admitting this and calling it impossible. Sartre exaggerates constantly, but I shall argue that he is not in the last resort a pessimist, though at times he may seem to be, and that he does not present a genuinely tragic view of life. He does offer a hope of rational moral activity, even though it be hard to attain, and of some sort of happiness for man. At all times he is far from the attitude of Camus, who regards the universe as absurd and the only possible human response to it a proud but doomed defiance. Sartre's Marxism is proof of his optimism, in spite of the degree

[1] N. N. Greene, *Jean-Paul Sartre: the Existentialist Ethic* (Ann Arbor, Mich., 1960), 13.

to which it admits violence. I suspect that some English critics, living in an atmosphere of political compromise, have forgotten that political action may involve violence and death. It would be harder for a Frenchman who has lived through the period 1939 to the present day to do so. Much of what an Englishman might see as gratuitously tragic may only be a just appreciation of a situation where irreconcileable parties confront each other with no possibility of compromise; it is worth remembering that it is not long since the O.A.S. made several attempts on Sartre's life. It has been said that real tragedy is impossible on a Christian view of life, and it seems to me that the same is true of a Marxist view.

Part at least of Sartre's exaggeration is only apparent, and arises from his passionate concern with moral issues. It has been remarked that "there are few opportunities for heroic virtue or heroic vice in the life of an Oxford don". In those tranquil backwaters it may be possible to regard morality as a matter of keeping dinner engagements or returning borrowed books; I have never seen a discussion in a philosophical journal of a moral problem of the type that many of our students now face: should I sleep with this girl whom I have no intention of marrying? What Sartre has to say is relevant to issues like this, to a world where there is a possibility of total annihilation. This constitutes his strength and importance. This does not mean, as I hope to show, that he is woolly-minded on these topics. His thought is hard to follow because the problems he is trying to deal with are difficult. The major one is that of producing a moral system which does justice to the facts and does not fall into the traps which Sartre thinks all previous systems have failed to avoid.

Before starting on a detailed analysis it may be helpful to give a brief indication of the two poles between which Sartre's ethical thought seems to oscillate. First, there is Marxism; I shall be dealing with the strictly political aspects of this in a later chapter. Here I only want to point out that, like Marx himself, Sartre sees ethics and politics as closely linked. Dubreuilh, who represents him in de Beauvoir's novel *Les Mandarins*, says at one point:

In a curved space, it is impossible to draw a straight line. You cannot lead a correct life in a society that is not itself correct. You are always caught from one side or another. Another illusion that must be got rid of, he concluded, that personal salvation is possible.[1]

At one stage he said that his morality would be Marxist. One writer reports:

One of his most assiduous readers and admirers has told me that, in the course of a lecture given at Frankfurt-am-Main in 1950, Sartre replied to a question about the direction of this morality by saying that it would be Marxist, but 'the real Marxism'.[2]

This Marxist ethic would presumably be that indicated by the "unsurpassable philosophy" of *Critique de la raison dialectique*, which will absorb the "existentialist ideology" (*CRD*, 17–18). In his latest pronouncement it would seem that he has placed the construction of a moral system after the Marxist revolution: "First all men must be able to become men by the improvement of their conditions of existence, so that a universal morality can be created."[3]

The other pole of Sartre's ethical thought is that represented by 'existential psychoanalysis', particularly in the form of 'purifying reflection' which will lead to the discovery of authenticity. (Sartre talks of 'purifying' reflection because there is also 'impure' or 'accessory' reflection; there is a variety of introspection which may foster bad faith rather than get rid of it.) In this sense *Saint Genet* is his promised work on ethics. The form of the book has been described as 'paradoxical', which to those expecting something rather different from moral philosophers it certainly is. Jeanson, Sartre's devoted disciple and friend, in a passage which is not altogether clear, describes it as "the major work of contemporary philosophy; perhaps the only one which is—with complete lucidity and no reserve—the wager of a man on the resources of man."[4] Certainly it seems to be an important work, though the

---

[1] pp. 489–90.

[2] P. Asveld, *La Pensée religieuse du jeune Hegel* (Louvain, 1953), 228n.

[3] "A long bitter, sweet madness"; interview with *Le Monde* tr. by Anthony Hartley and published in *Encounter*, June 1964, 62.

[4] *Sartre par lui-même*, 184.

fact that it operates within the discussion of the life and works of an extremely aberrant individual makes it difficult to be certain that one has understood all the doctrines expressed in it. But perhaps Sartre's attempt should be welcomed by those who insist that philosophy involves above all detailed work.

The nature of *Saint Genet* should not mislead us into thinking that it is an example of what has come to be thought of in this country as 'existentialist ethics', an ethic of choice and decision in which the choices and decisions are not based on any universalisable rules. It has come to be believed that existentialism offers what can only be called a 'private morality', a tendency which has been encouraged by the reading of *L'Existentialisme est un humanisme*. One philosopher defends such a view of morality in the following way:

But, where a situation is too complex, phrases like 'someone like me' or 'this kind of situation', become vacuous. For I am the only person sufficiently 'like me' to be morally relevant and no situation could be sufficiently like 'this kind of situation' without being precisely this situation. But what situation could be complex in this way? The situation of Françoise in Simone de Beauvoir's *L'Invitée* or that of Mathieu in Sartre's *Les Chemins de la liberté* are examples that spring to mind, for part of their problem is to discover precisely what their problem is. And this brings out the point that it is because Sartre and Simone de Beauvoir are concerned with morality of this kind and in this way that they present and can only present their insights in the form of novels rather than of logical analysis.[1]

I have chosen this passage, as Mr MacIntyre is sympathetic to what he takes to be the existentialist claim. It seems to me, however, that the belief in the possibility of this kind of approach to morality is based on a confusion. There are cases, such as that used by Sartre in *L'Existentialisme est un humanisme* of the young man torn between the duty to look after his mother and that of joining the Free French in England, where it seems that conventional morality gives no guidance. There is a moral dilemma here, and it may be an agonising one. But there is no philosophical problem arising

[1] A. MacIntyre, 'What morality is not', *Philosophy*, 1957, 335.

from such a situation. For in any system of rules there are bound to be cases not obviously included under them, or even included under two contradictory rules. Such cases arise often in law, where every effort has been made by legal draughtsmen to avoid them. It is not surprising that they should occur with the less precise conventional rules of morality. Faced with such a situation, we might find it hard to advise or to act, but most people would have some idea of the lines on which to go about settling the difficulty within the framework of everyday morality. And when they did reach a decision it would be in principle universalisable, even though the situation happens to be unique. The universalisability will lie in the fact that the action or decision can be explained or justified to others, even though it may take the skill of a novelist to expound the justification. Behaving morally may be more difficult than might be thought from reading moral philosophers, with their natural and proper tendency to start with simple examples, but this does not mean that their descriptions are wrong in principle. If Sartre really is suggesting that 'true' morality is a purely individual affair, that there are no general counsels, only particular cases which each must cope with as best he can, then he is wrong. There can no more be a private morality than there can be a private language, and for reasons which are partly common to both cases.

It is of course possible to construct a private *code*—for example to use a certain combination of letters in a diary to represent a recurring sensation—but this code is itself parasitic on an already existing language; the code-word functions in the same way as ordinary words in the language and is, in fact, defined in terms of them. It is because the common language has been learnt that it is possible to use the code-word in accordance with similar rules. The code is only 'accidentally' private; it could easily be taught to another person. But a private language could only be something which does not have such a connection with an already existing language, the language which a Robinson Crusoe shipwrecked from birth might compose for himself. But what could be meant by 'composing a language for oneself'? We think we understand such a state of affairs because we can, in the context of public language, give a name to a new object or event. But this can only be done because the new word at once takes its place among all the other words of our language. Naming something is one of our normal linguistic activities. For the isolated individual there would be no such procedure possible. It might be thought that he could always utter the same noise (it cannot be called a word) when the same animal came by. Several difficulties at once arise. Why should he do this? What part would it play in his life? Without the apparatus of classification that a language provides, how would he know that it was the *same* (or *same kind of*) animal? Again, if he utters the sound in the presence of a different animal, what, if anything, has gone wrong? It is impossible to say whether he has made a mistake, changed his mind or extended the meaning of the word. We cannot understand what such an activity on the part of a linguistically isolated individual would be like. Only in so far as an individual is in communication with others do procedures like naming make sense.

Much the same appears to me to apply to the notion of morality, though perhaps not quite so obviously. One of the things that is expected of a moral man is that his behaviour should be consistent, that he should treat the same situation in the same way whenever it recurs. If someone who claims to be following a private morality does not behave in this way, we should accuse him of acting capriciously, not morally, for he has behaved in different ways in two similar situations. There would seem two lines of defence open to him. First he could claim that he had behaved in the same way each time. Unless he could show us, and convince us, that this was the case we should fail to understand him. Second, he could claim that the two situations were, in fact, different. Here we should want to have the difference pointed out to us before we should accept what he said. In both cases the same thing has been done in defence, namely the setting of the actions in a public context in terms of a justification that we, the observers, could understand. I do not wish to maintain that we should have to agree with or approve of what he had done; there is no reason why we should not *understand* the actions of a man who holds moral views that we abhor. But we should have to be able to understand the rationale of the difference in his behaviour. If we could not, then we should fail to understand him, be unable to classify his behaviour as moral. We should also fail to understand the man who said that he was doing what he ought to do, but that he didn't mean by this that anyone else like him in a similar situation should also act like him. Unless there is both constancy in behaviour and reference to reasons that can be explained to others, there is no difference between the so-called morality and pure caprice, or, in other words, it cannot be called a morality.

Part of the confusion about the possibility of a private morality may well have arisen from the fact that there do appear to be cases where a person's behaviour is described in these terms, namely the situation in which he is acting on moral principles which are different from those normal in his society. For to act on different moral principles must result in behaving differently in situations the critics think of as the same, or in the same way in situations the critics think of as different. If this were not so, there would be no call to talk of the underlying principles as different. To someone unsympathetic to the new morality, the behaviour of its follower may well appear capricious or even immoral. For example, what is often called the 'loose sexual behaviour' of the younger generation may well be governed by rules, but rules radically different from those observed by the older generation. But, and this is the point of importance here, the new morality is still universal in intention, relies on rules which are meant to apply to all cases. It may, if held by only one person, appear private, but such privacy is only accidental; in essence it is as universal as the old morality, and the imperatives or reasons for acting in which it issues are applicable to all people in the same situation. Otherwise it would make no sense to talk of it as a 'morality' at all.

Even to understand a person to any degree involves seeing his *reasons* for acting in the way he does, and this means that we are in the realm of universal public criteria. It may be that the novel 'gives us more understanding' of the behaviour of its characters than does a bald account in a philosophical or psychological text-book, but this is because there is room for a more detailed account of their reasons for acting. The two kinds of account do not differ in principle. It may be *easier* for Sartre to present his "insights in the form of novels rather than logical analyses", but if they are genuine insights then they must also be presentable in the latter form. If they cannot be, then they are not insights. In fact, I don't think Sartre is using his later novels to present insights which he cannot conceptualise; they have a very different function in the corpus of his work. I discuss the point at greater length below, confining myself here to saying that it might be useful to think of the novels as particularly detailed philosophical examples, but what they are examples of is to be found in the philosophical works themselves. And these latter are the bulk of Sartre's writing.

I have examined this view of 'existentialist morality' in detail because I think it is important not to misunderstand Sartre's radical approach to morality. First, a person who is undergoing a 'radical conversion' cannot rely on reasons, for what he is doing is changing what he is going to count as a reason, and it may well be impossible for a person who has not gone through a similar process to understand what has happened. On the other hand, two converts can obviously discuss the differences and similarities of their radical change. Although there can't be reasons in the strict sense for such a conversion, there must be some "considerations capable of influencing the intellect" which can perhaps be indicated. Indeed, the whole purpose of existential psychoanalysis in its application to an individual by himself is to bring about such a change. To understand what one's fundamental project is is to be in a position to change it for another; anyone who claims to have uncovered his original choice and to be unable to change it is in bad faith, which is evidence that he has not really reached the end of the analytic process. Further, the representation of the life of the *salauds* in all its unpleasantness is another way of affecting the intellect, though not by giving reasons. At this level the relation between ethics and aesthetics is close, for the artistic representation may well be the best way of making a criticism of a certain way of life, or of rendering intelligible a radical conversion. In the last resort, the reasons that are given to explain or justify a piece of conduct may not be expressible in simple terms, but to admit this is not the same thing as to deny their universalisability.

Some critics have misrepresented Sartre as equating every moral decision to a radical conversion; they have done so because they have failed to notice the radical nature of his attack on conventional views of ethics. For he regards ordinary morality as one of the main sources of bad faith, which in this context he frequently refers to as 'serious-mindedness' (*l'esprit de sérieux*). A passage from Nietzsche will indicate the type of criticism Sartre is making:

In all previous studies of morality, one thing was lacking, strange as that may sound: the problem of morality itself; what was lacking was the suspicion that there was anything at all problematic here. What the philosophers called a 'rational foundation for morality' and tried to supply was, properly considered, only a scholarly variation of a common *faith* in the prevalent morality; a new means of *expression* of this faith; in short, itself simply another feature of, or rather another fact within, a particular morality; indeed, in the last analysis, a kind of denial that this morality might ever be considered problematic—certainly the very opposite of an examination, analysis, questioning and vivisection of this very faith.[1]

Sartre would consider those attacked by Nietzsche as typically serious-minded, for they accepted the current morality without noticing that there was a problem involved. Serious-mindedness he defines as having "the double characteristic, in fact, of considering values as 'given' transcendentally, independently from human beings, and of transferring the character 'desirable' from the ontological structure of things to their simple material composition" (*EN*, 721). It is an attempt to look upon values as if they were qualities of the world, not in some sense the result of human choices. But if values were "written into the nature of things" it would seem that they would have nothing to do with us, no longer be 'values', in fact. To pretend that objects or deeds *are*

[1] *Beyond Good and Evil*, §186.

valuable without reference to human needs and situations is to attempt to escape from one's own freedom. The analysis of serious-mindedness reflects on the ethical level the earlier analysis of bad faith. Just as the waiter tries to identify himself with his social role, to be nothing more than a waiter, in order to escape from knowledge of his freedom, of the fact that he freely gets up at five in the morning, so the serious-minded man looks on moral choice as a kind of deduction from necessary premisses in order to conceal from himself the extent to which he is choosing the action. Morality for him is mechanical, never creative, and one of the elements that it seems to me Sartre wishes to give a higher value to is the very element of creativity in moral decision. Real morality cannot be static.

In some of his later works Sartre expresses the same idea by using the term "alienation"; the man in bad faith alienates his freedom by thinking of himself as a thing, or as compelled to act in certain ways. He uses the term to refer both to 'private' alienation, as in the cases just mentioned, where the individual himself is responsible, and also to 'public' alienation, where the social system imposes a certain view of himself on a particular individual. The latter sense has, of course, closer connection with the original Hegelo-Marxist use of the term. Genet is Sartre's prime example of the latter type. Caught stealing by his foster-parents at an early age, he found that they took precautions against further such acts on his part, with the result that Genet became convinced that he *was* a thief, that this was his nature and role. "By an inverted idealism, he applied the famous *esse est percipi* to himself, and only recognised himself as others saw him" (*StG*, 40). This is an extreme example of what we are all inclined to do in less obvious ways, to accept the judgment of our fellow men on our 'character', to feel as a consequence that we *are* such-and-such, to behave in the ways that are expected of us by our fellow men for the very reason that they do expect it. The realisation that bad faith may be caused in part by the social situation marks a stage in what might be called the 'politicalisation' of Sartre's thought, which I shall discuss in more detail below. Morality for many people, above all for the bourgeoisie, Sartre sees as a case of this second form of alienation; conscience, the 'moral law within' is merely the interiorisation of the rules and attitudes of society. This is reprehensible because the fact that at each step human decisions are involved has been forgotten; human freedom is ignored.

A further criticism of serious-mindedness is that it always involves oversimplification. By seeing human beings as classifiable in a small number of categories, by limiting the range of human possibilities, the serious-minded ignore man's nature. This for Sartre is the perpetual danger of any *system* of morality; hence he wishes to avoid recommending a set of fixed rules. Further, in present-day conditions it is more obvious than it used to be that simple categories are inadequate to cope with human relations in their richness. Sartre expresses this in a characteristically exaggerated passage: "Thus any morality which is not explicitly given as *impossible today* contributes to the mystification and alienation of men. The moral 'problem' arises from the fact that *for us* morality is at the same time inevitable and impossible. Action must be given its ethical norms in this climate of unsurpassable impossibility. It is from this point of view, for example, that we must look at the problem of violence and that of the relation between ends and means. For someone who survives being split apart in this way and who is at the same time compelled to choose and to decide, all beautiful revolt, all cries of refusal, all virtuous indignation will appear as out-of-date rhetoric" (*StG*, 177).

Sartre's statement of the moral problem for the philosophers, after it has been cut down to size and exaggerations removed, is thus very different from that which might be given by an English philosopher. He is concerned with the 'human condition' as a whole, the other would claim that the important thing is the analysis of moral notions. But a subject for analysis is something accepted as non-problematical; for example, it makes perfect sense to say that the object of the Philosophy of Science is to analyse the procedure and arguments of scientists because their work is, by other standards, on the whole successful. The case for morality might be similar if moral rules were regarded solely as means for obtaining conformity of behaviour—but then there would be little of philosophical interest about them. It is because many philosophers regard morality both as important and as, in its broad outlines, unproblematic, that we get the kind of books that outsiders find unhelpful and irrelevant, so being driven into a woolly version of 'existentialism' to satisfy their questions. There is an assumption that 'there is' such a thing as moral obligation, and the tricky question is to see what on earth it could be. There is no doubt that people do feel morally obliged to do things, but before any analysis can be given of this feeling, the following challenge must be met:

It certainly does not seem to me *self-evident* that the sense of moral obligation deserves any more respect than a neurotic compulsion: that is something which needs to be demonstrated, or at least shown to be reasonably probable.[1]

It is indeed an important fact which Sartre himself emphasises that the problem of moral *obligation* is a comparative new-comer on the ethical scene. Many of the traditional philosophers were not concerned with actions when they were discussing ethics. "In this sense, Kant's morality is the first great system which substitutes doing for being as the supreme value of action" (*EN*, 507). Aristotle, the Stoics and Spinoza, for instance, were more concerned with the 'right way of life', by which they meant the way of life which would lead to happiness or to blessedness, viewed as a particular state of *being*. For them, the justification of any rule lay in the effect that acting in accordance with it had on the agent, not in the consequences. Once the rule is divorced from the agent's desires and aims ethics is liable to become prey to some form of consequentialism. If the moral rule is thought of as a kind of unwritten law of the land, then clearly it must be justified, if at all, by reference to its consequences in the world outside the agent. In the eyes of the serious-minded such a rule may retain validity on the ground that it is a rule, but more sceptical spirits are bound to challenge it. In this case the only justification would

[1] A. M. MacIver, 'Good and evil and Mr Geach', *Analysis*, 18, 12.

seem to be the consequences of actions done in accordance with the rule. It is interesting to note the extent to which we are all utilitarians nowadays; it is hard to bring forward any view of, for example, punishment, without the question immediately being raised of the results of punishment. Only if those results are shown to be desirable do the majority think that punishment is justifiable. But earlier writers on moral philosophy brought forward very different justifications; Hegel and Bradley ignored consequences deliberately in their consideration of the topic.

Sartre is, in this respect, more like the traditional moral philosophers. They, for obvious reasons, tended to start their philosophising with an investigation of the nature of man: Sartre has done the same thing in *L'Etre et le néant*. The point of difference between him and other philosophers lies, as I have already indicated, in his denial that there is a simple essence of man. Consequently there is no possibility of discovering a right way of life based on coincidence with one's nature. "Existence is prior to essence" is meant to point to this fact. But, for Sartre, men do have something in common, even if they have no "essence"; they are beings who are not what they are and who are what they are not, in other words they are free. For if they had nothing in common, then the analysis of *L'Etre et le néant* would be merely a case-history, which it is certainly not intended to be. The denial of a human essence is a denial that happiness or the right way of life can be found in a fulfilment of a man's function. It is even possible that at the time of writing that work Sartre would have been willing to admit that there was more than one way of achieving happiness, though I am doubtful if he would now maintain that view.

That he did think in this way is borne out by a suggestion made in that work as a remedy for the serious-minded view of morality, that it should be regarded as a form of play. This liberates from the idea that rules are written in the nature of things because it is an activity in accordance with freely chosen rules. In addition, there are different forms of play, and hence it would seem different moralities. The serious-minded man starts from the fact that "life is real, life is earnest", or in Sartre's words that "there is more reality in the world than in oneself, or at least that one is real in so far as one belongs to the world" (*EN*, 669). The player, the man doing something for fun, finds himself to be more real the more he escapes from the world, the more he uses his freedom. Sartre uses this notion to contrast the desire *to be*, to be something fixed and stable, which is the essence of bad faith, with the desire to employ freedom which he sees as the central characteristic of the "authentic" man; the latter does not want to *be* any particular sort of thing, except perhaps a human being, whose nature has been shown in *L'Etre et le néant* to be ambiguous. But Sartre goes on to suggest that play could be made the basis of ethics, that there could be a moral system based on it (*EN*, 670). In a genuinely absurd universe, whatever that could mean, morality might well have the character of play, a game played by man against the absurdity of nature. Even then, it would have to be played by a solitary individual. Such an 'aesthetic' morality would escape the charge of being serious by becoming trivial. Playing games is relaxing because it permits us to make or accept rules which are only valid within the field of play, to perform actions whose significance is limited to the duration of the game. Play generally takes place in an area which is marked off, actually or conceptually, from that of everyday life, and this is why what is done during play does not have, or is not considered to have, effects outside its own sphere. This fact may account for the way in which games which are especially liable to have such effects, such as serious injury or large financial loss, are thought to be outside the ordinary category of play; Russian roulette is a limiting case of a game. For a solitary individual there would be no difference between play and morality, if either were possible for him, but for those who live in society there is; our actions have effects beyond, or even other than, our intentions. "Not only in history but even in everyday life the events transform our best intentions into criminal acts" (*StG*, 548).

This difficulty is not an accidental one, something which might be avoided if care is taken or luck on our side. Even in writing

L'Etre et le néant Sartre realised that all our actions involve other people, and many of them involve changing them, or at least constraining them. "This constraint, although it is not exercised always, or most frequently, under the form of violence, nevertheless regulates the relations of men among themselves. If I console, if I cheer up, it is in order to separate the other person's freedom from the fears or griefs that obscure it; but consolation or reassuring arguments are the organisation of a system of means designed to *act* on the other person and in consequence to integrate him as an object or utensil in the system. . . . It is no good however thinking that a *laisser-faire* morality or one of tolerance respects the other's freedom to a greater degree: since I exist, I build an actual limit to his freedom, I *am* this limit and each one of my projects draws this limit around the other person; charity, *laisser-faire*, tolerance—or an attitude of abstention—are my projects which commit me and also engage the other person's assent" (*EN*, 479–80). "No one governs innocently"; St Just's phrase is often echoed by Sartre, with the understanding that it is not only in politics that action involves violence to others. It may be more obvious in that sphere, but this is only because the scale of political action is that of everyday life magnified. Indeed, it has seemed to some critics that Sartre asserts the complete impossibility of human relations. This can be taken as the lesson of the section "Concrete Relations with Other People", but, as I have argued, Sartre's real claim is that failure to notice the extent and importance of violence is what really makes human relations impossible.

He does indeed paint a sombre picture of the 'human condition'; perhaps the most sombre is the conclusion of *Saint Genet*, which I will quote at length. Sartre mentions the Chinese sessions of condemnation set up by the Communist régime in its early years, which one writer has described as "one of the most abject inventions of our time". Sartre continues: "They are indeed abject. But why 'Chinese'? Or rather we are all Chinese without knowing it, at the same time Chinese victims and Chinese executioners, for I see in these meetings for accusation the image of our own condition: accusers with the rest, we are, at the same time, alone and accused by all. Because social relationships are ambiguous and comprise partial failure, because we are at the same time the Chinese crowd laughing and the terrified China-man who is dragged to execution, because every thought separ-ates as much as it unites, because every statement brings together by what it expresses and isolates by what it does not say, because an unpassable abyss separates the subjective certainty we have of ourselves and the objective truth of what we are for others, because we never stop judging ourselves guilty though we feel ourselves to be innocent, because events not only in history but in everyday life transform our best intentions into criminal acts, because we are never certain of not becoming traitors in retro-spect, because we ceaselessly fail to communicate, to love, to make ourselves loved and every failure shows us our solitude, because we dream sometimes of wiping out our criminal singu-larity by humble confession and sometimes of affirming it with defiance in the vain hope of taking it completely on our shoulders, because we are conformists in the open, defeated and wicked in the depths of our souls, because the only expedient and single dignity of the guilty person is obstinate stubborness, sulkiness, bad faith and resentment, because we can neither escape from the objecti-vity which crushes us nor cast off the subjectivity which exiles us, because we can neither raise ourselves to the rank of being nor bury ourselves in nothingness, because we are, in any case, *impossible nonentities*, we must listen to the voice of Genet, our neighbour, our brother" (*StG*, 548–9).

It is passages such as these, and there are many that could be found in Sartre's writings, that have led critics to see him as a pessimist or worse. The picture he paints is certainly sombre, and he seems to regard our own epoch as perhaps more distressing than previous eras; its problems, atomic war, poverty in the midst of plenty, colonial strife, more acute than in other times if only because we are more conscious of them and of our responsibility for them. To indicate that a view is depressing is not to deny that anything can be done to improve it. Christianity has generally taken a dark view of the human condition, and yet is a basically optimistic religion, even though its optimism may be qualified in that salvation lies for ever outside the world in which we must live and act. For characters in Sartre's novels there may be no way out, except the action of Mathieu symbolically destroying the world by shooting Germans in an engagement doomed to failure and leading to his own death: "He fired on Man, on Virtue, on the World; Freedom is Terror . . . he shot at the handsome officer, at all the Beauty on earth, at the street, at flowers, at gardens, at everything he had loved. . . . He fired: he was pure and all-powerful, he was free . . ." (*MdA*, 193). Mathieu is not Sartre; like most of the other characters in the book he has 'la mort dans l'âme', and there is an ironical contrast between the private reasons he has for joining the last defence of France against the Germans and the duty and sense of solidarity which lead the others on the church tower to continue the fight even though they know they cannot win. It is important to note that the defenders form a united group, and Sartre gives no indication that it is one founded on error or bad faith. There is a means of finding human solidarity in this world, even if the "morality of deliverance and salvation" mentioned above is generally beyond man. The case of Genet is important because even he attains liberation, improbable as this might have seemed from his background and early life. No "sinner" is irretrievably lost; there is a way, even though it may be hard to find. Ultimately Sartre is optimistic, though not facilely so.

I have discussed in Chapter VIII the way in which Sartre combines a belief in man's freedom with a desire to liberate him: "If man is not originally free, it is impossible even to conceive what his liberation would be" (*S.III*, 207). The method and approach to this goal I compared with Freud's. The name that Sartre gives to this liberating remedy is 'authenticity', a notion which has gained much popularity amongst those who consider themselves existentialists and which has consequently perhaps bulked larger in discussions of Sartre's ethics than it should have done. Nevertheless it is clear that he regards the notion as an important one. He defines it: "Authenticity, it is obvious, consists in having a lucid and truthful awareness of the situation, in bearing the responsibilities and risks which the situation demands, in taking it upon oneself with pride or humility, sometimes with horror and hatred" (QJ, 110). At first sight there appears to be little that is ethical about this notion, for it gives no guidance as to what responsibilities and risks are to be taken. A writer on Freud makes a similar point about both him and Sartre:

In this final suspension, Freud's ethic resembles Sartre's existentialism, which offers a related criterion, authenticity, as a way of judging what is good in human action ... [but] As a purely explanatory and scientific ideal, honesty has no content. Though the Freudian training involves intellectual judgment based on a calm and neutral appraisal of all the demanding elements of a life-situation, still, the freedom to choose must end in choice. Here, at the crucial moment, the Freudian ethic of honesty ceases to be helpful. Being honest, admitting one's nature, does not resolve specific issues of choice. To achieve greater balance in the psyche, to shift the relative weights of instinct and repression, instals no new substantive rules of decision.[1]

An equally serious criticism of Sartre's notion of authenticity is that often it seems as if he were advocating a kind of acceptance of one's lot. "Jewish authenticity consists in choosing oneself *as a Jew*, that is to say in realising the Jewish condition. An authentic Jew abandons the myth of universal man; he knows himself and wills himself to be in history as a historic and damned creature; he has ceased to flee from and be ashamed of his own people. He understands that society is bad . . . he knows that he is *apart*, untouchable, spurned, proscribed and he takes his Jewishness upon himself" (QJ, 169). There seems more than an echo of "Freedom is the recognition of necessity" in this passage; the Jew can achieve happiness only by recognising that he is a Jew and in consequence cut off from other men. Such counsel may be helpful, but it hardly seems particularly a part of morality. In defence of Sartre it must be said that he believes that the situation of the Jew is largely due to the behaviour of the rest of mankind.

[1] P. Rieff, *Freud, the Mind of a Moralist*, 312.

The Jew can choose authenticity: "that is true, but it must be understood that *it doesn't concern us*; the prisoner is always free to escape, if it is understood that he risks death in crossing the barbed wire; does this make the gaoler any the less guilty?" (*QJ*, 169). For certain people or in certain states of society, there may be no possibility of complete happiness; for them, morality may be both "inevitable and impossible".

For Genet, however, the search for authenticity was more than a search for a way of accepting his lot. The Jew is a difficult example precisely because there is a way of defining him in terms not of his character but of his inheritance; a Jew is a person born of Jewish parents, and this at once places special limits on him in a society with anti-semitic tendencies. But the remedy for anti-semitism and for the colour-bar lies in the hands of the non-Jewish and the non-coloured. Most of us are more like Genet in that we can undergo radical conversion, can change that fundamental project which, in so far as anything does, can be said to constitute our essence. To understand that one does possess a fundamental project is already to be in a position to change it. The detailed example of one case is the book *Saint Genet*, but in so far as this deals with the liberation of one person it is a work of moral pathology, just as the history of an individual Freudian analysis is one of psychological pathology. For ethics something more is needed. This extra is given in the case of psychoanalysis by the theoretical writings of Freud; as I have already said, Sartre nowhere sets out in full the equivalent theoretical ethics. That he does not do this is not because there are only particular cases; it is possible to show the fundamental cause of inauthenticity which is the same for all forms. It is that 'desire to become God' which has been mentioned in the last chapter.

Sartre means by this that the core of inauthenticity is the denial of what it is to be a man, a wish to be a complete being, one which is never affected by anything outside itself, and one which exists in itself with no desires; Spinoza's *Deus sive natura* would be an example. But a man cannot be like this, both because he lives in a world of other men who affect him and whom he affects, and because he can never *be* anything in the way in which a stone is a stone. For he is free, and hence can only exist by choosing courses of action. A complete being would have no need nor motive for choice. Authenticity consists therefore in the recognition of incompleteness, and hence of responsibility. Inauthenticity is the attempt to escape from such recognition, by claiming that one *is* of a certain nature, that one cannot do otherwise. Existential psychoanalysis functions by showing that this so-called nature is really itself the result of a decision or choice, and hence putting the inauthentic person in a position to change. The ambiguity of much of Sartre's writing on ethics lies in the fact that it is never clear whether this authenticity is a means to morality or its ultimate end. In 'Moral Perspectives' at the end of *L'Etre et le néant* he seems to adopt the latter view, and Jeanson, writing in 1947 with Sartre's approval, certainly takes this to be the core of Sartrean ethics. It is by no means clear what such an ethic would amount to; knowing oneself can hardly constitute the whole of moral behaviour, though it may be an essential preliminary to it. At first sight it would seem that *any* action could be done authentically. Nevertheless I think that Sartre would want to argue that there are limitations on what would count as authentic action. He regards it as impossible to act authentically and at the same time uphold a colour-bar. Authenticity must involve respect for other people. The reasons would be much the same as he gives for limiting possible subjects for novels: "But no one could suppose for an instant that it would be possible to write a good novel in praise of anti-semitism. For it cannot be expected of me, at the time when I realise that my freedom is indissolubly linked to that of all other men, that I should use it to approve of the enslavement of some of them" (*S.II*, 112).

–That the authentic individual must desire the liberation of other men would seem to follow from the definition of authenticity. To understand oneself is to understand to some extent all men, for we all partake of a common condition, in that we are all free individuals in a single world. A free man can only desire relations with free men. The pathological varieties of human relations analysed in *L'Etre et le néant* are all results of one of the partners refusing to recognise the other as a *person*, treating him as mere *means* to satisfaction. Similarly, Mathieu's relations with Marcelle are shown up as inauthentic when he is brought to realise that he has never really thought of her as a person. Authenticity might thus be seen as involving the Kantian imperative "So act as to treat humanity, whether in thine own person or in that of any other, in every case as an end, never as a means only". Though to act otherwise is not, as Kant thought it was, contradictory, Sartre is right in seeing something *inconsistent* in conduct contrary to this rule, for to behave otherwise is to demand a special position for oneself, and the man who knows himself, who is authentic, must know that there is nothing special about his own position.

The authentic man will be happy in that he is insulated from the vagaries of his situation, like the Stoic wise man. During the war years and those immediately following, Sartre thought that private authenticity was the solution of the moral problem, even if he never very clearly represented authenticity. With the decay of post-war optimism, he began to think that the structure of society itself might be an important factor in preventing men from achieving it. This is an aspect of that politicalisation of his thought that I have already mentioned, and would seem to date from about 1947. I must add that it is a change of emphasis rather than a 'radical conversion'; though it may be necessary to change society before individuals in that society can attain authenticity, the character of the authenticity to be worked for is still the same. It has been remarked that the

division among the ancient moralists parallels that among the psycho-analysts between those who (like Freud) seem confident that the exist-ing social order is all right, so that a man who was mentally healthy would be found behaving in ways considered laudable by his neigh-bours—sticking to one lawfully wedded wife and so on—and those who (like Eric Fromm) allow that a whole society can be 'neurotic', so that a healthy way of life might be one that was not socially ap-proved.[1]

[1] A. M. MacIver, ibid.

Sartre might be said to have passed from the first of these positions to the second, with the difference that he thinks of the second as necessitating a general revolution, a change in the whole state of society, rather than as only requiring individual non-conformity. Nevertheless, the 'existentialists' (*sales existentialistes*) who became notorious in Paris immediately after the war took Sartre to be advocating non-conformity as an essential feature of authenticity. Though Sartre clearly never thought that authenticity involved mere conformity, there is a great difference, which he would admit, between disagreeing with social standards because they get in the way of a genuine moral life and in revolting against them for the sake of revolt. It would be wrong to blame him for the actions of a lunatic fringe.

Authenticity involves relations between free men, relations themselves based on freedom. If society renders such freedom impossible, then it is useless for a single individual to work for it. As an example, he says that under the occupation no satisfactory attitude was possible to a man compelled to wear the Star of David. (He is thinking of meeting such a man in the street for the first time.) For sympathy and an offer of friendship, to the same degree as hatred, involved treating the wearer of the Star as an object, as a Jew to be sympathised with because one disapproved of the Nazi policy, was not an anti-semite and so on (*QJ*, 93–95). In other words, the behaviour was based on motives that had nothing to do with the individual towards whom they were directed. Also it might happen that the Jew did not desire the proffered sympathy, feeling that it was directed not to him but to a class of people. Sartre feels that this is an extreme example of something which is liable to occur in societies operating colour-bars, or even recognisable class barriers. These latter may not depend on anything as conspicuous as skin-colour, but accent or level of wealth may prove as effective obstacles if they are important in the society. The bourgeois who tries to ignore his class, even by living the life of a worker, may find himself marked off as a 'bourgeois-who-denies-his-class' for his fellow workers. They may regard his action as admirable, but even this will lead to a different relation with him to the one they would have with a member of their own class. Again, for the bourgeois himself the workers still constitute a *class* with whom he is trying to get into contact; he is not thinking of them as individual human beings. "In a curved space it is impossible to draw a straight line. . . ." Even if Sartre's examples seem to be exaggerated, he has got hold of an important point; dramatically expressed, it forms one strand of the conflict between Hugo and Hoederer in *Les Mains sales*.

The only remedy that Sartre sees for this situation is a classless society; hence his Marxism. But, as I have said, he reaches his form of Marxism by a moral route, not by an economic one. Man-made structures stand in the way of genuine human relations, therefore these must be changed. It might be said that the aim of both Marx and Freud was to liberate man from the burden of his past. Marx thinks of the past that bears on man and inhibits his freedom as the social constructions of earlier times which have outlived their usefulness and now only serve to restrict human contact. Freud thinks of the past of the individual which he tends to re-live in the present and so renders himself incapable of reacting in appropriate ways to new situations. Both regard bondage to the past as the repetition of behaviour patterns which may once have been desirable for the development of society or the individual, but which are now merely restrictive. Both see freedom and the possibility of rational action as dependent on escape from these sterile repetitions. Sartre thinks that both forms of liberation are necessary: the psychoanalytical, in his own existentialist form, is insufficient by itself, for its results may be upset by political conditions; the Marxist liberation, as it is usually stated nowadays, is inadequate in that it fails to take into account the actual nature of man. A Marxist is just as liable to fall into bad faith as anyone else who has not undergone a course of purifying reflection. The two doctrines, the Freudian and the Marxist, put the accent on subjectivity and objectivity respectively. Both are needed.

At the end of *Saint Genet* Sartre puts the issue in terms of two individuals he has discussed, one at great length, Genet, the criminal who chose to be a criminal and hence cut off from society, and Bukharin who 'confessed' to crimes he had not committed because he wished to remain a member of society. The dilemma lies in finding a middle way between these two extremes: "Bukharin or our desire *to be together* pushed to the point of martyrdom; Genet or our solitude pushed to the point of crucifixion. If we hope and intend to escape from this dilemma, if there is still time, by a last effort, to reconcile subject and object, we must, even if only once and in the imagination, realise that hidden solitude which erodes our acts and our thoughts; we spend our time escaping from the objective into subjectivity and from the subjective into objectivity; this game of hide-and-seek will only end when we find the courage to go to both these extremes at one and the same time" (*StG*, 549–50). He adds that in *Saint Genet* he has been mainly concerned with exposing the subjective side of the dilemma, which at the time of writing seemed the more important, though not so in itself.

X

Ethics II

I HAVE introduced a separate section at this point because I want to discuss Sartre's ethics in a more radical way. So far I have endeavoured to expound his view, and such criticisms as I mentioned I tried to dispose of in his terms and by means of his own statements. But in spite of the rejection in the last chapter of the doctrine of *L'Existentialisme est un humanisme*, it may well seem that Sartre has not really progressed beyond the position he there put forward, of telling the puzzled questioner to choose without giving him any concrete basis on which to do this. Part of the difficulty here is that we already recognise the situation in which the young man is placed as one needing a *moral* solution, and I think Sartre assumes that we will do this. In other words he is presupposing quite a lot of ordinary moral notions; the problems that he regards as central are those which have always been thought of as such, and his demand for a radical solution of them does not imply, though he sometimes fails to make this clear, a rejection of the web of human loyalties and duties which are the foundation of any morality whatsoever. Undoubtedly some of his critics, and even Sartre himself, have assumed that the object of his ethical discussion was to start with a clean slate, an ethical *tabula rasa*, and hence have supposed that the failure to produce a set of rules marks the failure of the whole enterprise. In so far as Sartre has thought this, he has fallen into one of the traps he criticises other thinkers for falling into, that of regarding morality as a single set of rules. If instead he had remained clear that authenticity was something already considered a value in existing moralities, and that his use of the notion involved a deepening and extension of ordinary moral notions, what he has to say about the topic would be less confused, and he would not think of himself as having failed in one aspect of his work. I believe he does regard himself as having failed here; in his latest pronouncement he says: "From the period when I wrote *La Nausée* I wanted to create a morality. My evolution consists in my no longer dreaming of doing so" (*Encounter*, June 1964, 62). But the remedy that he hints at, that of postponing the consideration of morality until after political action has rendered conditions suitable for it, seems a falling off from his earlier views which saw the two as inseparably linked. For, as Hegel saw, the danger of a purely abstract idea of freedom, one which was not linked with a network of relations to other people, was that it led to Terror. Sartre's criticisms of some actions of the Communist Party showed that he has been aware of this danger; I think that part of the reason for the unsatisfactory nature of *Critique de la raison dialectique* is that he has forgotten it.

Sartre certainly has succeeded in the sphere of moral criticism, both in his philosophical and his literary works. He has shown up the inauthenticity of many different types of people, both real and fictional. What he has not succeeded in doing is picturing a fully authentic individual in any detail, though some of the characters in his plays approximate to it. The most obvious example of his failure in this respect is the fact that he has been unable to write the fourth volume of *Les Chemins de la liberté*, which was to depict the authentic life of a group of people in the Resistance. I will discuss this in more detail in the next chapter. Part of the difficulty here is that it is much easier to show up inauthenticity than it is to give a genuine content to authenticity. Kant's Categorical Imperative, in its formulation of treating other people always as ends, never merely as means, is very similar to Sartrean authenticity and also suffers from being easier to express in negative form. It is possible to say that a certain action involves treating somebody as a means but much harder to say how to treat him as an end. Kant appears to have recognised this, for he remarks in his *Metaphysics of Ethics*:

It will be observed that in the foregoing chapter it is not virtues that are insisted on, but rather the contrary vices which have been reprehended; and this arises from the very notion of respect, which, as we are bound to show it towards others, is but a negative duty: I am not obliged to revere others (regarded simply as men), i.e. to pay them positive veneration.[1]

Some critics have felt that Sartre has failed in the same way that Kant may be said to have done, for his principles of authenticity and respect for others turn out to be hollow or parasitic on an already existing morality. I feel that the charge of parasitism is not so grave, for I fail to see how anyone could produce, or even try to produce, a moral system which bore no relation to our already existing codes, for these are related to those facts which constitute us human beings.

Sartre himself might claim that his attempt to be radical in his criticism of existing moral systems, coupled with his analysis of human 'nature', makes it impossible to produce a morality, for to do such a thing would be to deny the very facts on which his whole work is based. If there were any reasons that always justified an action, then it would be possible to be both serious-minded and moral. The whole attack on the notion of a human nature, the categorisation of man as the being who is not what he is and is what he is not, is aimed at destroying a belief in values embodied in the structure of the universe, and hence the notion that there is a single moral way of acting. The danger of this attempt to be radical is that it reduces moral action to the level of arbitrary decision. It is even doubtful if we could talk of 'decisions' here, for a decision can only be made in the context of a meaningful way of life. For Sartre it would appear that the meaning is subsequent to the decision, in which case it is impossible to know what is being decided. Similarly, if morality results from a bare project, it is hard to see in what sense it can be called a morality. Sartre, himself a highly moral man, is convinced that it is impossible to be an authentic anti-semite. This does credit to his character, but it is hard to see how he can really justify his position, at least if he

[1] Book II, Apotome II, sect. 44 note.

wishes to ignore existing rules and attitudes. The danger is that all we are given is a do-it-yourself kit, not a morality.

The basic error springs from that exaggeration that I have frequently mentioned; Sartre requires an absolute solution, an answer which is clear and distinct. "If I occupy myself in treating as absolute ends certain chosen persons, my wife, my son, my friends, the poor man I meet on my way, if I wear myself out in fulfilling my duties towards them, I shall have to *pass in silence* over the injustices of the age, the class struggle, anti-semitism, etc., and finally I shall have *to profit from oppression to do good*. . . . But, on the other hand, if I throw myself into a revolutionary enterprise, I take the risk of having no leisure for personal relations, and worse still of being brought by the logic of action to treat the greater part of men and even my comrades as means" (*S.II*, 296). Sartre often talks and writes as if what he hoped to do was to find the single solution to problems such as these. I think that there is also in the body of his work an answer, or a sketch of an answer, which does not demand a simple "either-or". For most of us, of course, the quotation above does not represent a problem, for we have come to terms with our lives to the extent that we can reconcile our duties to those near and dear to us with goodwill towards those in a worse position; we can salve our consciences by a donation to "Freedom from Hunger" or a South African Defence Fund. It is part of Sartre's importance for our time that he refuses to accept such a compromise, or, if he is compelled to, he still demands that it should be remembered that it is a compromise, and that a better individual would do more. If we face up to our situation, then we must feel guilty for failing, and, because of what we are, we are doomed to fail. We are "impossible nonentities". And authenticity, it seems to me, can only consist in the recognition of this fact, not in the finding of a way out. Sartre's desire for an absolute led him to talk as if there was a way out, and that he provided it; hence the confusions that I have mentioned in this section. But this other strand in his thought, and it is one which bulks large and in the last resort seems to be most in accord with his metaphysical position, does not require a solution, merely that we recognise our ambiguity and strive to live with it, even though there is no perfect way of doing so.

Sartre seems now to have seen this clearly; in reply to the question "What are we saved by?" he says "By nothing. There is no salvation anywhere. The idea of salvation implies the idea of an absolute. For forty years I was conscripted by the absolute, the neurosis. The absolute is gone." Later in the same interview, he says: "A Soviet citizen, an official writer, once said to me: 'The day when Communism (that is, well-being for everyone) reigns, man's tragedy will begin: his finitude'." Sartre adds, "It is not yet time to reveal it."[1] But, of course, he has revealed it, and, furthermore, shown the difficulties of living with the knowledge. But I do not think he regards it as fully tragic, in that there is a possibility of coming to terms with it. There may be no salvation anywhere, but this is only to repeat the point he has made elsewhere, that there is no transcendent solution to man's problems; it lies in man himself.

[1] *Encounter*, June 1964, 61.

XI

Paths to Freedom: Sartre's Novels

IN THE last chapter I have suggested that Sartre's literary works could be regarded in the light of detailed examples, playing a fictional role analogous to that played by the works of Genet and Baudelaire. This is not to deny that they are works of art in their own right, and on that ground alone worth examination; no study of Sartre which ignored them would be complete. Here I am mainly interested in seeing how they are related to Sartre's philosophy in a strict sense, but it should not be forgotten that they can be enjoyed by a wide public which knows little or nothing of Sartre's theoretical writings. If it is felt that I have failed to do justice to this fact, I must point out that it seems to me that their success has been due partly to the philosophic underpinnings which make them what they are, as well as to Sartre's skill as a writer, here more obvious than in his technically philosophical works. I suspect that Sartre's literary works have distorted his philosophy, rather than the other way about, as has been argued by some critics. For he does allow an independence to the novels and plays, so that there are dangers in picking out fragments to illustrate his views; above all, his irony may be forgotten, particularly when it is taken in conjunction with an impartial presentation. The distortion of his philosophy springs from the concentration on extreme situations, the neglect of the everyday and humdrum moral relationships which are the web of ordinary life but which find little place in literature, or at least in his literature. Extreme situations are the stuff of art, they may well be the cause of wrong emphases and of ignoring of details in philosophy. The criticisms I have made of Sartre's ethical views could be expressed by saying that he has tended to go direct from very general principles to particular cases, ignoring the ground in between. Morality can be impoverished and falsified by doing this as much as by talking only in terms of everyday examples, returning of borrowed books and so on. By thinking of the moral situation as one which would make a good novel or play, this element will be left out of account.

I have separated consideration of Sartre's novels from that of his plays because there is a difference between them in this context. The novel is more closely connected with morality, drama with politics. It has been remarked that the novel is the most 'philosophic' literary medium; one critic has said of the novelist: "He has always been, what the very latest philosophers claim to be, a describer rather than an explainer; and in consequence he has often anticipated the philosophers' discoveries."[1] What can be described includes the thoughts of the characters, not merely their reasons for their actions but also the potential reasons which they reject, the gap between intention and fulfilment, the perpetual conflict between public and private. Further, the novel is a 'free' form, the author can make his points in a variety of different ways. A play is different in that it has got to hold the audience in performance, which involves the observance of conventions. The protagonists of the play are inevitably 'characters' in the sense that they are what they do and say. The theatre is general rather than particular, and thus 'political' not necessarily in a narrow sense but at least in being concerned with a public statement, an issue which is common to a number of people. It is interesting to note that Sartre has stated that one of his reasons for writing *Les Séquestrés d'Altona* was that he found himself unable to complete a novel and so turned to the different mode of expression offered by the theatre. There, it seems, he could express in general terms what he had failed to work out in particular.

In one way the novel is particularly close to Sartre's philosophical views, for it has no need of 'characters', even though many novelists have used them. The essential nothingness of the pro-

[1] Iris Murdoch, *Sartre*, 8.

tagonists can be represented. In his own words, it is "unnecessary to create *characters*. I did not realise it by myself. It was Jean Vaudal who, commenting upon my collection of short stories, *Le Mur*, noted that at the heart of each of my personages there was an indetermination, nothingness, not a *character*. What I used to do spontaneously, I now do deliberately" (*Lettres Françaises*, 24 Nov. 1945). The personages in Sartre's novels develop 'dialectically' in that their actions can never be foreseen in the light of what they have previously done and the events that confront them, but when they have acted, it is possible to see that this was, in some sense, the only action open to them. They were not compelled to act in that way by their character; their character, their public face, consists in their having behaved in this way.

Les Chemins de la liberté comprises three published volumes, *L'Age de raison, Le Sursis, La Mort dans l'âme*, and a promised fourth volume, *La Dernière chance*. Of this last volume sixty-seven pages were published in *Temps modernes* (vol. v, 1949-50) under the title 'Drôle d'amitié'. It now seems unlikely that Sartre will ever complete the book; besides his own admission of difficulties in writing it, Gallimard no longer describe it as "À paraître" on the back of his works. His own comment runs: ". . . I'm having trouble finishing my novel. The fourth volume was supposed to deal with the Resistance. Then the choice was easy—even if later it took a lot of strength to keep it up. One was either for or against the Germans. It was black or white. Today—and since 1945—the situation has become much more complex. Perhaps it takes less courage to choose, but the choices are much more difficult. I can't express the ambiguities of our time in a novel set in 1943. And, on the other hand, this unfinished work weighs on me: it's difficult for me to begin another before I've finished this one" (Interview with *L'Express*). I have already pointed out that this failure to complete the series is partly the result of his failure to find a positive way of expressing his morality, and I shall enlarge on this point below, after briefly summarising the plot of the novels.

L'Age de raison is about Mathieu, who teaches philosophy in a Paris *lycée*, and his relations with a group of friends. These include Marcelle, his mistress who has become pregnant; Daniel, a homosexual who finally marries her; Boris, one of Mathieu's students and his sister Ivich, with whom Mathieu is in love; Brunet, a member of the Communist Party; Gomez, a painter who has become a general in the Spanish Republican Army. The action takes place at the beginning of the summer holiday and is centred on Mathieu's attempts to deal with the problem of Marcelle's pregnancy, a problem which is finally taken out of his hands by her marriage to Daniel. *Le Sursis* covers the period 23 to 30 September 1938, the Munich crisis. All the same characters appear in it, together with the historical personages involved and a host of minor figures whose lives are affected by the international events. It is an attempt to give a picture of the crisis itself, which involves analysing it into a 'logical construction' out of the events as they appear to particular individuals, for "The war only exists for God. But God does not exist. Nevertheless, the war does exist" (*LS*, 258). *La Mort dans l'âme* is divided into two parts, of which the first deals with the period of the French collapse in 1940. Mathieu is with the defeated army, but finally decides to join a small group of soldiers who continue to fight after the Armistice. He is apparently killed by the advancing Germans. In the second part, and also in 'Drôle d'amitié', Brunet becomes the central figure. Taken prisoner at the time Mathieu is killed, he spends his time in the camp organising a branch of the Party. Other Party members later arrive and reveal that his main confidant was thrown out of the Party before the war, and that Moscow has produced a new line radically different from that taught by Brunet. He attempts to escape with Vicarios, the supposed traitor, but the attempt fails and Vicarios is shot. The section concludes with Brunet's thought "Even if the U.S.S.R. wins, all men are alone" (*TM*, v, 1039).

A little more is known about the rest of the book than is mentioned in the quotation on page 169. Mathieu had not been killed, only wounded. After his recovery he worked with the Maquis

and found there true comradeship and that authenticity and freedom which had been the goal of all the other major characters.
Clearly external factors had some influence on Sartre's failure to
complete the series. He was contemplating the conclusion in the
time of post-war optimism when it seemed possible that men of
goodwill could unite as they had done in fighting the Germans.
With the return of political divisions to France and the beginning
of the cold war, Sartre obviously became aware that it was not
so simple a matter as he had thought. Further, there are considerable difficulties in writing a novel about a character whom the
author regards as ideal, particularly when the opposite parts are
played by the execrated Nazis and Militiamen. Ultimately the
trouble springs from the difficulty of giving a positive content to
authenticity. There are an infinite number of ways of being inauthentic, only one path to freedom.

It can be said in a general way that freedom consists in avoiding
the varieties of bad faith that he has portrayed in the other characters. But it is always possible to fall into a new kind of bad faith
in the effort to escape from another; Brunet avoids all Mathieu's
errors but develops others of his own. Hoederer in *Les Mains
sales* (*Crime Passionel*) may represent a man who has found freedom, but the problem of representing such a person in a novel is
greater than that of doing so on the stage, where it is only necessary to portray major events, situations where authenticity can
be clearly demonstrated. In the smaller details of life which are
required in the novel the problem is much greater, though this is
not just an accident of literary form. Hoederer respects men,
treats them also as ends, doesn't protect his own life by humiliating Hugo; he can say "For me, one man more or less in the world
matters" (v, iii). In the kinds of situation in which he is represented
it is fairly clear what this means. It is not clear what it means when
Mathieu is wondering whether he should marry Marcelle now
that she is pregnant. The emptiness of 'respect for persons' as a
guiding principle is manifested in more everyday situations, those
which do not involve death. For both marriage and a refusal to
marry might be seen as treating Marcelle also as an end. It is clear

in the pages of *L'Age de raison* that Mathieu's relation with her is inauthentic; he has an abstract desire for freedom which leads him to wish to be uncommitted and unattached. But it is not clear how he could have established an authentic relation with her; marrying her, leaving her, agreeing to an abortion and carrying on as before could all be considered appropriate courses of action.

The difficulty in dealing with *Les Chemins de la liberté*, both from a literary and a philosophical point of view, arises from the fact that it is unfinished. If we were faced with three separate novels, linked only by common characters, each could be considered on its merits; the linking of all of them by a common title destroys this possibility except perhaps in the case of the first in the series. *L'Age de raison* does seem complete; the series of events that have taken place in the few days covered by it have revealed Mathieu, the dilemma with which the book began has been solved by Daniel's proposal to marry Marcelle. At the end, Mathieu can reflect not just on what has happened, but on his whole life. "He yawned: he had finished his day and with it he had finished his youth. Already some well-tried moralities discreetly offered their services; epicureanism free of illusion, smiling indulgence, resignation, serious-mindedness, stoicism, any of these would allow him to enjoy as a connoisseur, minute by minute, his spoilt life. He took off his jacket, began to untie his tie. Yawning, he repeated to himself: 'It's true, it really is true. I've reached the age of reason'" (*AdeR*, 315). In addition it is written in standard 'novel' form, divided into chapters each of which represents a single stage in the development of the situation which is the core of the whole story. However much we may, as readers, be interested in the other characters for their own sakes, in the end it is because of their relation to Mathieu that we follow their behaviour. We are, I think, justified in thinking that the author has put into the book just this set of people because only with them could all facets of Mathieu be brought to the eyes of the reader. There is no reason why the reader should expect a sequel. But the fact that there is a sequel compels us to restrain our moral, if not our literary, judgment of the book. Mathieu and the others are

given a further chance to emerge from the bad faith in whi
they are enmeshed.

For any of the major characters in the book would serve as an
example for the discussion of bad faith. There is even the barman
who behaves in the same way as the waiter in the example given
in *L'Etre et le néant*: "Around him it was the same. There were
some people who didn't exist at all, mere breaths of air, and there
were others who existed too much. The barman, for example.
Just now he was smoking, vaguely; at present he had woken up,
he was a little too much a barman, he brandished the shaker,
opened it, poured a yellow liquid into the glasses with a superfluous precision: he was playing at being a barman" (*AdeR*, 181).
But this is not merely a philosophical example inserted into the
text; it also serves the purpose of emphasising Mathieu's growing
realisation of the emptiness of his own life, of the extent to which
he does the same thing. The realisation of Mathieu's bad faith
comes to the reader as a result of reading the novel itself, it is not
necessary for him to be explicitly aware of the theory Sartre has
expounded elsewhere. The further point that sincerity can also be
a form of bad faith is illustrated a little earlier: "He added with
irony, as if for himself: 'I am a thinking reed.' As if for himself.
But that wasn't true, he was not sincere; at bottom he wanted to
please Ivich. He thought: 'Then I've got it?' He had profited from
his downfall, he didn't mind getting small advantages from it, he
used it to be polite to little girls. 'Salaud'. But he stopped, frightened; when he treated himself as a salaud, he still wasn't being
sincere, he was not really indignant. It was a trick to redeem himself, he thought he could save himself from abjection by 'lucidity',
but this lucidity cost him nothing, it amused him rather. And even
this judgment he made about his lucidity, this way of climbing
on his own shoulders . . . 'one must change to the very bottom.'
But nothing could help him to do this; all his thoughts were con-
taminated from their birth. Suddenly, Mathieu opened up like a
wound; he saw himself completely like a yawning gulf: thoughts,
thoughts about thoughts, thoughts about thoughts about thoughts;
he was infinitely transparent and infinitely decayed. And then it

faded, and he found he was seated opposite Ivich who looked at him oddly" (AdeR, 176).

The central irony of the book is that the man whose bad faith is most clearly represented is the one who ought to be most self-aware, the philosopher Mathieu, though, as I remarked in the first chapter, we are given little enough evidence of his philosophising. We are told that this is his job, and we are also told that Boris is one of his students, but he is never seen in action. I suspect this is because Sartre wished to avoid the charge of stuffing the book with philosophy. For the points Sartre wishes to make are revealed in the course of the story, not added on to it. The irony is brought out by what happens and what is said, not by the intervention of the narrator. The greatest irony of all is perhaps the fact that the one character who sees through Mathieu and puts the case for authenticity in the clearest form in which it is expressed in the book is Jacques, Mathieu's bourgeois brother, who deliberately decided to conform to custom after a youth that was more bohemian than Mathieu's own. After Mathieu has asked him for a loan to pay for Marcelle's abortion, Jacques criticises his way of life: "You know, I don't understand you; you're so quick at getting indignant when you hear of an injustice and yet you keep this woman in a humiliating position for years, for the simple pleasure of telling yourself that you are acting in accordance with your principles. And if even that were true, if you did live in accordance with your ideas. But, I repeat, you are to all intents and purposes married, you have a stylish flat, you regularly get a tidy salary, you have no worries about the future since the State guarantees you a pension . . . and you like this sort of life, calm and ordered, a real civil servant's life." Mathieu claims that he is only worried about keeping his freedom; Jacques continues: "I would have thought that freedom consisted in facing up to situations into which one has freely entered and accepting all the responsibilities" (AdeR, 113-4).

Sartre is engaged in criticising bad faith, not wickedness. Mathieu is not represented as an immoral character; he seriously believes that Marcelle and he are in agreement about the abortion, and indeed about the whole character of their relationship. He is not even aware, at the beginning of the book, that their original love has disappeared. The full admission of this comes right at the end. "If he took her in his arms, if he said that he loved her, everything would be saved. He would marry her, they would have the baby, they would live side by side for the rest of their lives. He had got up, he was going to say to her 'I love you'. He staggered a bit and said in a clear voice: 'Well, it's true . . . I no longer love you.' Long after the sentence had been uttered he still heard it, stupefied." Even at this stage, Mathieu still contemplates "doing his duty by Marcelle" in the traditional sense. By ordinary standards there is little to say against him, though I think Merleau-Ponty exaggerates his goodness. After commenting on Sartre's good moral character, he says:

This kind of goodness passes into the characters of the novels. Mathieu, in the *Age of Reason*, is willing to become a husband and father. Marcelle has only to say the word. If he does not seduce Ivich, it is because he despises the ceremony of seduction. . . . It is finally because he thinks he has no rights over her, that he respects her and wants her to be free. There do not occur in his novels, except for the purpose of satire and in the persons satirised, chiaroscuro, complacency and sensuality. Sartre's favourite characters are men of good-will and of an uncommon cleanliness.[1]

Sartre's own character is clearly good; he has shown considerable personal courage in standing up both to the French government and the O.A.S. on issues where he felt that a moral point of view should be taken. If the characters of his novels are frequently shown up, it should be remembered that this is by the highest of standards; authenticity is clearly meant to be the acme of morality, a development out of the normal moral code, not a substitute for it.

The danger that Sartre runs in expressing his philosophical views in the way and to the extent that he does in the novels is that his point will be missed, that people, knowing he is a philosopher, will take certain things to be expressions of his views when

[1] *Sens et non-sens* (Nagel, 1948), 74–5.

they are meant quite otherwise. *Les Chemins de la liberté* is a novel and not a text-book. In fact his plays and novels contain few explicit philosophical points; it is only because we know what to look for from other sources that they can be discovered. Some critics seem to have fallen into the trap not only of taking his literary works as accurate expressions of his philosophy, but even of attributing to Sartre the views put forward by characters in their own person. The example I am going to use to illustrate this point has been chosen because it is fairly typical and also brings out some extra features of what Sartre is doing. Mr Cranston, in his book *Sartre* says: "He is revolted also by women. There is something sickening about all the female characters in Sartre's plays and stories. Woman is seen as corrupt and corrupting. . . . Sexual congress is invariably depicted by him as a charmless exercise."[1] Even if it were true that all females in his work were depicted as sickening, it would not follow that Sartre is revolted by women. But it is not true that all women are seen as sickening *by the author*. Mathieu does find Marcelle nauseating when he learns she is pregnant: "In her belly there was a small undefined upsurge which was swelling gently, eventually it would be like an eye. It will spread out in the filth she has in her stomach, it's living" (*AdeR*, 24). That he finds her so is partly due to his own feeling of guilt for her condition, partly to the fact that he no longer loves her. Sartre is not expressing an attitude to pregnancy as such, but developing the feeling of a man like Mathieu in such a situation. That so many of the men have unsatisfactory relations with their mistresses is a part of Sartre's criticism of the characters themselves; they are not seeking a genuine human relation in their love-making, or are incapable of such a relation. This is why few of them find sexual intercourse satisfying. Boris sleeps with Lola because he thinks that he ought to have a mistress as part of his 'experience'. He doesn't want one and is always thinking of how he can get away from her. Hence it is hardly surprising that after making love with her he is disgusted with the "physiological" and thinks of becoming a monk (*AdeR*, 41). In most instances of this

[1] *Sartre* (Oliver and Boyd, 1962), 112.

sort the reason for the failure clearly lies in the characters themselves. The two proletarians in *Le Sursis*, Maurice and Zezette,
have no such difficulties. Simone de Beauvoir reports that in the
fourth volume Mathieu and Odette were to have a successful
affair: "Mathieu and Odette were to fall in love, she was to leave
Jacques, they were to experience the fullness of a mutual passion."[1]
Sex between authentic persons is normally satisfying.

It is the authenticity, the realisation of what it is to be a human
being, that is central here; Mr Cranston's attitude to Sartre is
confused, though less so than that of other critics.

If there is such a thing as a tender heterosexual relationship in all
Sartre's writings (something to compare with the homosexual relationship between Brunet and Vicarios), it is between Charles, the cripple
on his trolley, holding hands with Catherine, a fellow-patient who has
just defaecated near him; humiliated, but *purged*, Catherine has the
purity that others lack. For the rest, the phrase of St Bernard about
women being 'bags of excrement' might well have been spoken by
Sartre.[2]

Incidentally, there is no evidence that there is anything homosexual in the relation between Brunet and Vicarios; it is meant as
an instance of masculine comradeship. The passage Mr Cranston
is referring to (*LS*, 200–2) is really designed to show that the
"physiological", even in this extreme form, doesn't matter.
Charles doesn't think that Catherine has been "purified" by de-
faecation, it is he who feels purified because the incident has, for
the moment at least, enabled him to come to terms with himself,
no longer to think of himself as an invalid. He continues to think
of Catherine as one: "She's an invalid, her beautiful sleek skin is
stretched over liquefying vertebrae, over festering intestines." His
grasp of freedom, momentary though it is, comes from his ability
to love her as she is. In a book where the majority of the characters
are being treated like things by forces beyond their control, it is a
part of the irony that the character who is most a thing should get
nearest to freedom. If Sartre had uttered St Bernard's phrase, he
would have meant it quite differently from the saint, as a simple

---

[1] *La Force des choses*, 213.   [2] *Sartre*, 112.

descriptive fact which, besides applying to men also, would not make any difference to a normal or authentic person. No human relationship which *denies* the physiological can be genuine or lasting. It must be accepted as a part of human existence.

Mr Cranston thinks that the attitude he attributes to Sartre about sex is a reflection of a wider disgust in face of the world:

It is a religious sensibility which shrinks from the external world, and perceives it, as Sartre does, as entirely viscous, sticky, messy, nauseating. The humanistic sensibility rejoices in nature; but Sartre sees natural objects as 'vague', 'soft', 'flabby', 'creamy', 'thick', 'tepid', 'dull', 'sickly' and 'obscene'.[1]

Sartre does indeed talk of the category of *le visqueux* and connects this with feelings of nausea. It is an interesting fact that there seems to be an almost universal horror or dislike of the viscous and sticky, and that such objects give rise to nausea, as he explained in *L'Etre et le néant*. Sartre certainly makes use of this in the novels. I have discussed in Chapter I the way in which Sartre employs the 'thinginess' of things, the contemplation of an object as it is in itself without reference to its normal context or possible uses. That Sartre makes fictional characters feel such sensations in an extreme form is no evidence of his own reaction to the world. If the passages where such terms as Mr Cranston mentions occur are examined closely, it will be found that it is the reaction of a character, not of the author, that is in question. Sartre may not like natural scenery, but it is clear that he likes people. Merleau-Ponty stresses this fact about him. He gets on well with a wide variety of types and is (or was in the immediate post-war period) always willing to try and help by discussing problems brought to him. (This fact was represented in the film *La Vie commence demain*.) "It's all very well, he said one day in front of the crowded Gare de Luxembourg, these chaps interest me."[2] Sartre is, in some sense of that abused word, a humanist. This sympathy for the man in the street is brought out in his description of the French Army awaiting the arrival of the Germans after the defeat of June 1940.

[1] *Sartre*, 111.   [2] *Sens et non-sens*, 80.

Whilst awaiting their captors, some at least of the soldiers fall into a state of primal innocence, wander through the fields with bunches of flowers and greet each other gravely (*MdeA*, 135–7).

Before dealing with the rest of *Les Chemins de la liberté*, I will continue with this discussion of the theory of philosophic literature, both because it will help to show how Sartre avoids the difficulties and because *Le Sursis* and *La Mort dans l'âme* are more closely linked to a philosophic programme than is *L'Age de raison*. (Although both the latter work and *Le Sursis* were published in the same year, 1945, I suspect from internal evidence that the times of writing were significantly different.) From what has already been said, it is clear that Sartre's fictional works are closely related to his philosophy; they cannot be ignored by philosophers in the way that Bertrand Russell's *Satan in the Suburbs* can be. Sartre, in his discussion "What is literature?" has described himself as a "metaphysical writer", defining metaphysics as "a living effort to embrace from the inside the human condition in its totality". He continues: "The questions which our time puts to us and which remain *our* questions are . . .: how can man be made in, by and for history? Is it possible to make a synthesis between our unique irreducible consciousness and our relativity, that is to say a synthesis between dogmatic humanism and a perspectivism? What is the relation between morals and politics? How can we be responsible for the objective consequences of our actions beyond our actual intentions? It would be strictly possible to tackle these problems in the abstract by philosophical reflection. But we, who want to experience them, that is to say to justify our thoughts by those fictitious and concrete experiments which novels are . . . (*S.II*, 251–2). (The French word which I have translated 'experiments' is *expériences*, meaning either 'experiment' or 'experiences'.) It is because these questions are his concern that he talks of "committed" or "engaged" literature; I will not here raise the question of the validity of this as a general theory; it clearly does represent Sartre's programme for the novel as a continuation of philosophy by other means. But he is well aware that the means are different: "After all the novel is not a studied application of the American technique, nor an illustration of Heidegger's theories. . . ." (*S.II*, 43). He would agree with Merleau-Ponty's remarks on the function of philosophic ideas in the novel: "The task of the novelist is not to illustrate these ideas, but to make them exist before us like things."[1] The novel is in the first place a work of art, and hence must be judged by artistic standards. It may be based on, and even reflect, philosophic thought, but this thought must be exhibited in the happenings of the book. A reader who is learned or skilful may be able to extract the philosophy, but it must not obtrude.

Sartre is thinking of this fact among others when he says that the engaged writer must construct his work "*as if* it will have the widest possible following. He never ought to say to himself 'Oh, I shall be lucky if I have three thousand readers' but rather 'What would happen if everyone read what I have written?'" (*S.II*, 73–4). The writer of novels has a responsibility to the reading public in general. The philosopher has a different responsibility; in the first place it is to the argument. He must consider his readers, but is entitled to demand certain levels of knowledge and concentration on their part. He knows that he is writing for a specialist public. I have argued that Sartre's first novel really only appeals to experts; in *Les Chemins* he has succeeded with a wider public. This is due partly to the fact that he has succeeded in 'making his ideas exist before us like things'; for example, the passage quoted on p. 175 above, where Mathieu suddenly expresses his true sentiments towards Marcelle, describes an event which we feel with the same shock as Mathieu does. It is a genuine event, but could also be used as an example of the way decisions 'come into being' rather than are made. It may even lead readers to think about decision. But it is not a mere intrusion, it is a vital part of the structure of the novel. It is because Sartre manages to incorporate philosophical insights in this manner that the novels have commanded the body of readers they have. To this extent Sartre has succeeded in combining the tasks of the philosopher and the novelist.

[1] *Sens et non-sens*, 45.

I have said that the object, or rather one of the objects, of *Le Sursis* is to analyse the Munich crisis in terms of the experiences of a large number of individuals who are affected by it in different ways. This is because the reality of such an event as a war or crisis lies only in particular consciousnesses, those of the led as well as those of the leaders, which was what the philosophers of the 1930s meant by calling such events "logical constructions". Besides this general purpose, Sartre also uses *Le Sursis* to continue the stories of Mathieu and the rest of his associates, and, of course, to bring out the same kind of points that he has already been making in *L'Age de raison*. In order to carry out the first object he wrote the book in a style that was radically different from its predecessor. It might be described as a 'stream of consciousness' style in which the consciousness is continually shifting from one person to another, sometimes remaining with one person for a long period of hours, sometimes switching with bewildering rapidity. Sartre is trying to capture the international event which affects various lives differently, and at the same time to show that this event is the feature which unites them. This leads him to include 'linking' passages in which the different characters are mentioned one after another: "Daniel put his napkin on his knees, Hannequin knotted his round his neck, Brunet took the paper napkin from the table, crumpled it and wiped his lips, Jeannine pushed Charles into the big empty dining-room and spread a napkin on his chest . . ." (*LS*, 95). This passage is clear; often we are not informed in which consciousness we are meant to be. This is deliberate; elsewhere he has argued that the kind of novels he wishes to write involve a change in the technique of novel-writing "from Newtonian mechanics to generalised relativity; we must fill our books with consciousnesses that are half lucid and half obscure, of which one or the other may be considered with more sympathy but of which none will have a privileged point of view either on himself or on the events" (*S.II*, 253). Because of the nature of the crisis there can be no privileged point of view, though of course some people, for instance the politicians Chamberlain, Daladier and Hitler, are in a better position to appreciate the full sweep of events than the illiterate shepherd Gros-Louis, who cannot even read the notices of general mobilisation.

Sartre's general object has largely escaped the critics' notice; it has been thought that he was experimenting with the style of Dos Passos, of whose *1919* he wrote an appreciative review in 1938 (*S.I*, 14–25). But a writer as conscious of what he is doing as Sartre does not simply take over a style from another author; the remark I have already quoted, "a novel is not . . . a studied application of the American technique", is probably intended to rebut this charge. I think the book does succeed in creating a powerful impression of the Munich crisis, particularly as it affected France; apart from the politicians and a family of Sudeten Czechs all the other characters are French or living in France, chosen to represent as wide a range of reactions as possible. Some, such as Gros-Louis and Charles the cripple, have their lives disrupted by forces outside their control; others react in ways which they later come to regret. For different reasons not all of them are glad that peace is signed, Ivich because she has given herself to a man she despises, Boris because he has joined up for three years, M. Birnenschatz, a Jew, because although he wanted peace he sees that the war should have been fought. For Sartre is not only describing an event, he is also criticising a society which preferred "peace at any price". The conclusion brings together Daladier, convinced the mob will tear him to pieces for his betrayal of Czechoslovakia, and Milan Hlinka, a Sudeten Czech: "The aeroplane had landed. Daladier got out with difficulty and stepped on to the ladder; he was pale. There was an enormous shout and people started to run, breaking the police cordon, carrying away the barriers; Milan drank and said laughing: To France, Long live England! Long live Peace! Then he threw the glass with all his strength against the wall; they shouted:—Long live France! Long live England! Long live Peace! they carried flags and bouquets. Daladier had stopped on the first step; he looked at them stupefied. He turned to Léger and said between his teeth 'The silly bastards' " (*LS*, 350). The technique, analogous to cutting in films, is an effective vehicle for Sartre's irony; the way in which one event is reflected differently in the consciousness of another person, or a set of other people, allows him many opportunities for it. Whether or not in the last resort it can be judged a success, it is clear that the book represents a considerable technical feat in combining the general view of the crisis with the development of the individual histories of those characters who appeared in *L'Age de raison* and who were to appear in the later volumes. I myself find it a worthy successor to the first book.

La Mort dans l'âme is less successful, because the book falls into two halves, the first concentrating mainly on Mathieu and the other characters with whom the reader has grown familiar, the second having as central figure Brunet, the Communist official who had appeared briefly in the two previous volumes as a friend of Mathieu. He is also the main figure in 'Drôle d'amitié', the extract from the fourth volume published in *Les Temps modernes*. It almost seems as if this extract is the conclusion of a single novel which starts on page 195 of *La Mort dans l'âme*, and which is about Brunet; the reader finds it hard to connect with what has gone before. It is at this point, I think, that Sartre has allowed his philosophic ideas to intrude disastrously, though this effect might have been mitigated by the publication of a complete *La Dernière chance*. Before examining this further, I will deal with the first part of *La Mort dans l'âme*. The style is reminiscent of that of *Le Sursis*, though it is not so extreme and its purpose is different. The action covers the period 15 to 18 June 1940, but Sartre is not trying to give a picture of the fall of France; there are too few incidents for that. Rather his object is to give an ironic counterpoint to Mathieu's activities, and at the same time to bring up to date the lives of some of the more important characters, to show their reactions to the events of the period. This latter narrative would have been an essential preparation for *La Dernière chance*. The difference in intention between *Le Sursis* and *La Mort dans l'âme* is marked by a difference in style. The characters appear for longer periods in the latter book, and in most cases the place and time is given as a kind of chapter heading.

In spite of this, Mathieu is plainly the central character of the first part; he appears in ninety-nine out of the 193 pages. (He had also occupied more space than any other single character in *Le Sursis*, seventy pages in all, twenty-two more than any one else.) He had, perhaps, advanced a little in genuine self-knowledge in the course of *Le Sursis*. After peace had been proclaimed he thinks: "And nothing would have happened, nothing at all. His domestic life was waiting for him, he had left it in his sitting-room, in his bedroom; he would flow back into it without any trouble. No one would be any trouble, no one would mention the Munich Interlude, in a month it would all be forgotten—there would only be a little invisible scar on his life's continuity, a little break, the memory of a night when he thought he was setting off to a war. 'I don't want to' he thought whilst gripping the bars with all his strength. 'I don't want to! It must not be!' He turned sharply, and looked smilingly at the windows sparkling in the sun. He felt strong; inside of himself he felt a little anguish with which he was beginning to get familiar, a small anguish that gave him confidence. No matter who, no matter where. He no longer owned anything, he no longer was anything. The dark night of the evening before last would not be lost; this massive house-moving would not be entirely useless. Let them re-sheathe their swords, if they want to; let them have their war or not have it, I don't care. I'm not a dupe. The accordion fell silent. Mathieu continued his walk round the square. 'I will remain free' he thought" (*LS*, 349).

Without the possibility of a definite course of action, it is not easy to see how far he has really grasped his freedom. The one concrete action he does perform in *La Mort dans l'âme* remains, in that novel, ambiguous. After the defeat and surrender of the French Army Mathieu and his friend Pinette join a group of soldiers who are continuing the fight; they make a final stand on a church tower. Mathieu is the last left alive. " 'God, he said aloud, they won't say we didn't hold out for a quarter of an hour.' He went to the parapet and began to fire standing up. It was an enormous revenge. Each shot avenged one of his old scruples. A shot for Lola whom I didn't dare rob, a shot for Marcelle whom

I ought to have chucked, a shot for Odette whom I didn't want to sleep with. This for the books that I didn't dare write, that for the journeys that I didn't take, this for all the people whom I wanted to detest and whom I tried to understand. He fired and the laws flew up into the air, thou shalt love thy neighbour as thyself, bang in that bastard's face, thou shalt not kill, bang at that scarecrow opposite. He fired on Man, on Virtue, on the World; Freedom is Terror; fire blazed in the *mairie*, blazed in his head; bullets whistled, free as air; the world will explode and me with it, he fired, he looked at his watch: fourteen and a half minutes; he asked for nothing more than thirty seconds respite, just the time to shoot that proud handsome officer who was running towards the church; he shot at the handsome officer, at all the Beauty on earth, at the street, at flowers, at gardens, at everything he had loved. Beauty made an obscene dive and Mathieu went on firing. He fired: he was pure and all-powerful, he was free. Fifteen minutes" (*MdeA*, 193).

This seems a grand romantic gesture, doomed to futility, rather than a prototype of an authentic action. There is no real point in holding up the German advance for fifteen minutes and killing a few of their soldiers. The war is already lost and the Armistice signed. The Hegelian slogan of "Freedom is Terror" with the rest of the rhetoric shows the hollowness of Mathieu's motives. The other soldiers fought for different, less personal, reasons. " 'And what makes you fight?' asked Pinette. 'With us it's not the same thing; we are *chasseurs*.' 'Well, then?' 'If you are a *chasseur*, you fight' " (*MdeA*, 169). Brunet, hidden in a cellar in the same village and waiting to surrender to the Germans in order to carry on with the work of the Communist Party in the P.O.W. camps, has made a more sensible decision. The natural assumption to make is that Mathieu has been killed with the rest of the group. The discovery that Sartre did not mean this to have happened destroys whatever value we might have seen in the gesture. In any case, it is not the behaviour of an authentic individual, at least in the sense in which Sartre meant the term at that stage of his thought.

The awkwardness about Mathieu's disappearance from the scene is that it leaves the reader with no central character to hold his interest. Brunet's previous appearances have in no way qualified him for the role of 'hero'. Mathieu clearly has a high regard for him, feels himself judged by Brunet's presence. " 'You are really real' said Mathieu. 'Whatever you touch seems real. Since you've been in my room it seems real to me and so disgusts me.' He added sharply, 'You are a man' " (*AdeR*, 126). The reader is willing to accept Mathieu's feelings about Brunet because he knows Mathieu; he is not convinced that Mathieu's feelings are justified. Brunet is a shadowy figure in the first two volumes; supposedly he is a high official in the Communist Party and has been an intimate friend of Mathieu. We are given no evidence of these facts; Sartre, contrary to his usual practice, tells the reader about him instead of allowing him to reveal himself through words and actions. To emphasise the difference between the two parts of the novel even more, Brunet's appearance is marked by an abrupt change of style. All the previous parts had been in the normal past tense for narration; the second half and 'Drôle d'amitié' are written in the present, though the English translation does not follow the French here. It does read awkwardly, but Sartre has clearly done it deliberately. I think that the explanation lies in an attempt to bring out the difference in character between Mathieu and Brunet; the latter, as a dedicated Communist, exists not in himself but in the Party. His ego is that "grammatical fiction" which Koestler talks of in *Darkness at Noon*. Brunet only has a present consciousness. This is another facet of Sartre's attempt to make Brunet a foil to Mathieu. He fails through excessive subjectivity, through too much interest in himself. Brunet fails because he has too little desire for freedom, is too convinced of the Party line. Seeing others only from a deterministic viewpoint, he is unable to have any genuine relationships with them. It is significant that the friendship that develops between him and Vicarios in this book and in 'Drôle d'amité' is at the expense of his strict allegiance to the Party. The literary device could be compared to the philosophic juxtaposition of

Genet and Bukharin quoted in the last chapter. But as a literary device it fails, whatever its philosophical interest, because it demands a more conspicuous and a more interesting Brunet to carry it off. This failure is emphasised in the structure of the novel because the group of men that Brunet gathers around him in the prison camp are seen as types rather than as individuals. Sartre, in accordance with his change of moral outlook, seems to have become more interested in the way in which groups form and maintain their solidarity than in the adventure of individuals. This might well form the subject of a novel, but not of a novel in which one figure has previously played such a conspicuous part.

Both in making Brunet central and in changing his style, Sartre has allowed his philosophic idea to distort a literary form, to the detriment of the latter. From the description Simone de Beauvoir gives of Sartre's plan for the final volume, it is unlikely that it would have succeeded in redeeming *La Mort dans l'âme*, though I must add that she prefers it to the two others. She further claims that the main reasons that led Sartre to abandon work on the fourth volume were that the important points had already been covered, that Sartre only had to "pick the fruits he had so carefully ripened". And that he was by that time more interested in the present than the past. I will quote her description of *La Dernière chance* at length. After the failure of his escape with Vicarios, Brunet "decided to make a new attempt. He had heard of a prisoner who directed an escape organisation, he found it was Mathieu who, at the moment of their meeting, was helping to execute an informer. . . . Thanks to his help, Brunet escaped and got to Paris; he learnt with stupefaction that,—by a reversal like that which at the end of *Mains sales* drove Hugo to suicide—the U.S.S.R. had entered the war, the Communist Party was condemning collaboration. Having succeeded in rehabilitating Vicarios, he became again a militant, this time in the Resistance. But doubt, scandal and solitude had taught him about his subjectivity; by engagement he had found his freedom again. Mathieu took the opposite path . . . tired of being free 'for nothing', he had at last cheerfully taken to action. . . . In the Stalag, his project had still been that of an individual adventurer; now, submitting to collective discipline, he had attained true engagement. Starting, one from alienation in a Cause, the other from an abstract freedom, Brunet and Mathieu both came to represent the authentic man of action as Sartre conceived him. Mathieu and Odette fell in love, she left Jacques, and they came to realise the fullness of a mutual passion. Arrested, Mathieu died under torture, heroic not by essence but because *he had made himself* into a hero. . . . Everybody died, or nearly everybody; there was no one left to raise the problems of after the war."[1]

The final sentence seems to represent a new twist to the fairy story "They all lived happily ever after". Nevertheless the fact that authenticity can only be represented in such extreme situations as this sketch describes is an important fact about Sartre's thought, and serves to confirm the diagnosis I gave of the failure of his morality in the last chapter. It also shows that what appears to be an increasing concern with the philosophical aspects of the tetralogy has led to a literary failure in the third volume and the virtual impossibility of completing the fourth, for it is hard to see that the sketch given by de Beauvoir could have been turned into a successful novel. But this failure is not evident at all in the first two volumes, though they are in some ways 'philosophical novels'. There the thought content is always at the service of the story. I regard the first two books as considerable achievements for any novelist, and even the third is by no means negligible from a purely literary point of view. All three can be appreciated by those who know little or nothing of Sartre's philosophic views. Those who are versed in his philosophy will find them even more rewarding intellectually and, I think, more immediately fascinating as novels. Some of my criticisms have been severe, but they are not meant to imply that *Les Chemins de la liberté* is other than a major achievement.

---

[1] *La Force des choses*, 213–14, with some passages omitted and one sentence moved to a different place.

XII

Sartre's Politics

I HAVE already suggested that Sartre's development can be viewed as starting from an individualist position and passing, by stages, into a collectivist one which emphasises the social nature of man; here I must stress it. Some of the failure of the later parts of *Les Chemins de la liberté* is due to the attempt to concentrate on groups rather than individuals, and the major fault of *Critique de la raison dialectique* is that it moves at such a level of generality that the individual is lost sight of in the group, which becomes the fundamental structure, man almost an epiphenomenon. The difficulties which became evident in talking about his moral theory are connected with this change from individualism to a more political view. In one of his latest pronouncements Sartre has said: "But I discovered suddenly that alienation, exploitation of man by man, under-nourishment, relegated to the background metaphysical evil which is a luxury. Hunger is an evil: period. . . . I believe, I desire, that social and economic ills may be remedied. With a little luck that epoch may arrive. I am on the side of those who think that things will go better when the world has changed."[1] This passage might be linked with one from *La Force des choses*. "This year [1949?] Sartre abandoned his morality properly so-called, because he became convinced that 'the moral attitude appeared when technical and social conditions made positive behaviour impossible. Morality is a collection of idealist devices to enable one to endure what the shortage of resources and lack of techniques imposes on one'."[2]

[1] *Encounter*, June 1964, 61–62.
[2] *La Force des choses*, 218. Simone de Beauvoir notes that the passage comes from an unpublished MS of Sartre's.

189

This shift from one view to another on the philosophical level parallels, and is closely linked with, Sartre's change of political views, using the word in a practical, rather than a theoretical, sense. It is hard to see which attitude caused the other; I suspect that not even Sartre himself could answer such a question. In politics he has travelled from a position, to use his own words, of "belated anarchism" to a full-blooded Marxism and a qualified support for the Communist Party itself on many issues. Before the war he was not sufficiently interested to vote; after it he helped to found the *Rassemblement Démocratique Révolutionnaire* (R.D.R.) to promote certain political ends. As a result, a large part of his post-war writing has been concerned with political questions, often with what now seem to be ephemeral issues. Such activity is less surprising in a Frenchman than it would be for an Englishman in a comparable position, for every eminent French writer is expected by the Press and the public to have views on the major issues of the day and is given an opportunity of putting them forward. Sartre has also had his private outlet in *Les Temps modernes*.

The main topics discussed in this chapter are Sartre's Marxism and his relations with the Communist Party. Concentration on the latter in Anglo-American discussions has falsified understanding of Sartre's actual views and positions *vis-à-vis* Marxism. To many critics *any* remarks in favour of the Communist Party or of the U.S.S.R. seem treasonable or wilfully eccentric, a last effort to 'épater les bourgeois'. Sartre has an acute mind; hence it is *a priori* improbable that his political views are merely silly on the theoretical level. He may not be sensible in practical politics, where different qualities are needed, but his intellectual judgments must be listened to with care, even if they can be refuted in the last resort. That Sartre supported the Communist cause on certain occasions is clear; what are interesting are his reasons for doing so and the qualifications he attached to his support.

On the intellectual plane anti-Communism is as corrupting as outright adherence to Communism; both render serious thought impossible, because both accept certain conclusions as given before any discussion can be started. Just as many Soviet attacks on the West omit reference to its virtues, so many exposures of Communism make it quite incomprehensible why anyone should ever have come to hold the doctrines of Marx, so foolish are they made to sound. It is useless to criticise any political doctrine unless the reasons for its attractiveness to its adherents are established, and hard to criticise it unless the critic has been sufficiently under the influence of the doctrine to feel its attractiveness, to see the point of it. A purely abstract analysis of a political doctrine always omits something. Sartre, talking of his own days as a student, remarks: "Certainly we were permitted to read Marx; we were even advised to do so: one had to know him 'in order to refute him'. But without any knowledge of Hegel and without Marxist instructors, without a programme or any instruments of thought, our generation, like those before and the one after, remained ignorant of historical materialism. . . . It was about this time that I read *Capital* and the *German Ideology*; I understood everything clearly and I understood nothing" (*CRD*, 22–23). Many of Sartre's critics in the West would seem to have had similar experiences; they are superficial anti-Marxists as so many intellectuals in the 1930s were superficial Communists. Some have even passed direct from one to the other without any mental upset.

In England it is, of course, difficult to take the Communist Party seriously; it is a small minority with little hope of ever having any substantial effect on the structure of British democracy. In France, where in the 'forties and 'fifties the Party was numbered in millions, though manipulation of electoral machinery prevented them from getting a fair proportion of deputies elected, it was a serious political factor. The attraction of Party membership is real, especially to intellectuals. To understand Sartre's (and Merleau-Ponty's) political views, this attraction must be understood. Both these philosophers were strongly drawn to the Party, though both found it impossible to become card-carrying members. But their conversions were to Marxism, not to Communism. In France any left-wing socialist had to come to terms with the Communist Party, the more so because of the part that it had played in the French Resistance Movement, which seemed in the early post-war period to provide a pattern for similar co-operation in peace-time. This was what Sartre hoped to do with the R.D.R., which might be described as an attempt to revive the pre-war Popular Front, rather than as a political party in the full sense. The point of the word *Rassemblement* was to indicate that it intended to group already existing organisations, not to supplant them. "We are obliged to get our membership from several already existing parties which have gathered together the social groups we are addressing. As a result, we have to say to these people 'Come to us and see, freely and whilst remaining members of your party, whether a regrouping is possible.' We do not claim to fill a gap in society that does not exist. The lack we are trying to óvercome is rather a lack at the level of action" (*EP*, 15).[1] The Communists, Sartre soon found, worked on the principle 'He who is not with us is against us', and talked as if the R.D.R. was an attempt to infiltrate the Communist Party from the right and to destroy it. This attitude was manifested in attacks on the motives and honesty, and even on the private lives, of all concerned in the R.D.R. If Sartre had any illusions about the ways in which the Communist Party conducted political action, he soon lost them. About this time a Communist Congress declared existentialism "ideological public enemy No. 1". Sartre commented: "That was perhaps the only day when the Communists showed a little bit of courtesy towards me, or, shall I say, were less rude. I am used to attacks on my private life and insinuations about my honesty. There all that was in question was the stupidity of the doctrine and the danger which it constituted. I was pleasantly surprised" (*EP*, 78).

It is now obvious that such an attempt as the R.D.R. represented was doomed to failure. Whether or not this was equally obvious at the foundation of the movement is hard to say. Even if it were, the motives were admirable; all Sartre can be convicted of is a lack of political realism, which does not disqualify a philos-

[1] *Entretiens sur la politique* (Gallimard, 1949). This book is a series of discussions between Sartre, David Rousset and Gérard Rosenthal, and was intended as a manifesto of the R.D.R.

opher from discussing politics. Some critics have suggested that
the result of the failure of the *R.D.R.* was to drive Sartre into the
arms of the Communists. Mr Cranston says, "From the collapse
of the *R.D.R.* Sartre drew one lesson: that henceforth he must
collaborate with the Communist Party, and this, without actually
joining the ranks, he has since steadfastly done."[1] It is not made
clear why the treatment he had received at the hands of the Communists should have driven him to co-operate with them. In fact,
he has since been careful to mark the limits of his agreement with
the Party in all of his prepared remarks. Sartre has frequently felt
the same way as have the Communists, though his reasons for
his attitudes have often been different from theirs. "It is true: the
aim of this article is to declare my agreement with the Communists on certain limited subjects, reasoning from *my own*
principles and not from *theirs*" (*TM*, VIII, 706). Such statements
as this have not prevented the Party from continuing its campaign against him, though there have been variations in its
virulence. Sartre has stuck to his own principles and has not
hesitated to condemn the Party when it appears to have acted
wrongly. He is under no illusions about the way in which the
French Communist Party is run; he has seen the extent to which
it is a centralised dictatorial body frequently operating in the
interests of the U.S.S.R. without regard to French national
interests or even the actual situation in France. This unfortunate
consequence of "socialism in one country", with the resulting
machiavellian employment of local parties by Moscow for its own
ends has destroyed many of the intellectuals who joined the Party
from idealistic motives. Sartre discusses one case of a man so
destroyed, that of Paul Nizan. Though he was killed in 1940, the
Communists have continued their attacks on him. It is probable
that the story of Brunet and Vicarios-Schneider in *Les Chemins de
la liberté* is based on the case of Nizan; the description Sartre gives
in his preface to *Aden Arabie* tallies in many points.

Sartre may be in agreement with the Communists on some
issues—it is hard for anyone at all politically aware not to be—

[1] *Encounter*, April 1962, 44.

but he is too conscious of the faults both of the Party and of the U.S.S.R. ever to be a naïve fellow traveller. Indeed, he demands from the Communists a higher standard than is to be expected from other parties, precisely because their claims are so much greater. His articles on the Hungarian uprising make this clear. "When Soviet politics puts socialism in danger, contradicts its principles and its aims, when the means it uses threaten to destroy the ends it serves, we reserve all our indignation for it. It is no longer a matter of fighting an enemy nor of eliminating a system; the method and those who direct it must be condemned. The greatness of their enterprise and the weight of their responsibilities are such as to rob them *in every case of the defence of extenuating circumstances*. . . . But when Russian tanks fire on buildings in Budapest, when they transform, as Césaire has rightly said, social-ism into a nightmare, when State police arrest and deport Hun-garian youths and workers, it is the hope of mankind—its only hope—which is put in question. . . . If the U.S.S.R. is worth no more and no less than capitalist England, then there remains noth-ing for us but to cultivate our gardens. To preserve that hope, the opposite must be done; recognise, through the barrier of errors, of monstrous acts and of crimes, the privileged position of the socialist camp, and condemn with so much the greater force those policies which endanger those privileges" (*TM*, XII, 677–8).

It is often said that the Communists believe that the 'end justifies the means'. Even if they have taken over this slogan from its Jesuit inventors, Sartre will not accept it, though he does not reject it on the basis of an absolute morality. Rather his point is that it is impossible to make a clear separation between means and ends; the analogy, so often lying behind Utilitarian discussions, of means as a kind of money that can be used indifferently to pur-chase any one of a number of different ends, does not satisfy him. ". . . in the majority of cases, the means used make a *qualitative* difference to the end." He explains this: "Let us imagine a revolu-tionary party which lies systematically to its members to protect them from uncertainties, crises of conscience, enemy propaganda. The end pursued is the abolition of oppression; but lying is itself a form of oppression. Can oppression be perpetuated under the pretext of ending it? Must man be enslaved in order to liberate him? It will be said that the means are transitory. No, not if they help to make mankind *lying* and *lied* to . . . for then the reasons that existed for abolishing oppression are destroyed by what is done to abolish it" (*S.II*, 308). Both here and elsewhere Sartre explicitly refers to the Communists: "Now if socialism does not determine the nature of the methods which it is claimed will protect it, if it is believed that it can be defended by methods which are closely related to Tsarist repression, it becomes a passive indifferent object, an ideal term of reference which could be replaced anywhere and at any time by some other abstraction" ('Le fantôme de Staline', *TM*, XII, 674). All means are not equivalent, because many of them are incompatible with the ends sought; in particular a just society cannot be founded by unjust methods. It is for this reason that Sartre ultimately rejects the methods of the Communists.

But he does not condemn violence *per se*; indeed, it even seems that he revels in its necessity, with what has been described as a typical intellectual's feeling for it, though, given the greater violence of French politics, Sartre's attitude may seem less surprising. His theoretical argument is that all political action rests on the possibility of compelling others to act or refrain from acting, and that this constraint involves violence. This doctrine is held by others besides the Marxists; Miss Anscombe, writing from a Catholic position, says

In a peaceful and law-abiding country such as England, it may not be immediately obvious that the rulers need to command violence to the point of fighting to the death those that would oppose it; but brief reflection shews that this is so. For those who oppose the force that backs the law will not always stop short of fighting to the death and cannot always be put down short of fighting to the death.[1]

The comparable passage from Sartre occurs in his articles on the Hungarian Revolution, 'Le fantôme de Staline': "One of my

[1] 'War and Murder', in *Nuclear Weapons and Christian Conscience*, ed. W. Stein, 46.

correspondents said 'Only the supporters of absolute non-violence have the right to judge'. Which means: Only those who above all else refuse to shed blood have the right to take up a *moral* position. Certainly. But that is precisely because they condemn *a priori* all *political* action . . . politics is necessary and no one can take part in it—not even the simple citizen who votes every four years for a party—if he does not accept in advance that violence, in certain cases, may be the lesser evil" (*TM*, XII, 579). Some misunderstandings of Sartre's position may arise from an uncritical acceptance of passages from the plays; for example, Hoederer says in *Les Mains sales*: "How frightened you are of dirtying your hands. Oh well, stay pure! What good will it do anyone and why did you join us? Purity is a fakir's or monk's ideal. You intellectuals and bourgeois anarchists, you make it an excuse for doing nothing. Do nothing then, stay still, fold your arms, wear gloves. As for me, I've got dirty hands. Dirty up to the elbows. I've dipped them in blood and shit. And then afterwards? Do you think it's possible to govern innocently?" (Tableau V, scene 3). Hoederer is speaking as a member of a revolutionary party in a revolutionary situation, not as an average man.

Nevertheless, the idea that all politics involves the possibility of violence sounds odd to English ears, though, as I have remarked, in France since the Algerian War the notion is not so hard to understand. But Sartre, like other French intellectuals, wants to make this fact more central. Indeed, it seems possible that his conversion to Marxism depended on his acceptance of this point of view. In so far as it is possible to name a time and an event which precipitated such a conversion, it would seem to be the reading of Merleau-Ponty's *Humanisme et terreur*, published in 1947, which is a defence of the Moscow Trials and a reply to Koestler's novel *Darkness at Noon*.[1] Merleau-Ponty argues that violence is an essential part of human life, at least of political life. He says

To respect someone who does not respect others is ultimately to despise them, to abstain from violence towards the violent is to make

[1] The French title is *Le Zéro et l'infini*.

oneself their accomplice. We do not have the choice between purity and violence, but between different sorts of violence. Violence is our lot in as much as we are creatures of flesh and blood. . . . Violence is the common point of departure for all régimes. Life, discussion, political choice all take place against this background.[1]

Merleau-Ponty further argues that the reason why Western society is free from violence is that it took place at times and places removed from that society, either in the colonies or during the Industrial Revolution. His conversion of Sartre was not, of course, the making of an anti-Marxist into a Marxist; clearly Sartre was always on the socialist side of the fence, supported the Government in Spain, disliked the bourgeoisie, and, on an intellectual level, by this time was acquainted with the works of Marx and Hegel. What Merleau-Ponty did by his book and his conversation was to bring a number of previously isolated points of view together and to fit them into Sartre's existing philosophical framework. "He revealed to me that I was making history in the way that M. Jourdain made prose" (TM, Nos. 184-5, 324).

This conversion might be said to be to a belief in politics rather than to a belief in Marxism, a belief that collective action can be effective and that it can change the individual as well as the society. I have already quoted Sartre's remark, from the same passage as the quotation in the last paragraph, about his "belated anarchism"; henceforth his philosophy is no longer a private creed but also a political doctrine. That the political doctrine should be Marxism is already, as I have argued, implicit. Merleau-Ponty made this explicit and thereby changed Sartre's philosophic attitude. At the end of Humanisme et terreur he talks of the difference between "bad existentialism" and the genuine variety; the former "merely describes the clash of reason against the contradictions of experience, and concludes with the consciousness of failure. But this is only a refurbishing of classical scepticism."[2] True existentialism, on the other hand, recognises that contingency is a fundamental feature of the world and that errors and violence are inevitable. But there is no fatality in history; men can work

---

[1] Humanisme et terreur, 117–18.   [2] ibid., 205.

towards rational goals, even though these may not be easy to achieve and may themselves involve further violence.

The popular image of existentialism has been that of Merleau-Ponty's "bad" variety, and the man who most obviously held the view was Camus. His attitude of revolt was a protest against the *universe as a whole*, not against any particular feature of it. He was struck by the contradiction between the rationality of man and the absurdity of things. Consequently his attitude was forced to remain individual and private; the condition was irremediable and man showed his stature by recording his vote against the inevitable. Sartre, with his more empirical approach, confined his protest to those features which seemed to him alterable, the relations between man and man. The famous quarrel between Sartre and Camus was ultimately motivated by this divergence in their philosophical views, though certain external incidents were its occasion. Although earlier writings of Sartre may appear to put forward a view similar to that of Camus, a close study will reveal essential differences; even in *La Nausée* it was the absurdity of man's behaviour rather than the absurdity of the universe as such that struck Roquentin. Sartre was never a "bad" existentialist in the sense that Camus was.

In the essay *Matérialisme et révolution* Sartre distinguishes between revolt and revolution; the former is the activity of an oppressed section of society, of slaves, Negroes, Jews for example, to attain the *same* rights as other members of that society. It does not involve any attempt to overthrow that society, indeed only makes sense in terms of the values of that society itself. The revolutionary, on the other hand, wants to establish a new society and a new kind of man. "Thus the revolutionary, because he is aware of the social structure on which he depends, demands a philosophy which comprehends his situation, and, as his action has no meaning unless it questions the lot of mankind, this philosophy must be total, that is to say it must illuminate the whole of the human condition" (*S.III*, 180). But the revolutionary desire to "invent man" anew depends on the existence of a contingent world. "The philosophers have only *interpreted* the world in various ways; the point, however, is to *change* it." Sartre several times echoes the XIth thesis on Feuerbach. But the change in his philosophy which is here under discussion consists in seeing that it is social, not individual change, which is the vital feature. Coupled with this goes a new feeling for the philosophy of Marx; in his open letter to Camus he says: "I do not have to defend those [ideas] of Marx, but let me say that the dilemma by which you claim to refute them (either his 'prophecies' are true or Marxism is only a method), leaves out the entire Marxist *philosophy*, and everything which is for me (who am not a Marxist) its profound truth" (*TM*, VIII, 343n.). I have already mentioned the different face that Marx presents to his French students and critics; it is a more Hegelian Marx, studied by those whose acquaintance with Hegel is wider than that of most English philosophers. Kojève's pre-war lectures on Hegel, presenting him in a very 'existentialist' light, as well as Hyppolite's *Études sur Marx et Hegel*, have had a great influence on Sartre and his contemporaries.

Though the 'existential' interpretations of Marx tend to rely heavily on the *Economic and Philosophic Manuscripts of 1844*, I think they are consistent with the rest of Marx's writings, and make it possible to claim that he was first and foremost a philosopher. This has been denied or ignored for two reasons, first, Marx's own greater concentration on practical and economic matters in the later works, and second the distortions of his original doctrine by Engels. (Sartre remarks: "This, again, is the view of Marx in 1844, that is to say before the ill-starred meeting with Engels", *S.III*, 213.) In Chapter IX I mentioned that Sartre made use of the term 'alienation' to describe the nature of bad faith. This might be called 'personal alienation'. At this stage of his thought it is 'public alienation' with which he is mainly concerned, and this is the alienation that forms the core of Marx's philosophic position. The bridge between the two Sartrean positions is partially provided by *Saint Genet*, in which he recognises that social conditions may force the individual to 'reify' himself, think of himself as an object. Sartre's acceptance of Marxism consists in seeing this reification as a necessary feature of present society. Marx's most vivid description of this occurs in the following passage:

As a result, therefore, man (the worker) no longer feels himself to be freely active in any but his most animal functions—eating, drinking, procreating, or at most in his dwelling and dressing up, etc.; and in his human functions he no longer feels himself to be anything but animal. What is animal becomes human and what is human becomes animal. Certainly, eating, drinking, procreating, etc., are also genuinely human functions. But in the abstraction which separates them from the sphere of all other human activities and turns them into sole and ultimate ends, they are animal.[1]

For Marx this alienation is twofold; first man is alienated from his work, which is seen as labour, something external and imposed by necessity, instead of being seen as what makes man human, the thing which distinguishes him from the animals: ". . . the *entire so-called history of the world* is nothing but the begetting of man through human labour. . . ."[2] Second, man is alienated from his fellows because the capitalist system of production leads to a class-structure, which prevents men from treating all human beings as fellows.

If Marx's analysis is taken as a correct diagnosis of the ills of society, then it follows that an improvement in the economic lot of the workers will not *solve* the problem; reduction in working hours and more money to spend on leisure will only increase the alienation from work, while doing nothing to remove class-barriers. Although the *physical* unpleasantness of the life of the lowest level of society has obviously decreased since Marx's time, Sartre would, I think, argue that it is by no means obvious that there has been a corresponding reduction in *mental* unpleasantness; the Marxian analysis of alienation is still applicable to all capitalist (and perhaps to most socialist) societies. Just as bad faith consisted in the denial of one's human nature, so alienation involves the

---

[1] *Economic and Philosophic Manuscripts of 1844* (Foreign Language Publishing House, Moscow), 73.

[2] op. cit., 113. Marx's italics.

same. Marxist revolutionary movements are 'humanist', Sartre thinks, because the affirmation "we *too* are men" lies at their base; they are attempts to bring all men to equality because only in that way can the external features of alienation be avoided. During the 1950s it seems that Sartre almost believed that the successful revolution would also solve the 'existential' problems of the individual, though, as the passage quoted at the end of Chapter IX shows, he is now doubtful about this.

It has been argued, both by Marxists and non-Marxists, that Sartre cannot accept Marxian materialism, that his theory of mind is clearly 'idealist'. It seems to me, on the contrary, that Marx's materialism has itself been misunderstood, particularly by the Marxists themselves; Lenin in *Materialism and Empirio-criticism* seems a conspicuous offender. This work seems to hark back to a pre-Marxian type of materialism which Marx explicitly criticises in the *Theses on Feuerbach* and elsewhere. Marx's own view of mind would seem not to be very different from that of Ryle or of Sartre himself. Merleau-Ponty, for example, describes Marx's analysis as

demanding at the theoretical level a new conception of consciousness, which explains both its autonomy and its dependence by describing it as a nothingness [*néant*] which arises in the world and which cannot keep its freedom without committing itself at every instant.[1]

Marx was engaged in fighting on two philosophic fronts; his theory was designed to avoid both the traps of idealism and those of the old materialism. Many of his followers have talked as if idealism were the only enemy, that any doctrine that could be called 'materialist' was correct. But there seems no reason to believe that Marx regarded consciousness as a mere epiphenomenon. Indeed, his whole emphasis on work as that which makes man truly human would be senseless if human consciousness were reduced in status. For work consists in altering the form of inert matter in accordance with a preconceived idea. It is in this sense that work is connected with human freedom. Sartre, echoing

[1] *Sens et non-sens*, 143.

Hegel's words on the relation between master and slave, words that were of great importance to Marx's thinking, says "In other words, it is the determinism of matter which gives him [the workman] the first image of his own freedom" (*S.III*, 199). Marx's theory of consciousness is not as elaborate as that of Sartre, but there is nothing necessarily inconsistent between them.

Sartre's quarrel is with the Marxists, rather than with Marx himself. For the followers have tried to claim that Marx gave a complete account of man. "The Marxists of today only take account of adults; in reading them one would be led to believe that we are born at the age when we get our first pay-packet; they have forgotten their own childhood and everything happens, according to them, as if men first experienced their alienation and their reification *in their own work*, whereas everyone experiences it *first*, as a child, *in the work of its parents*" (*CRD*, 47). They have ignored the part played in the shaping of the individual by those factors that the psychoanalysts have stressed. These latter have likewise, according to Sartre, ignored economic factors. The Marxists explain away Flaubert as a bourgeois writer; but, Sartre argues, there were many bourgeois in the same position as Flaubert both socially and economically; only he wrote *Madame Bovary*, *Salammbo* and the other books. Hence more than economic factors are required to account for him. In the early sections of *Critique de la raison dialectique* Sartre sketches some of these factors, the concrete situation of Flaubert in his early life and the 'fundamental project' which made him into the man he was. He has suggested that he may complete this study at a later date. Implicit in such studies is the belief that more is necessary than most Marxists think to deal satisfactorily with man. For Sartre, Marx's philosophy is a series of "directive principles, indications of tasks, problems" rather than a collection of "concrete truths" (*CRD*, 33). It is for this reason that Sartre says, at the end of the first part of the *Critique*: "These considerations make it understandable why I can declare both that I am in deep agreement with Marxist philosophy and provisionally maintain the autonomy of the existentialist ideology" (*CRD*, 107). Existentialism will only 'wither away' when its fundamental insights have been incorporated into Marxism, when, in Sartre's words, the latter takes "the human dimension (that is to say the existential project) as the foundation of anthropological knowledge" (*CRD*, 111).

In spite of these reservations, Sartre maintains that Marxism is "the unsurpassable philosophy of our time", though precisely what he means by this phrase is not easy to grasp. He divides the history of modern philosophy into three periods, the "moment" of Descartes and Locke, that of Kant and Hegel, and finally that of Marx. "These three philosophies become, each in its turn, the soil of all particular thought and the horizon of all culture; they are unsurpassable as long as the historical period of which they are the expression has not passed. I have often noticed that an 'anti-Marxist' argument is only the apparent rejuvenation of a pre-Marxist idea. Any claimed 'surpassing' of Marxism will be at worst a return to pre-Marxism, at the best a rediscovery of a thought already contained in the philosophy which it is claimed has been surpassed" (*CRD*, 17). Such remarks seem to make philosophy into the mere reflection of the prevailing modes of production of the age, an example of Marxist dogmatism rather than a contribution to the subject. If one looks at the history of thought in a general manner it is possible to characterise it as divided into 'periods', but any closer examination will reveal that these are only superficial aids, not true analyses. Further, even if it is possible to characterise past ages in these ways, it is too early to be sure how the future will view our own, what trend of thought it will regard as the dominant one. If Sartre is claiming, as he appears to be, that all discussion is carried on in Marxist terms, even by those who are not Marxists, then he is clearly wrong. In the *Critique* he defines a 'philosophy' as the "totalisation of contemporary knowledge" (e.g., *CRD*, 15). This would appear to be a return to the old view of philosophy as the science of all sciences, the system into which all knowledge can be fitted, and as such to be an error. Here again Sartre has allowed himself to be carried away by enthusiasm into maintaining a position which is untenable. Marxism may have much to offer the world at the present time, but the way to establish this is by detailed analyses of particular problems, not by grand 'metaphysical' claims.

However, there is something to be said, though not precisely in Sartre's terms, about the refutation of philosophic systems. Historians of philosophy often talk as if the subject consisted of a series of battles between rival schools, with victory for a time going to one of the contenders. This is largely the result of viewing the events from the outside. From within the situation is quite different; certain ways of dealing with problems, indeed certain problems themselves, are dropped because they no longer seem appropriate or interesting. Certainly there are published 'refutations' of a certain way of doing things, but those who adhere to the refuted system generally feel that these miss the point altogether. For example there have been plenty of such refutations of 'linguistic philosophy', but these have had little or no effect on the linguistic philosophers themselves. And most of those who practise this method would not claim that they did so because the previous philosophies had been decisively refuted by a set of arguments. Old philosophies are not killed in battles between rival schools; they just fade away. Sartre's own conversion to Marxism was not the result of a refutation of his previous views; indeed, as has been seen, these are to a large extent incorporated in his later work. Further, Sartre's Marxism now (1965) seems less eccentric than it did ten years ago; the climate of the age is, perhaps even partly as a result of his writing, more sympathetic to Marx as a thinker. This is shown by the increasing number of books about him published, not all of which are 'refutations' or shots in the cold war.

Sartre's political philosophy is as rationalist as the other parts of his work. To many it appears that his political commitments are also rationalistic, based on theoretical grounds rather than on close consideration of the present political facts. Certainly some of his pronouncements on actual events have sounded rather silly, though perhaps never as silly as some of his critics have made out. There is something 'idealistic' in the foundation of the R.D.R. and his recent (1962) attempt to form an 'anti-Fascist league'. But it is not silly or idealistic to stand out for justice and freedom at a time when one's government and a large section of the populace seems bent on ignoring them, particularly when it is clear that such a stand involves personal danger. Though Sartre's personal character is strictly irrelevant to a study like the present, it seems clear that he cannot be lightly dismissed as a mere intellectual meddling in politics. The stand he has had to take in the practical sphere demonstrates that the theoretical bases of politics in the Western democracies at least need constant examination.

XIII

Dialectic

Critique de la raison dialectique is a monumental book. It contains 755 pages, slightly more than L'Etre et le néant, but it is printed in smaller type, so it is, in fact, about half as long again, with 390,000 against 250,000 words. To daunt the reader further, he is told that it is only the first of two volumes. Apart from the sheer bulk, it is by no means easy to read; the writing is turgid with few of the flashes of wit which enliven L'Etre et le néant. The sentences are long and tortuous; the paragraphs ramble, many running to three or four pages. The examples, so often a source of delight and illumination in reading Sartre, tend at their best to be detailed analyses of sections of French history; to be dubious at their worst. After the first 111 pages, previously published under the title 'Questions de méthode' in Temps modernes, and under the title 'Existentialisme et marxisme' in a Polish journal, the reader is liable to feel lost. And even if he does manage to finish the book, grave doubts will arise in his mind as to the validity of the conclusions reached. Those who do succeed in this herculean task will feel inclined to echo the words of one reviewer: "The time has come for us to say to Sartre that what we need from him are fewer theories and more plays."[1] Although the section 'Questions de méthode' precedes the body of the work, Sartre complicates matters by stating in the preface that logically it should follow the main portion, for the latter provides the foundation for its more general conclusions. This is particularly regrettable in that the argument of 'Questions de méthode' can be followed comparatively easily; it was, after all,

[1] A. MacIntyre, 'Sartre as a Social Theorist', The Listener, 22 March 1962, 513.

206

written independently. Finally, though Sartre talks in the first section of an 'existentialism' which would appear to be that of his earlier writings, it seems that the notion of 'scarcity' in an economic sense has now become the central term. Human beings are, it seems, reduced to something like the "economic man" of the early economists. "Thus the scandal lies not, as Hegel thought, in the simple existence of the other person, which would refer us to an original unintelligibility. It lies in experienced (or threatened) violence, that is to say in interiorised scarcity" (*CRD*, 752). It is no longer the look which reveals the existence of another person, it is the possibility that he will take what I want. The dominance of scarcity also leads Sartre to curtail drastically the province of freedom: "Above all let no one interpret me as saying that man is free in all situations, as the Stoics claimed. I want to say exactly the opposite, namely that all men are slaves in so far as their experience of life takes place in the realm of the *practico-inert* and in the exact measure in which this realm is originally conditioned by scarcity" (*CRD*, 369).

Marx tried to define the area in which men were bound by their own and their ancestors' actions, the extent to which freedom is diminished by what has been done. Sartre's term *practico-inert* names this area in which previous free actions restrict present behaviour. He uses as example the way in which the Chinese peasants, seeking wood and increased land for cultivation, cut down all the trees and so exposed themselves and their descendants to disastrous floods and famines. Clearly the term is a useful one; in many spheres the economic and technical sins of the fathers are visited on the children. As far as the Chinese peasant of today is concerned, the state of the countryside is a given factor, though actually the result of past '*praxis*', human action; *practico-inert* describes this admirably, and Sartre is clearly justified in talking of the "hell of the *practico-inert*". Marx realised that the *practico-inert* presented an important limitation on human action and freedom; instead of following Marx, Sartre seems to leap to the conclusion that there is no freedom because of this feature. Even in the new formulation, his old exaggeration comes to the fore.

Nevertheless, the problem which he is attempting to deal with in *Critique de la raison dialectique* is an important one, though presented perhaps in a misleading way. He calls it the problem of the relation between 'existentialism' and Marxism, but, reduced to concrete terms, it is that of the relation between sociology and psychology, between explanations in terms of social forces and those in terms of individual motivation. This may well be seen as one of the central problems of contemporary social theory, and that Sartre has attempted to tackle it shows that he is well aware of what needs to be done in the field. What is unsatisfactory is the way he tackles the problem. Some critics have suggested that this is because he fails to pay sufficient attention to the facts.[1] My first impression on reading the work was that the mass of detailed facts, together with the special terminology Sartre introduces, effectively conceals what he wants to say. Certainly some of the conclusions are extreme, both from a general point of view and from that of arguments he has used elsewhere. But there are interesting and important points to be extracted from the work, if the extremism that Sartre shows here, as elsewhere, is neglected.

Throughout this study I have been at pains to avoid using passages from Sartre's literary works to illustrate his philosophical theories, but I think an exception is necessary at this point. There are many verbal echoes of *Critique de la raison dialectique* in Sartre's latest play, *Les Séquestrés d'Altona*, and these are clearly more than coincidences. Frantz's last speech contains the words "The century would have been good if there had not been lying in wait for man his cruel, immemorial enemy, the flesh-eating species who had sworn to destroy him, the hairless and malignant beast, man himself." This can be compared with such passages as: "In fact nothing—neither wild animals nor microbes—is more terrible for man than that intelligent, flesh-eating and cruel species which can understand and thwart human intelligence and whose aim is precisely the destruction of man" (*CRD*, 208). There are other similar comparisons which can be drawn between the two works. But *Les Séquestrés d'Altona* is not about *scarcity* in the economic

[1] e.g. A. MacIntyre, loc. cit.

sense at all; its subject is guilt. That this coupling should exist seems to me of great importance. Sartre is still concerned with what is for him the central problem—what it is to be a human being and how human beings can have with each other the relations they ought to have. The ostensible purpose of *Critique de la raison dialectique* may well be to provide a foundation for the dialectic, to give 'Prolegomena to any future anthropology' (*CRD*, 153), but the real subject is the one that has haunted him throughout. Man is a single species, yet his relations with other men, both as an individual and in groups, seem to involve conflict and opposition. It would seem that Hegel's life and death struggle is a natural state for man. But for Hegel this was a fact about human beings, an inevitable part of their make-up. Sartre wishes to understand it and bring others to understand it; hence to assist men in living together peacefully. Some of the obstacles to human relations were analysed in *L'Etre et le néant*; here Sartre is trying to carry the process a stage further.

The stages in Sartre's thought might be expressed in this way; the traditional philosophers tended to talk about human relations as if they were between disembodied spirits. In *L'Etre et le néant* Sartre 'embodies' the spirits; he discusses human relations as if they took place between creatures having desires, particularly sexual desires, that depended on their possessing bodies. Human conduct is seen by him as essentially involving animal bodies. But the material world remains, in that book, a kind of neutral backcloth against which human activity is carried on. In *Critique de la raison dialectique* the material world itself is seen to be a central element in the relationship of man to man; both in itself and as modified by human action it is an essential part of our 'world'. There is no denial of the distinction so fundamental to *L'Etre et le néant* between *l'en-soi* and *le pour-soi*, merely a widening of its scope. Throughout the central issue is human existence itself. Thus it is no accident that the most abstract of his theoretical works and a concrete drama echo one another. Two things seem to follow from this. First, in spite of what Sartre says, more is at issue in the *Critique* than an attempt to bring Marxism up to date.

Second, it is clear that Sartre cannot accept any simple utopian solution, such as many Marxists seem to hope for; the roots of human conflict and alienation lie at a deeper level than the economic (cf. p. 200 above). *Scarcity* may be the new key-word, but it is not simply a shortage of consumer goods that the term implies; it is a reflection of man's finitude. Thus the solution lies in the acceptance of scarcity rather than in its total abolition, though, of course, Sartre is enough of a Marxist to demand an improvement in the standard of living of mankind. It is this recurrent emphasis on finitude and on the various possible means of living with it, authenticity, art, Marxism, which has led some writers to consider Sartre a religious thinker.[1] Of course, if all that is meant by a 'religious thinker' is one concerned with fundamental problems, then the description is just. But it seems to me that a necessary condition for talking of religion is the recognition that it is concerned with something transcendent to man, something infinite in contrast to man's finitude. There is nothing of this in Sartre; he is everywhere concerned with the relation of the finite to the finite. To talk of him as in any way religious is either to have misunderstood him or so to have widened the scope of the term as to make it useless for descriptive purposes.

The use of the word 'critique', together with his characterisation of the work as 'Prolegomena to any future anthropology', clearly invites and is meant to invite a comparison with Kant. Sartre has turned from conceptual psychology to conceptual sociology—or to conceptual history, for it is not clear how far Sartre regards these two as distinct—and finds certain steps necessary in the latter case that were not required in the former. For there is, in the latter area, a lack of an appropriate terminology for dealing with the material. A terminology cannot be conjured out of thin air; it must be shown to be suitable for the subject-matter. This involves a *deduction* of the kind that Kant gave in his *Critique of Pure Reason* under the title of the 'Transcendental deduction'. The two volumes of *Critique de la raison dialectique* are intended to provide a similar basis for sociology. Sartre argues that the pro-

[1] cf., for example, M. Cranston, *Sartre*, 112–13.

blem is more complex than Kant's because of the double nature of the dialectic in its Hegelo-Marxist sense; the term "dialectic" applies both to our knowledge of history and to history itself. "You are aware that the dialectic of history was the first to appear. It originated as a simultaneous discovery on the one hand of the law of development of historical reality, and on the other hand of the law of development of knowledge of history" (*ME*, 1–2).[1] Sartre will not accept the Stalinist thesis that all nature is dialectical, an idea which in any case seems to derive from Engels rather than from Marx. For him the essential point about dialectic is that it involves *understanding* what is happening, and "there is no *intelligibility* in the sciences of nature" (*CRD*, 160). Science, in this sense, may enable accurate predictions to be made and control to be exercised over things, but it does not tell us why they should be thus. Any feeling that we have achieved understanding when a theory has been established is for Sartre illusory; all scientific explanation ultimately must arrive at the point where it says, "It just does happen in this way, and that is all we can say about it." Sartre's arguments are here much the same as those he used to disprove the possibility of a scientific psychology; understanding human beings, either individually or in the mass, involves being able to *see* their reasons for acting, to be able to put oneself in their place. What Sartre is seeking is a set of concepts which apply to social phenomena and at the same time make them intelligible. That such a search is possible he regards as due to the fact that the reality which they are to describe is itself dialectical, and does not proceed by the operation of fixed causal laws, but everywhere depends on the choices and decisions of human beings, even though these choices are themselves restricted and influenced by what has previously been done. Hence the facts can be genuinely explained and understood.

We are still in the realm of human freedom, but it is a freedom

---

[1] *Marxisme et existentialisme* (Plon, 1962). This is the text of a discussion between Sartre and Jean Hyppolite and three Marxist thinkers on the subject "whether dialectic is only a law of history or whether it is also a law of nature" (ibid., introduction). Thus the title is misleading; there is no actual 'existentialist' thesis at issue.

rather different from that which Sartre celebrated in his early works. On the literary side this is particularly clear; Orestes, in *Les Mouches*, achieves freedom by what could be called an 'acte gratuit' which, at least as far as he is concerned, ignores the social situation that had hitherto existed. In the later plays the heroes find themselves increasingly forced to be aware that what they thought were free acts were largely the result of social forces. They are still to be held responsible for what they do; in fact, the responsibility may even be heavier than Orestes', because the decisions are more complex. Sartre has learnt that freedom is not as simple or as unitary as he once thought. He has come to see what Marx described in the *Eighteenth Brumaire of Louis Napoleon*: "Men make their own history, but they do not make it just as they please; they do not make it under circumstances chosen by themselves, but under circumstances directly encountered, given and transmitted from the past. The tradition of all the dead generations lies like a nightmare on the brain of the living." But the attempt to deal with this problem is not entirely new for Sartre; the programme of the *Critique* is similar to one he sketched in *Qu'est-ce que la littérature?* in 1947: "Human enterprise has two sides it is both success and failure. In order to understand it, the dialectic is inadequate. We must make our vocabulary and our intellectual framework more supple. One day I shall attempt to describe this peculiar object called History, which is neither objective nor entirely subjective, in which the dialectic process is checked, penetrated and worn away by a kind of anti-dialectic, which itself is nevertheless dialectic. But this is a task for philosophers . . ." (*S.II*, 86). The corresponding description in the *Critique* runs: "This leads us to the main divisions of the first volume: *productive dialectic* (as it is understood in abstract clarity through the *praxis* of the individual) is limited in its operation and transformed into *anti-dialectic*" (*CRD*, 154). Sartre uses the pair of terms 'la dialectique constituante' and 'la dialectique constituée'; I shall translate the former by 'productive dialectic', the latter by 'dialectic as product'. The word '*praxis*' is used by Sartre almost as a technical term to describe human activity in general. An early use may serve to introduce the term: "Thus the world and men are revealed by *ventures*. And all ventures that we talk about can be reduced to a single one, that of *making history*. (In the sense that 'Men make their own history . . .'.) Thus we are brought to the moment when we must abandon a literature of *exis* in order to make one of *praxis*" (*S.II*, 265).

One of the main problems that strikes Sartre is how it is that men can act as a group, given that they are, and must remain, separate individuals; he still will have no truck with 'group minds' or organic theories. In his terminology, the dialectic of history depends on individual *praxis*, and yet at the same time history is a "*totalisation*", in some sense a single whole. But this whole is not a true unit; Sartre distinguishes a "*totalité*", a dead and completed whole, and a "*totalisation*", something which is always in the process of becoming a totality without ever reaching a final and static form (cf. *CRD*, 137, 165 and 279). To describe how this "*totalisation*" is possible, he distinguishes between a *collection* of people and a genuine *group*. A collection is a grouping of people brought together as a result of the way in which each is pursuing his own separate aims; Sartre instances people waiting for a bus, not, of course, in an orderly queue. The potential passengers are separated rather than united by the fact that they all intend to catch the *same* bus; each can be seen as a potential rival for a place. It does not matter who he is nor what his intention is, he represents one unit of accommodation less and hence less chance for anyone else of achieving his project. Such a collection of people, like so many in modern society, is a *serial* one; any 'unit' could be replaced by any other. *Serialisation* is the enemy of genuine grouping, of real contact between individuals (cf. *CRD*, 307–20). An important source of serialisation is the *practico-inert*; in this case the fact that there is a bus of such a size running at such times on this particular route. The individual often regards such facts more as laws of nature than as the result of human decisions: "The last tram leaves the Town Hall at 11.5 p.m." (*N*, 198. Cf. the whole passage, quoted above, Ch. I, p. 10.) Indeed, in a complex industrial society they are only to a minimal extent the result of human decisions; the interlocking of so many different factors is such that one cannot be now changed in any simple way. A city or large organisation has "a life of its own" sometimes in conflict with the individual desires of those involved in it. Such a situation is due to the way in which the intentions of past organisers have been "inscribed" in material objects. It is not simply the "tradition of past generations" that holds us in thrall, it is their acts as well.

Sartre is describing a phenomenon which is a common source of complaint in modern society; more and more the individual feels that he is being treated as a mere unit in a complex mechanism rather than as a human being. This might indeed be considered the commonest form of alienation. But Sartre does more than simply point out this fact; he writes as if serialisation vitiated *all* human relations, as if only collections existed in capitalist society, never human contacts freed from the oppressive influence of the *practico-inert*. In some passages he even seems to suggest that the abolition of capitalism would mean the end of all alienation (cf. *CRD*, 349 n.). His procedure here is very like his earlier treatment of bad faith; in *L'Etre et le néant* by the aid of a series of brilliant examples he succeeded in showing that many human relations and activities were vitiated by bad faith. Instead of drawing the obvious conclusion that one should seek ways of obviating it, he went on to talk as if all human beings were 'doomed' to suffer from it. Similarly, instead of showing how serialisation menaces human relations, he talks as if it were unavoidable in present society. As it was clear from what he said about bad faith that some people were victims of it to a greater degree than others, so it might seem that some forms of serialisation were deplorable, though others might be less serious or even beneficial. Indeed, without some serialisation no complex social machinery could function. There are numerous situations in which what needs to be done demands that people should be considered only as units. As long as there remain other areas where people are more than units, areas where genuine human relationships are possible, there seems nothing wrong with the existence of some serialisation. Sartre, in demanding the abolition of serialisation, seems to be asking for an impossible Utopia; the only one that I can imagine satisfying him would be that represented by William Morris in *News from Nowhere*. (Sometimes I think that Morris's Utopia *is* a true representation of what Marx envisaged after the "withering away of the state". A passage from the *German Ideology* points in this direction. "In communist society where nobody has one exclusive sphere of activity but each can become accomplished in any branch he wishes, society regulates the general production and this makes it possible for me to do one thing today and another tomorrow, to hunt in the morning, fish in the afternoon, rear cattle in the evening, criticise after dinner, just as I have a mind, without ever becoming hunter, fisherman, shepherd or critic." Sartre is often accused of a lack of political realism; in this passage Marx seems to have suffered from the same want.)

But these flaws in the use of the concept of serialisation should not be allowed to obscure the concept itself, for it is clearly an important one, or the examples Sartre gives of its operation. The picture he paints is one where the 'tools' of *L'Etre et le néant* have become, like the robots of *R.U.R.*, things that manipulate men by means of man's very manipulation of them. Even language, that most essential of tools, sometimes now behaves in this way, and, Sartre adds, this occurs also in the so-called "socialist states" (cf. *CRD*, 348 n.). Every time men alter the material world to serve their own present purposes there are liable to be effects other than those intended, some of which may have a long-lasting influence on men themselves. Sartre uses the phrase "We've been had" to sum up this situation. He instances the soldiers who have fallen into an ambush; by their own free action they have brought about their downfall. They are responsible for the result and yet they by no means intended it. Examples from the sphere of the *practico-inert* are easy to find, from the large-scale events such as dust-bowls and floods to smaller ones. In all such cases men have been "caught in their own trap". Certainly there are many cases in which we might want to say "We've been had" in the way Sartre indicates; for a finite being this is a standing risk. In his earlier analyses Sartre was willing to treat the consequences of human finitude as conditions for the exercise of freedom; here he seems to come close to denying all meaning to the term.

A collection of people is necessarily serial, and no relations of a genuine kind are possible within it, Sartre argues. But there are also groups, sets of men with common intentions and common actions. More than this, however, is required to distinguish a group from the collection of men at the bus stop, who might also be said to have a common intention and to act in the same way. Sartre attempts to bring out the difference by describing the first stage in the formation of a group, its coming together (*CRD*, 381–435). What is essential is that the sense of being a group should be present to all the members, in other words that each should feel that all the others are necessary to the task in hand. He instances a small group of strikers who realise the impossibility of breaking a police cordon. If their number grows, the time will come when the group *as a whole* can risk attacking. In such a case the numerical size of the group is present to each member of it. "Here, on the contrary, the individual attacks *in so far as he is many*, that is to say his action already involves multiplicity by its very *praxis*. He doesn't begin to attack *in isolation* nor as a *hundredth* [of the whole group], but by freely using the power which is given to him by the fact of *being*, here and everywhere, *the material strength* of one hundred men" (*CRD*, 419). There is nothing mystical in this description; Sartre warns that "in fact, the group is not a metaphysical reality but a certain practical relation that men have to an object and between each other" (*CRD*, 427 n.). This "interiorisation of multiplicity" is only possible in so far as there is a common aim, one that can only be attained by united actions. Sartre takes his examples from violent behaviour not because of any preference for it, but because only at such moments can a group coming into existence be observed. When there is a stable social situation, groupings are normally imposed by the structure of the society. Nevertheless, it does seem possible to find instances where a group which has arisen spontaneously could say of itself, "*We* did so-and-so." The admission of the possibility of a genuine 'we-experience' corrects the doctrine of *L'Etre et le néant* that such an experience is purely subjective (*EN*, 502).

But there is nothing permanent about such a group; once the aim has been achieved, it is liable to disintegrate, to fall back into a collection again. Sartre next discusses the devices for keeping the group in being, for maintaining the "interiorisation of multiplicity" (*CRD*, 436–60). One factor that will help to maintain the group is the pressure of an opposing force, an enemy to be guarded against. But whereas in the heat of the battle it is easy to see that everyone is involved in the activity, when it is a question of mounting guard or carrying out other operations where the individual is separated off from the group, more is needed. This more is the *oath*: "A free attempt to substitute the fear of all for fear of oneself and of the other in and through each person, in so far as it re-establishes sharply violence as an intelligible means of overcoming individual alienation by common freedom: such is the oath" (*CRD*, 450). The group is thus kept in being by terror; it becomes a group under pressure of opposition, but it can only continue to exist in so far as the fear of everyone else in the group is stronger than the desire for one's own safety. That unity is founded on fear may sound an appropriate doctrine for the bastard mercenary Goetz, in *Le Diable et le bon Dieu*: "We shall be assured of victory when the men fear me more than they fear the enemy" (closing scene), but it hardly seems an appropriate means for understanding all collective action. Sartre nevertheless does mean this, for he talks of it as "the beginning of humanity" (*CRD*, 453). He adds: "Let me be understood: this is not just a matter of referring only to the great times of revolution when, in fact, everyone has the feeling of producing and experiencing man as a new reality. Every organisation with a reciprocal oath is a first beginning, because it is a victory of man over seriality, of whatever sort, by common freedom. It is true that this first happens at the level of the group coming together, but it is by the oath that the group asserts itself . . . as a means of obtaining a more or less distant objective; *hence* it also asserts itself as its own immediate aim" (*CRD*, 453 n.). This state of affairs is for Sartre an improvement on seriality, because it is an escape from bondage to matter, to the *practico-inert*. Man can no longer create humanity by his individual action, as he seems to have argued in his earlier works; it is a co-operative enterprise in this odd sense. Ultimately, Sartre thinks, it is possible to understand a group only in so far as one is a member of one, something that, of course, no man can avoid.

The oath is in no sense a "social contract"; the origin of the group is not that of the State. Even society is not a group, not even a collection of groups; it is rather a collection of both groups and collections, unified by some feature external to it, such as the habitation of the same area (*CRD*, 608). I have not here followed in detail Sartre's description of the development of institutions within the group, and of the rise of "sovereignty", "alienation to avoid alienation" (*CRD*, 603), because it is at this stage of the argument that he seems most unclear. This is because he bases his argument on too little empirical evidence and on the use of terms, such as 'sovereignty' itself, which require more careful handling than he gives them. Even the relation between examples and conclusions is puzzling. For instance, he gives a lengthy analysis of an American "Pick of the Pops" programme (*CRD*, 615 et seq.), in which he rightly points out that the mere fact of a record being played as one of the "Top Ten" increases its sales in the following week. There is clearly a fruitful field here for empirical research into similar phenomena. But Sartre applies his conclusions direct to democratic government: ". . . the candidates elected no more represent the *will* of the country than do most popular discs reflect the *taste* of the purchasers. The only possible manifestation of 'will' in the masses is a revolutionary regrouping against the inertia of institutions and against that sovereignty which is founded upon their impotence. The ballot, a passive method, can indeed make insignificant changes in the composition of the governing body; *in no case* can it claim to modify the policy of the government (unless the very circumstances which accompany it are of a kind which themselves modify that policy)" (*CRD*, 624 n.). The argument has moved into a different realm, that of

Marxist propaganda at its worst. The governing group is entirely determined by its class interests, and consequently *cannot* change its policy unless those very interests change. "[The State] embodies and realises the general interest of the dominant class over and above the antagonisms and conflicts of particular interests" (*CRD*, 611). The State becomes the personification of class, and, in this great determinist movement, even the dictatorship of the proletariat seems to have become impossible because of the play of historical forces (*CRD*, 629–30)!

Apart from the obviously unsatisfactory nature of this way of dealing with the problem, a flaw which ought to have been manifest to Sartre, still more surprising is the way in which it contradicts the very path he had earlier sketched out. Such an analysis would hardly seem to be taking "the human dimension as the foundation of anthropological knowledge" (*CRD*, 111), but rather to be ignoring human actions altogether. It is the problem of freedom which causes Sartre most of his trouble in this book, and this accounts for the apparently contradictory statements he makes about it, one of which I have quoted above (p. 207). Sartre wants to say, "Man is born free, but everywhere he has forged chains for himself, or has met chains already forged." It is at this point that the radical freedom of 'existentialism' and the strict determinism of Marxism pull him in opposite directions. What is needed is not a descent on either side of the fence, but a detailed investigation of the extent to which freedom exists *in any given society*. All societies limit freedom, but there is no reason to assume that they all limit it by the same amount or in the same direction. Sartre does not have the necessary knowledge of societies other than his own, nor even the empirical interest, to investigate these questions. Consequently much of his analysis remains in the air, presenting a picture which bears little relation to any facts. An obvious example is his claim that the ballot in a democratic society is powerless to influence the policy of the government. In recent years in France this may well have seemed to be the case, but there are other states where the situation has been different.

If Sartre had subsequently considered the film script he wrote in 1948, entitled *L'Engrenage*, he might have arrived at a more balanced view of some of these problems. The plot concerns the overthrow of the old revolutionary government by a new one; the reason for their overthrow was that they had failed to carry out their stated aims, the nationalisation of the oil-wells on which the wealth of the country depends. The new government soon find themselves in the same position as the old, for the neighbouring Great Power informs them that any attempt at nationalisation will be followed by an immediate invasion. They 'cannot' act in the way they promised. But the whole problem lies in the nature of the impossibility facing them; this is contingent on their wish to preserve the independence of the country. In the majority of cases where we say that we "cannot act otherwise" there is a reference to some wishes or needs on our part. This is the sense which Sartre ought to be, and sometimes is, discussing. It is not the "objective" class interests, but those interests as seen and interpreted by the members of that class which compel them to behave in certain ways. In the case of a government, their actual policy is always a compromise between their interests, in this sense, and the pressures from underneath. The whole tension of the position of the revolutionaries in *L'Engrenage* resides in this fact. The trouble with the *Critique* is that Sartre often fails to consider such issues in realistic detail.

It has been suggested[1] that Sartre's old hatred of the bourgeoisie is one of the factors that has blinded him. Certainly they are often attacked in the *Critique*, and in terms reminiscent of those used by orthodox Marxists. It is not, however, clear that the bourgeois here used as a target are the same people as those attacked in *La Nausée* and *L'Etre et le néant*. In the early works the term referred to the smug, comfortable people who were convinced that everything was right with the world and themselves, the traditional target of French artists. In the *Critique* 'bourgeoisie' is an economic classification, and they are under fire not in themselves but as part of a morally wrong economic system. For Sartre not the least of the

[1] In the *Times Literary Supplement*, 5 May 1961, 276.

faults of capitalism is that it produces a bourgeoisie, a class cut off from the greater part of the nation; this division is a manifestation of the *practico-inert*. But instead of being content with exhibiting the unfortunate division between bourgeoisie and proletariat, and with examining ways in which it might be overcome, Sartre rushes into what Merleau-Ponty called an "ultra-Bolshevik" position, one that is elsewhere described as "anarchism and nihilism".[1] A specimen of his more extreme sentiments runs: "On this level, we find the roots of bourgeois humanism; this is abstract violence and oppression because it identifies the bourgeois with man in contrast to *the other species*, that is to say *the anti-man* or workman. Humanism is the pendant of racism: it is a piece of exclusion. But, at the same time—like racism—it is the product of external conditioning, that is to say of seriality" (*CRD*, 702). In addition Sartre seems to be committed to the view that *any* organisation will reproduce similar features once it has departed from the purity of the group coming together; only at that moment can men really act freely together without the constraint of the oath and its accompanying terror. Thus government and organised society become impossible without serialisation and alienation. Here it would seem that it is not so much his Marxism as his retreat from Marxism that is the source of his errors. The search for a form of society where serialisation and the "hell of the *practico-inert*" do not dominate becomes a proof of the impossibility of any form of social organisation whatsoever.

The fundamental error seems to lie in the very nature of *Critique de la raison dialectique*, the double attempt to discuss how social phenomena are to be understood, how we can get from individual actions to social laws, and at the same time to criticise existing societies. There is good reason for saying that 'dialectic' reason, in contrast to analytic, or scientific, reason, is the correct way to understand social phenomena. This, as I understand him, is the thesis of Mr Peter Winch in his *Idea of a Social Science*,[2] though he might disapprove of this way of putting it. Both Sartre and

[1] By A. MacIntyre, *The Listener*, 22 March 1962, 513.
[2] Routledge, 1958.

Winch argue that it is impossible to understand a society entirely externally; understanding other ways of life is possible because we are ourselves social creatures. But Sartre's desire to reform his own society leads him to assert more than this, to lay down an *a priori* pattern of how societies must develop. It is here that the failure to look at a wide range of examples takes its toll; Sartre's excessive reliance on reason has prevented him from paying attention to the facts. (Those examples that he does discuss are generally taken from French history from 1789 to the present day.) He has not taken to heart Marx's lesson of the *18th Brumaire*, that every historical situation must be considered in detail.

The failure of the book springs from an attempt to do more than any philosopher is entitled to do. Sartre has not produced a metaphysical system so much as an *a priori* account of society. The extreme conclusion that can be drawn from this failure is that Sartre is not a philosopher at all, but an artist who has strayed into the wrong field, an opinion which is supported by the similarities in language between *Critique de la raison dialectique* and *Les Séquestrés d'Altona*. But in my opinion the failure does not spring from this; even in this work there are philosophical insights of importance and, as I have argued, elsewhere Sartre has made genuine contributions to philosophy. I suspect that one important reason is the fact that he has deserted the field of philosophy for so long that he has forgotten the discipline required. This book has the air of being written against the clock, as if it were an article for the next issue of *Les Temps modernes*. There is no evidence that he has discussed the ideas he presents with others working in the field. Where he has put forward interesting and sound ideas they are not related to each other by arguments that will stand up to criticism; sometimes they are even contradictory. It has been said that "Sartre uses fiction as a philosophical workshop".[1] If this is true, and there is evidence at least in this case, the ideas in the *Critique* have been transferred from the workshop of *Les Séquestrés d'Altona* too quickly and without adequate checking. In this sense the failure might be put down to a flaw in character;

[1] Professor J. Cruickshank, personal communication.

Sartre has come to think of himself as a great philosopher and hence as not needing to consider other men's views or to ask for their criticisms of his own. Ultimately, however, he is too much of a rationalist to be only an artist; he wants to learn the reason for violence in human affairs, to explain what the audience of a play is forced to accept by the dramatic presentation of a situation. In watching the play we are willing to believe in Frantz and the rest of the characters, to see *their* reasons for their actions. Sartre wants to understand *the* reasons for their behaviour, and, he thinks, it is possible only to understand *rational* behaviour. "What counts, in fact, for a dialectical understanding of another person is the rationality of his *praxis*. Now this rationality appears in violence itself in so far as it is not merely contingent ferocity in man but a comprehensible interiorisation of the contingent fact of scarcity in *each person*; human violence is *meaningful*" (*CRD*, 752). This central theme of *Critique de la raison dialectique* connects it with the rest of his work and provides a limited degree of justification for its 755 pages.

XIV

Action and Identity: Sartre's Plays

S ARTRE's plays, though apparently diverse in content, possess a single theme, are centred round one basic problem. This problem arises from his philosophic concern and provides, if one is needed, a justification for the treatment of his drama in a philosophic study. To a casual reader this may not appear to be the case, because the dramatic skill of Sartre manifests itself in producing dramas which can interest those who have no knowledge of his philosophical views. There is no reason to think that he has written plays in order to express his philosophy in another medium. Indeed, he has himself pointed out that writing for the theatre alters his style: "It's a change, it makes me speak *differently*" (interview with *L'Express*, 1959).[1] That there is a single theme, as well as the exact nature of it, will become clear, I trust, in the course of this chapter. It can be briefly characterised here as 'the problem of Action and Identity', because the hero (or heroes) of every Sartrean play is concerned with the question "Who am I?". This concern arises from an uncertainty about what he ought to do or about what he has done. If the action lies in the future, then the protagonist in acting is also choosing more than the action itself, a whole life is in question. If the action has already been done, then the character is uncertain about the exact nature of his deed, in the sense that he is unclear whether he has acted freely or has been manipulated by external forces. This doubt reflects an uncertainty about the nature of his whole personality. There are other important themes which vary from play to play

---

[1] Extracts in *Evergreen Review*, vol. 4, no. 11, Jan.–Feb. 1960, pp. 143–52. I have quoted from this version, p. 144.

and which may even conceal this central concern. But the interest and power of Sartre's drama lie largely in the presence of the problem of action and identity.

Hence it is an error to divide his drama into the 'political' plays and the others, for the theme is as manifest in the comedies *Kean* and *Nekrassov* as it is in *Le Diable et le bon Dieu* or *Les Mains sales*. The only play which cannot be characterised in this way is also Sartre's only failure. I refer to *La Putaine respectueuse*, written as a curtain raiser to *Morts sans sépultures*. It is an ill-tempered little play, a violent attack on racism in the southern states of the U.S.A. Sartre's presentation at times seems more akin to propaganda than to anything else. The original version has an unhappy ending; the white prostitute lies at the instigation of a Senator and so causes the death of an innocent Negro. She then becomes the mistress of the Senator's son. Lizzie, the prostitute, is too 'respectful' of the established order to stand out against its pressures in the cause of truth and justice. It might have been easier to take this work seriously if Sartre himself had not been willing to rewrite the ending into a happy one for performance on the other side of the Iron Curtain and also for the film version. His justification was apparently that the workers would see the film, and that they needed optimism and hope, which could only be given if Lizzie finally acted 'in the interests of mankind' rather than selfishly. In so altering the ending, Sartre appears to have acted in accordance with the official Soviet view of the nature of literature, rather than in accordance with his own theory of committed or engaged literature, which is more subtle.

Though there is one theme in the rest of his dramatic works, the alterations in the treatment of it reflect the changes in his philosophic thought that have already been discussed. In some cases the connection between a philosophical work and a play is obvious, both from the point of view of style and of date; *Les Mouches* is obviously linked to *L'Etre et le néant* and, as became clear in the last chapter, *Les Séquestrés d'Altona* to *Critique de la raison dialectique*. In other cases there is no single philosophical work with which the play can be connected, but the relation between philosophy and dramatic practice is none the less evident. I must stress at this point that it is not a matter of looking at the plays to find *illustrations* of Sartre's philosophy. Though he has said that the play is a "public object", that "In the theater intentions don't count. What counts is what *comes out*. The public writes the play as much as the author does" (interview with *L'Express*, loc. cit., 146), nevertheless we should not be justified in ignoring the dramatic element. Sartre is a dramatic craftsman of no mean stature, and has seldom allowed philosophical purposes to affect adversely the play he was writing. It is unfortunate that his plays have not been well translated into English, though it is a tribute to them that they are so successful when viewed through such distorting glasses. When asked to produce an amateur *Huis clos* I found it necessary to make a new translation in order to attain something approximating to the original.

Sartre's first play was *Les Mouches*, first performed during the German occupation of France in 1943. Some critics have treated it as if it were a call to resist the Germans, an assertion of freedom in time of oppression. A calm reading of the work, coupled with the fact that the Germans allowed the play to be performed, may make the reader suspect this interpretation. I have discussed the evidence in an appendix to this chapter. The plot of the play is the classical story of the murder of Clytemnestra and Aegisthus by Orestes and Electra, the children of Clytemnestra and Agamemnon, the husband she and Aegisthus murdered. Sartre converts the story into a discussion of human freedom; but the kind of freedom in question is very like that sought by Mathieu in *L'Age de raison*. Its chief characteristic seems to be an escape from the customary bourgeois views of religion and morality. Orestes finds freedom in committing what is normally thought of as a crime and yet not suffering from remorse. The Flies, and the Furies, have no power over him because he refuses to accept their power, or even that of Jupiter, whom he taunts with the fact that he has created man free. Orestes shows his freedom by accepting what he has become by his own action, for "the most cowardly of assassins is he who suffers from remorse" (Act III, scene 2). This acceptance of his crime is equivalent to an authentic action, to taking it upon himself and "making it his own". Orestes says "A crime which the doer cannot bear is not anyone's crime, is it? It's almost an accident" (Act III, scene 6). Only by accepting what he has done can a man 'become himself'. Electra, his accomplice in the murders, almost succeeds in escaping from her bondage in the same way, but at the last moment Jupiter brings her to repentance; she relapses into inauthenticity by accepting the standards of ordinary society, in this case those of Argos. She welcomes her punishment as a means of salvation and the Furies fasten on her. She cannot accept herself nor what she has done.

For men are not held in check by the gods, but by their own created rules. Jupiter knows this; he tells Aegisthus that they both have the same secret, "the painful secret of Gods and kings; it is that men are free. They are free, Aegisthus. You know it and they don't" (Act II, tableau II, scene 5). Orestes discovers this freedom, and presents one of Sartre's most 'existential' statements of it: "A stranger to myself, I know I am. Outside nature, contrary to nature, without any justification, with no help except from myself. But I won't accept your laws; I am doomed to have no laws other than my own. I won't accept your nature. In it there are a thousand paths that lead to you, but I can only follow my own road. Nature finds man horrifying, and you, the King of Gods, you also find men horrifying" (Act III, scene 2). This has little relevance to the situation of France under the German occupation; Aegisthus is a usurper, but the point about his usurpation that interests Sartre is that he maintains his hold on the people by convincing them that they are guilty in the eyes of their own dead and of the Gods. However, Jupiter is not the classical deity, but the Christian God, creator of an ordered universe into which man has brought evil. Orestes' speech that I have just quoted is a reply to a long one by this Jupiter; the theme of it is that the universe is good, being a divine creation. It is full of echoes of Christian, rather than classical Greek, religious doctrine. For although Orestes' assertion of freedom involves the commission of a murder, what is important in Jupiter's eyes, and in the play itself, is the religious revolt which is involved in failing to feel guilt for this action; Orestes becomes a full human being by breaking the religious chains, by seeing himself as an individual instead of a created being.

Thus the central theme of the play is far removed from any possible relation to the actual situation of the time; Orestes, the individualist hero from outside the oppressed town, is hardly the type of hero for the Resistance. He attempts to save Argos by his single act, and, in the situation as sketched, no more is needed. Indeed, it is possible to see something not entirely contrary to Fascist thought in Orestes; the more intellectual Nazis might find the doctrines implicit in the play not unacceptable. For at this stage of his thought Sartre's view of action seems close to Gide's 'acte gratuit'. A man changes himself by acting, but no reasons for acting are suggested. It is clear that Sartre means us to approve Orestes' conduct, but this approval seems somewhat arbitrary because, although Orestes has chosen himself, there are other selves he could have chosen and these, presumably, would also have led to freedom. For the freedom represented in Les Mouches seems, in the last resort, to involve merely the escape from the accepted norms of society. Any act which broke the normal pattern would have done as well to establish Orestes' individuality. This is a consequence of Sartre's apparent stress on the negative criteria of the action required for freedom; to reject the bourgeois-Christian view of life is to become an individual, to assert one's freedom. Hence there is no room for any positive method of comparing different actions, or different reasons for action. For those who think in the Gidean way more is, in fact, involved—the action is always one that must shock—but this is not expressed in the theory itself. Lafcadio's 'acte gratuit', in Gide's Les Caves du Vatican, is to push a man out of a railway train; but if no reason for the action is needed, as Gide seems to argue, then any other action would have done as well.

Dramatically, the play fails for reasons closely connected with the points I have just made. Orestes is a hero from outside Argos, and the interest centres on him. Hence the situation of Argos has an air of being set up solely as a kind of backcloth against which he can act. As I have said, there is no adequate reason for his action at a philosophical level; this lack is reflected at the dramatic level. In removing the drama from the situation of the classical Orestes and setting it in a modernised Argos, Sartre has removed the power of the original motivation without providing one that will dramatically carry the play. Its interest resides in the expression of Sartre's ideas, not in the dramatic situation itself. It is no accident that it has been probably the least popular of all Sartre's plays, for the lack of dramatic motivation has driven him to rely on philosophic argument to fill the gaps. The debate between Jupiter and Orestes is a fine piece of dialectic, but it is not dramatic, does not satisfy an audience who are watching a play on the stage, however interesting it may be to analyse in the study. I suspect that those who have praised it have been thinking primarily of its intellectual, not of its dramatic, interest.

Sartre avoided both the dramatic and the philosophic flaws in his second play, *Huis clos* (1944). Dramatically, it is excellently constructed; the actual skill in putting the dialogue together for stage purposes could serve as an example to many dramatists. Its success as a play is shown by the frequency with which it has been performed, both on stage, on radio and as a film. One of the reasons for its success is that Sartre set himself the task, simpler both dramatically and for his philosophic outlook of the time, of analysing how three people have become what they are by past action, rather than that of showing them actually in the process of becoming. The play is set in Hell, so that there is no possibility of change, only the gradual revelation of the reasons that brought the characters to their present condition. I have pointed out earlier in this book that the notion of authenticity is one which it is easier to apply to what has been done than to use for solving the problem of present action; the dramatic success of *Huis clos* would seem an illustration of this fact.

The three characters soon discover that there are no torturers employed in Hell, that "the clients do it for themselves, as in a self-service restaurant" (scene 5). For this purpose, they are ideally selected; a flirt, a Lesbian, and a man who makes love to any woman. Estelle, the flirt, is sometimes described as a nympho-maniac; the casualness of her own description of her adultery and her dismissal of her lover seem to show that only a failure to take human relationships seriously is involved, not a pathological dis-order. Inès, the Lesbian, is also in Hell, not because her love is per-verted, but because of the cruelty she showed in that love. The setting is not the Hell of orthodox Christianity; Sartre does not believe in damnation for sins in the traditional sense. His point is rather that failure to respect others as human beings is ultimately self-destructive. In this sense, Garcin's final cry of "Hell is other people" is a most damning piece of self-criticism. None of the characters can have genuine relations with others, because none can see himself clearly. And because they are not clear about their own identity, none can act authentically. They can only see themselves, and others, in a distorting mirror, and by this means have constructed their own hell. Hence, when the door of their room suddenly opens, they are all afraid to step outside, to face the possibilities of a real life of choice, which will involve the admission that their previous behaviour was wrong. Their bad faith is by this stage so deeply developed that they cannot escape it, or rather do not want to undergo the radical conversion that would involve the denial of all their past lives. Garcin is told by Inès that his final act of cowardice has *made* him into a coward for all time, and this would seem an instance of "Death changes life into destiny". But this is not one of the philosophic doctrines of the play. For Garcin is not in Hell for cowardice, but for his treatment of his wife; part of his bad faith is manifested in his failure even to see what he has done and what he has made him-self. His final act of cowardice is relevant because he had always played the tough, again in bad faith. Each is tortured by the others because of his or her own bad faith; one fragment of authenticity would lead to escape. Hell is the dramatic device to bring this across: if there were an issue, such self-torture might be considered morbid. Thus in spite of the necessities of dramatic representation, the philosophic doctrines are those of *L'Etre et le néant*. But the success of *Huis clos* as a play does not depend on knowledge of these doctrines; Sartre has achieved the feat of expressing them in dramatic form in a way which will 'exhibit' them to a non-philosophic audience.

Morts sans sépultures (1946), translated under the title *Men without Shadows*, is a more complex play. Sartre has made an interesting comment on the object of the play and its flaw. "The time was 1944. Some members of the Resistance were being tortured by Militiamen [Frenchmen working for the Germans]. I wasn't interested in showing the physical reality of the torture, but the relationships and conflicts between these two groups of men. And the actors and director knew what I wanted. The rehearsals had gone off well, in a relaxed atmosphere. Vitold, who directed the play and had the leading role, never had time to eat dinner and waited till he was off the stage to devour a sandwich. While he was in the wings eating he was supposed to cry out in pain, and the fact that he did it with his mouth full prevented us from 'believing' in the scene. On the night of the dress rehearsal [French 'répétition générale', normally with a large invited audience] certain people in the audience found it intolerable. It was through them, and I admit I was dumbfounded, that I discovered the real meaning of classical discretion. One can't reveal everything" (*L'Express,* loc. cit., 145). Certainly the lack of 'distancing' is a serious weakness, and tends to conceal from the audience the true subject of the play. Our sympathy is liable to go out to the Resistance group and so to ignore the very subtle portrait of the Militiamen and their different reasons for wanting to get the group to reveal the vital information, even though it is no longer of any use to them. Indeed, the operation of pride on both sides is skilfully observed. The original group of prisoners numbers five, Canoris, Sorbier, Henri, Lucie and her 15-year-old brother François. They believe that their chief, Jean, has escaped, and at first their object is to hold out long enough to give him time to get away. Soon after he is brought in, though not thought by the Militia to be a member of the Resistance. The situation now has changed, they all have something more important to hide. François shows signs of weakening under the strain, so Henri, on Lucie's instructions, kills him. Jean is released. Sorbier commits suicide to avoid further torture. The remainder are finally shot after 'revealing' the whereabouts of their chief.

The complexity of the play springs from the fact that the Resistance group are continually altering their assessments of themselves under the impact of what happens to them. Because of the situation they are in, they cannot, at the end, tell what they have done; everything is in suspense because the outcome, Jean's escape and delivery of a warning to other groups, is what will decide their success and failure, and consequently the true nature of their action. The situation is one in which normal moral standards are destroyed because there is no future, only the outcome of this particular fragment of the struggle, which is at issue. After the murder of François, Henri has doubts about his action, whether he killed from pride, the desire to defeat the Militia. Canoris tries to reassure him: "He had to die; if he'd been nearer me, I'd have done it. As for what went on in your head, that doesn't matter. Nothing matters between these four walls. He had to die, that's all" (tableau III, scene 2). And as long as there seems to be no future for them, this satisfies Henri. When, at the end of the play, there appears to be a genuine prospect of living, Henri realises that he cannot continue with a doubt of this kind; he would prefer death. Lucie had been Jean's lover; when she returns from her 'interrogation' she, too, has the single object of revenging her rape by not giving in to the Militia. There is no room for any love, because she has no future, only one 'project', that of holding out. Jean calls her "a desert of pride". She agrees, and says she is nearer to the torturers now than to Jean, the one who is going to escape because of their suffering. He has become, in the eyes of the rest, a thing rather than a comrade; he has one function, to warn the other sixty men who will be coming to the village. Nothing he can do will restore the old comradeship between them.

The problems of identity that face all the characters in this play are difficult for them, because none is certain how far they can act and how far they can only 'suffer', have things done to them. The normal human possibilities disappear with the disappearance of the future, and consequently questions of identity hardly make sense. Nevertheless, things are done and they change as a result of them. *Morts sans sépultures* differs from *Huis clos* in that the characters are not revealing what they have become, they are becoming something different, but it is not clear how far their own actions and how far the situation is responsible for the change. In this sense, none of them has an identity. Part of the trouble is that the 'extreme situation' in which the play is set renders it hard to apply the tests of more settled times; moral judgments are inevitably distorted by sympathy for the characters' plight. Thus, in spite of the dramatic skill Sartre shows in the construction of the play, the audience is liable to leave a performance with a merely negative impression.

Les Mains sales (1948) has been translated under the curious title of *Crime Passionel*. The plot was taken from the story of Trotsky's assassination, and this has confirmed the view that it is an anti-Communist play. Sartre has denied that this was his intention, and I think a careful reading will show that, although the action partly takes place at the political level, the situation is not one into which Communism as such enters at all, but is concerned with the conflict of characters. A summary of the plot will demonstrate this. Hugo, an intellectual Communist, is ordered to murder Hoederer, one of the Party leaders, because he is thought to be trying to reach agreement with the Regent of the country. Hugo is made Hoederer's secretary and finds that this indeed is his policy, though only because Hoederer regards it as in the Party's best interests. Nevertheless, Hugo cannot bring himself to kill Hoederer for ideological reasons, though he does so when he finds his wife in Hoederer's arms. Even after his release from prison, Hugo is unclear about his real motives. Olga, a dedicated Communist in love with Hugo, tries to get him to say that he killed from personal motives, so that he can be received back into the Party, for Hoederer's policy has, in fact, been carried out, and Hoederer 'rehabilitated' posthumously. Hugo refuses her assistance and goes to meet his death at the hands of the Party.

I have already pointed out how Hoederer is the 'existentialist hero'. a man willing to act and to take responsibility for his actions. Hugo is the opposite; an 'abstract' character who joined the party from principle, not, as Hoederer did, from love of men. Incidentally, some of the arguments that Sartre puts into Hoederer's mouth are those he condemns in 'Le fantôme de Staline'. The basic tension of the play is between these two characters, Hoederer who understands what it is to act, and Hugo, who, even when it appears that he has acted, can't bring himself to integrate that action into his life. He tries to justify himself to Olga thus: "Was it only I who did it? I didn't kill, it was chance. . . . Chance fired three shots, as in bad detective novels. And with chance the 'ifs' started coming in. '*If* I had stayed by the chestnut trees a little longer, *if* I had walked to the end of the garden, *if* I had gone back into the summer-house. . . .' But me myself. What do I become inside? It's an assassination without an assassin" (tableau VII). Basically, he wants to be what his act has made him, an assassin, but he can't make himself feel this. His 'purity', for which Hoederer criticised him, demands that he should make the act a part of his essence; the pressure from the Party is intended to make him say that it was personal and hence trivial. Here again action and identity are joined together. Hugo's tragedy is that he cannot bring himself to accept one and say he accepts the other. Sartre's comments on *Le Diable et le bon Dieu* also apply here: "The play deals throughout with the relation of man to God, or, if you prefer it, the relation of man to the absolute" (blurb to *Le Diable*). Sartre does not mean this in the conventional sense; he is referring to the ultimate relation between a man and himself, a relation which involves the right assessment of his own actions. Hugo's abstractness or 'purity' consists in his demand to see everything in terms of black or white. In this respect he is like Goetz, the hero of *Le Diable et le bon Dieu*, in the earlier parts of that play. There is little temptation to think of the latter play as about the Peasant Wars; these are only the backcloth against which the characters reveal themselves. The Communist Party has the the same role in *Les Mains sales*, though Sartre naturally uses the opportunity to make comments on it, just as he comments on the Church in the other play. But in both cases the comments are only subsidiary to the main themes.

Sartre has himself made the comparison between the two plays in the blurb on the back of *Le Diable et le bon Dieu*. He says of the latter: "This play might be considered as a complement, a sequel to *Mains sales*, although the action takes place four hundred years earlier. I tried to show a character as far distant from the masses of his time as Hugo, the young bourgeois, hero of *Mains sales*, was, and one equally mixed up." The couple Nasty-Goetz reproduces the couple Hugo-Hoederer. But the later play is on a much bigger scale; there are subsidiary issues and characters which exist in their own right, whereas in the earlier play it might seem that the rest of the characters are only there for the sake of the conflict between Hugo and Hoederer. *Le Diable et le bon Dieu* is also, in spite of its length, a much better play; in my opinion the best that Sartre has written. Here I will confine myself to indicating only the philosophical aspects which are relevant to my main theme. Goetz, the hero, is a bastard, a man who has no natural place in the world, and hence no proper sense of his own identity. In a vain attempt to find one, he decides to become absolutely evil, to do evil for its own sake. Unfortunately, he discovers that his attempts do not succeed in destroying society, though, as commander of the army, he can kill men. The objective result of his activities is to weaken the peasant forces and strengthen the power of the princes. Convinced by a priest that every man, in fact, does evil, he decides to do the impossible, good; but to satisfy his ambition it must be absolute good. He founds the "City of the Sun", a community of equals, on his own lands, but quickly finds that the peasants prefer the old system. Goetz's absolutism fails to take account of human individuality; he remains 'abstract'. In spite of the sacrifices he makes, his attempt to love men purely, he cannot get them to love him. In a contest between him and a priest selling indulgences he loses because he cannot see that to love men one must see them as they are with all their weaknesses, hence one must meet them on their own terms. Even his attempt to show his love for mankind by kissing the leper fails; the leper comments: "Here's another one who wants to kiss a leper. . . . If it's for your salvation, I can't refuse, but be quick about it. You're all the same; it looks as though God gave me leprosy just to give them the opportunity of going to Heaven. (*Goetz goes to embrace him*) Not on the mouth! (*Kiss*) Pouah! (*He wipes his face*)" (tableau v, scene 2). The priest's offer of a free indulgence is taken by the leper and the rest of the peasants as better evidence of love.

The failure of Goetz's universal love is reflected by a corresponding failure at the individual level. In an effort to compel God to love him, he undergoes a long period of asceticism and rejection of the body. The genuine love that Hilda has for him shows up the falsity of his attempt at this level. I will quote two relevant speeches in full:

GOETZ. Give me the eyes of a Boeotian lynx so that I can see through your skin. Show me what is hidden in those nostrils and ears. How can I, who can't bring myself to touch a dung-hill with a finger, bring myself to desire to hold in my arms a mere sack of excrement?

HILDA. There is more filth in your soul than in my body. It's in your soul that the ugliness and dirt of flesh exist. I have no need of a lynx's eyes; I've looked after you, washed you, learnt the smell of your illness. Have I stopped loving you? Every day you get more like the corpse that you soon will be and still I love you. If you die, I shall lie down beside you and stay till the end, without eating or drinking; you will decay in my arms and I will love you as carrion. For if you don't love everything you don't love at all. (Tableau x, scene 2.)

These speeches will serve incidentally to reinforce the remarks I have made about Sartre's opinions on physical love; it is clear that Hilda states his view. In the context of the play they show up what is wrong with Goetz's attitudes, his failure to realise human finitude and failure as an essential part of action. To be a genuine human being or really to act involves realising these facts. In this sense the play deals with "the relation of man to the absolute".

Goetz finally realises what is needed; Nasty appeals to him as the only man who can save the peasants in their premature revolt. Without a captain of Goetz's stature, their defeat is inevitable. He agrees to abandon his 'abstract' ambitions and to lead the army. His first action is to kill an officer who refuses to serve under him. The play ends with this speech:

> (*Goetz kicks the corpse*) That's the beginning of the Kingdom of Man. It's a good start! Well, Nasty, I'm going to be an executioner and a butcher. . . . Don't worry, I won't give in. I'll horrify them because I've no other way of loving them, I'll give them orders because I've no other way of obeying, I'll remain alone with this empty sky above my head because there's no other way of being with everybody. There's a war to fight and I'll fight it.

Goetz succeeds where Hugo failed because he comes to terms with himself and the real world, reaches authenticity by a realistic assessment of his own situation. His realisation of the limitations of the possibilities of action open to him, and his acceptance of those limitations, enable him to become a real person, to find a true identity (Hugo, in *Les Mains sales*, fails because he is never sufficiently in contact with reality) in the course of this play Goetz passes through stages similar to those of Hugo, but finally gets beyond them.

Sartre's next two plays, *Kean* (1953) and *Nekrassov* (1955), tend to receive less attention from critics concerned with his ideas because they are lighter in tone. This is a pity, both because they are good plays and because their lighter treatment of the same set of problems as the rest of his drama serves as a foil to the view that existentialism is inevitably gloomy in outlook. Sartre's wit and high spirits come to the fore in them. *Kean* is an adaptation made, at the request of Pierre Brasseur, of one of Dumas' plays. Gallimard have printed Dumas' text in the volume containing Sartre's version, and it is an interesting exercise to compare the two. The skill with which Sartre has refurbished the old play whilst retaining its outline is remarkable. Kean himself is changed from the hero of a melodrama to an existentialist hero, though on a smaller scale than Goetz. But his problem is analogous to Goetz's; an actor is like a bastard because he is necessarily uncertain of his real position in the world; Kean is never sure whether his actions are those of Kean the actor or of Mr Edmond the man:

> To act, you must take yourself for somebody else. I took myself for Kean, who took himself for Hamlet, who took himself for Fortinbras. . . . Yes, Hamlet thought he was Fortinbras. But hush! That's a secret. What a shower of misunderstandings. Fortinbras didn't take himself for anybody else. Fortinbras and Mr Edmond are of the same kind; they are what they are and say what is so. You can ask them the state of the weather, what time it is or the price of bread. But above all don't try to make them act in a play (Act v, scene 2).

This uncertainty of his position is emphasised by his relation to the Prince of Wales; is he a friend or a subject? Even in his love affair with the Countess of Koefeld, Kean is not sure if he is acting a part or is genuinely in love. The whole play is constructed around this game of mirrors: Kean loves Elena, the Countess. The Prince of Wales loves Elena because he thinks Kean loves her. Elena loves Kean the actor, not Mr Edmond the man. But who is Kean? Which of the loves is genuine? The entry of Anna Damby, an authentic person who falls in love with Kean, helps to precipitate the crisis. Kean, playing Othello to Anna's Desdemona, sees the Prince of Wales in a box with Elena. He has a breakdown on the stage, confusing Elena with Desdemona, reality and appearance. The result is scandal, an insult to the Prince and to the audience. The next morning Kean (or Mr Edmond) is still uncertain what he has done:

KEAN. Well, what have I done?

SOLOMON. You have insulted the Prince of Wales, a peer of the realm and seven hundred and eighty-two people.

KEAN. Yes, yes, I know. But what was it?

SOLOMON. They say it was a crime, the crime of lèse-majesté.

KEAN. That wasn't what I was asking, idiot. Was it a gesture or was it an action?

SOLOMON. I don't know.

KEAN. It was a gesture, don't you understand? The last one. I took myself for Othello, and her, laughing in her box, I took for Desdemona. A gesture with no significance for which I owe nothing to anybody. Sleepwalkers are not responsible.

SOLOMON. That's what I said. You're not guilty and for that reason you must be defended.

KEAN (*in a loud voice*). You lie! It was an action! It was an action because it ruined my life. Ten years in prison, eh? That's not too dear, since I really frightened them. Oh, Solomon, an action or a gesture? That's the question. Seven hundred and eighty-two people saw me commit a crime; therefore it was a deliberate act. But me? Did I will this crime or did I dream it? Did I want to risk my wealth and my life? Didn't I still think I had a clown's immunity? Well, it was suicide in jest. But someone had loaded the pistol, and the great Kean really killed himself. (Act V, scene 2.)

However, with Anna's aid, Kean comes to accept his ambiguous situation as an actor, and also to see that his previous troubles over his identity were a means of escape from himself. He had played a part in real life just as he did on the stage; his love for Elena only existed in so far as she was unattainable. She was also playing at love, and for the same reason; she knew they could not marry. When, after the disaster, she comes to offer herself to Kean, they both soon realise the true situation. The Prince gets Kean's prison sentence commuted to a year's exile. He agrees to marry Anna, but they both join in pretending to the Prince that Kean still loves Elena. The play ends happily. At the appropriate level both Kean and Anna have achieved authenticity. What is interesting is that it is an authenticity in a minor key, suitable to those in their station and hence milder than that of the tragic hero of the type of Goetz. But it is of the same kind. Apart from providing a virtuoso part for an actor and being well worth production, the play is interesting in suggesting that authenticity can occur at different levels. Perhaps it is a pity that Sartre has not paid more attention to situations of this type in his theoretical work.

Nekrassov is a satire on anti-Communism, but there is nothing solemn about its treatment of a serious subject. It is Sartre's funniest play, with elements of pure farce in it. Some parts are reminiscent of Shaw's comedy of ideas, for example the opening scene where the hero attempts suicide in the Seine and is reluctantly rescued by two beggars, or the scene where he welcomes the sane reaction of the 'ordinary' man who, finding de Valera hiding in his flat, wants to hand him over to the police, rather than hide him as the Communist daughter had wanted to. The plot is simple; Georges de Valera is a confidence trickster wanted by the police. After his suicide bid, he hides in a journalist's flat. This latter is frantically trying to find a new anti-Communist angle for his paper, the semi-official *Soir à Paris*. Georges pretends to be Nekrassov, a Soviet minister who has fled to the West. He convinces the staff of the paper and produces a string of sensational revelations about life in Russia and her plans for the conquest of France. Gradually Georges finds that he is not in control of the situation, as he first thought, but is being manipulated. He is threatened with deportation if he does not testify against two innocent Communists who have written against the rearming of Germany. Finally he escapes and tells the truth about his imposture to the Communist paper, *Libérateur*. But even this action is stolen from him; *Soir à Paris* goes to press with two headlines "Georges de Valera sells himself to the Communists" and "Nekrassov kidnapped by the Russians". "Will they believe us?" asks one of the staff. "No, but they won't believe the story in *Libérateur* either," replies the chief. In the Cold War truth is unimportant, the effect of the story on the readers all. The play is set in contemporary France, with numerous references to actual incidents and people. When the editorial staff is looking for a new writer, someone suggests Thierry Maulnier: " 'He's got a distinguished mind and is very frightened of Communism.' 'Yes, but he can't communicate his fear; I've known two people who read his articles and went straight away to join the Communist Party'" (tableau v, scene 1).

The satiric nature of the play compels Sartre to deal with the questions of action and identity at a very different level from the rest of his dramatic works. It is not the fundamental identity of the actors that is in question so much as their public one; action has the restricted meaning of what appears to the rest of the world. Motives are hardly in question. For example, if the editor of *Soir à Paris* cannot find a good anti-Communist item, he will lose his job:

GEORGES (*ironically*). You really need me to be Nekrassov.

JULES. Unfortunately.

GEORGES. Therefore I am Nekrassov.

JULES. What do you mean?

GEORGES. Have you forgotten the catechism? There the existence of God is proved by man's need of him. (Tableau v, scene 2.)

More elaborate, but in the same vein, is Georges' proof of his identity to Sibilot, another journalist who knows he is an impostor. Georges asks him to establish his own identity:

SIBILOT. I've got my papers.

GEORGES. I've got some too.

SIBILOT. Mine are genuine.

GEORGES. So are mine. Do you want to see my residence permit given to me by the Prefecture of Police?

SIBILOT. It's worth nothing.

GEORGES. Why not?

SIBILOT. Because you're not Nekrassov.

GEORGES. And your papers are valid?

SIBILOT. Yes.

GEORGES. Why?

SIBILOT. Because I am Sibilot.

GEORGES. So you see, it isn't the papers that prove the identity.

SIBILOT. Well, no, it isn't the papers.

GEORGES. Well, then. Prove to me that you are Sibilot.

SIBILOT. Everyone says I am.

GEORGES. Everyone? How many people is that?

SIBILOT. A hundred, two hundred, I don't know, a thousand. . . .

GEORGES. A thousand people take you for Sibilot and you want me to take their word for it and yet you reject the witness of two million readers who take me for Nekrassov?

SIBILOT. It's not the same thing.

Later in the same scene:

GEORGES. How can I make you understand? Look, on one side take forty million Frenchmen, our contemporaries, all convinced they are living in the middle of the twentieth century, and on the other a single individual who swears that he is the Emperor Charles V. What would you call that man?

SIBILOT. Mad.

GEORGES. And that's what you are if you claim to deny truths founded on universal consent. (Tableau v, scene 4.)

The whole play is a wry comment on what happens when it is believed that the end justifies the means; ultimately the result is a general loss of authenticity. Because effectiveness of the propaganda is the only test of 'reality' in the world of the newspaper, all the characters are at the mercy of impersonal forces, the public reaction to what they say. They think they are acting, really they are manipulated, become puppets rather than human beings.

Les Séquestrés d'Altona (1959) is certainly the most difficult of all Sartre's plays. Although many critics received it enthusiastically, others found it incomprehensible, full of inflated language and vague symbolism. It is a dense construction, and can be considered on several different levels. One of these is clearly the question of the use of torture by the French in Algeria, a subject on which Sartre has been outspoken elsewhere. But Frantz, the hero, does not represent France; such symbolism is foreign to Sartre's design. In this case, above all others, a bare summary would distort the complex relationships of the characters, all of whom live on the others by a kind of emotional cannibalism. I have already mentioned the extent to which the language of this play echoes that of *Critique de la raison dialectique*; perhaps Sartre tries to express in the play some part of what he failed to get across in that overlong work. But the echoes of this and other prose writings are fully integrated into a dramatic structure which leaves a powerful, though perhaps vague, impression on the audience. Most of the major themes of Sartre's thought are touched on. The final speech on stage summarises in part the play as a whole. It is Frantz's tape-recording, played after his suicide. Half is spoken to an empty stage. The intended audience is the tribunal of Crabs, Frantz's imagined inhabitants of the thirtieth century who occupy man's old position.

Centuries, here is my century, alone and shapeless, the accused. My client disembowelled himself with his own hands; what you take to be lymph is blood; there are no red corpuscles, for the accused is dying of hunger. But I can tell you the secret of his manifold wounds; the century would have been good if man had not had his immemorial cruel enemy lying in wait for him, that flesh-eating species which had sworn to destroy him, that hairless, malignant beast, man himself. One and one make one, that's our mystery. The beast lay hidden; we suddenly caught its glance in the depth of our neighbours' eyes. So we struck; legitimate self-defence. I surprised the beast, I struck and a man fell. In his dying eyes I saw, still living, the beast: myself. One and one make one; what a misunderstanding! From whom, from what comes this rank and insipid taste in my mouth? From man? From the beast? From myself? It is the taste of the century. Happy centuries, you have forgotten our hatreds, so how can you understand the terrible power of our fatal loves. Love, hatred, one and one. . . . Acquit us! My client was the first to know shame; he saw he was naked. Happy children, you spring from us, our griefs have created you. This century is a woman, it is giving birth. Can you condemn your mother? Eh? Answer then! (*a pause*)

The thirtieth century no longer answers. Perhaps there are no more centuries after ours. Perhaps the Bomb has blown out all the lights. Everything is dead, eyes, judges, even time itself. Night. Oh tribunal of night, you who have been, who will be, who are, I have lived! I have lived! I, Frantz von Gerlach, here, in this room, have taken up the burden of this century and have said 'I will answer for it'. In this day and for evermore. What? (Act v, scene 3).

Sartre comments on one aspect of this speech: "The whole play is constructed from the viewpoint of a future which is simultaneously false and true. The recluse's madness lies in considering himself—in an effort to avoid feeling guilty—the witness of a century which is in the process of disappearing and in addressing himself to a superior tribunal. All he says is absurd, to be sure, and not a true commentary on this century, but I wanted the spectator to feel himself to some degree in the presence of this tribunal.... Or, quite simply, in the presence of centuries to come. ... I would like the public to see our century from without, as a disinterested witness. And yet they participate, since they are making this century. There is, moreover, something singular about our time: we know we will be judged" (*Evergreen Review*, loc. cit., 152. I have substituted "they" for "he" in both places in the penultimate sentence). The tribunal of Crabs also represents a transcendent God; Frantz's bad faith lies both in seeking consolation from such a source and in trying to take more responsibility than he really bears. Part of the motivation for his suicide is the discovery that his father has long been aware of the action for which he feels guilty, the torture of Russian prisoners during the war; his father does not regard this as very important. Frantz wants to believe that it was a genuine action with real consequences and that hence he is right to feel guilty, that he *is* a torturer. Further, not only is he punishing himself and being punished for it, but also he believes that Germany is being systematically destroyed by the victors. The revelation that Germany is the most prosperous nation in Europe, with its own armed forces and, in his father's words "Tomorrow the Bomb", helps to destroy the identity he has constructed for himself in the locked room. "Loser wins" is indeed an account of the situation. His father had educated him to be a power in the great von Gerlach shipyard, but, in fact, he never had any power over events. The 'Enterprise'—the shipyard, Germany, the march of History—for it is all of these things, in fact had manipulated him. His father explains: "I gave you all the virtues as well as my bitter taste for power. It was no use. What a waste! In order to act, you took the supreme risk and, you see, it transformed your acts into gestures. Finally your agony pushed you into crime and it even wiped out your crime; it grows fat on your defeat" (Act v, scene 1). Frantz learns at the level of tragedy what Kean and Georges de Valera learn at the level of comedy. His last despairing cry "J'ai été", I have been (or lived), is the final irony. For he has never "been" anything, only an agent of forces that he didn't understand; all he thought were actions turn out to be, in the original sense, 'passions', things done to him. He realises that he was "destined to impotence", that what he thought he had done could just have well have been done by anyone else.

I have only considered one strand of this complex play, but it seems to me the central one; in different ways the other characters reflect the same set of conflicts that occur in Frantz. And, at another level, all that happens reflects what has happened in the world in the last twenty-five years. The "rank and insipid taste" is not only that of the body, it is also the taste of the whole century. This points to the main new element in this play, the presence of the *practico-inert*. Even on a political level, Goetz could act; in *Les Séquestrés d'Altona* it is doubtful if anyone can act even on a purely individual level. All the characters might be adjuncts of the 'Enterprise', their freedom circumscribed by that complex machine that they and their ancestors have created. To this extent it is the most pessimistic of Sartre's plays, for individual action is no longer sufficient to attain authenticity. This is, it might be said, the fundamental problem of *Critique de la raison dialectique*. To know whether Sartre has a solution, we must await the next volume of that work or his next play.

The Performance of *Les Mouches* in 1943

Mme de Beauvoir is one of the sources of the story that this play was a testament of the Resistance. In *La Force de l'âge* she writes: "Impossible to mistake the meaning of the play; coming from Orestes' mouth, the word Freedom exploded with violence. The German critic of *Pariser Zeitung* understood it, and said so, whilst handling the play with kid gloves to give it a favourable notice. In the clandestine *Les Lettres Françaises* Michel Leiris praised *Les Mouches* and underlined its political significance. The majority of critics pretended to have seen no such reference; they pitched into the play, but claimed that this was on purely literary grounds. They said it was unfortunately inspired by the works of Giraudoux, that it was verbose, over-subtle and boring. They recognised Olga's talent; for her it was a great success. In return they attacked the production, the décor and the costumes. The public did not flock to see it. It was already June and time for the theatre to close. Dullin put *Les Mouches* on again in October, alternating it with other plays."[1] As I have argued in the chapter, the kind of freedom that Orestes sought was more that of the solitary adventurer than that of a Resistance fighter. Sartre's disciple Jeanson is clearly worried about this and discusses the question in *Sartre par lui-même* at some length (150–1, also quoted in Cranston, *Sartre*, 37–38). But he still seems to accept the Resistance story, as does Sartre himself.

But the facts as Mme de Beauvoir presents them are surprising; if the Germans did see that the play was a call to Freedom, then it is surprising that they allowed it to be performed. And even if the Germans did, it appears that the Parisians didn't, or were not at that time ready to respond to such an appeal, for the play was not a success. It looks as if Dullin only kept it on for the sake of friendship. The only review of the play in *Lettres Françaises* did not appear until some time after the opening, and contains no reference to any political significance. Mr J. N. J. Palmer, to whom I owe this information, wrote to Mme de Beauvoir, who replied that she had made a mistake, and that the

[1] *La Force de l'âge*, 553–4.

original review of Leiris did contain political references, but these must have been deleted before publication. This may well have been the case, but it does seem likely that the other critics did not see any political reference in the play. Given the climate of 1943 in France this is very possible. Unfortunately the review in *Pariser Zeitung* cannot be consulted. Mr Cranston, in talking of what political significance the play could have, says: "All this (although the Nazis did not see it until their French collaborators pointed it out to them) might seem plain enough" (37). I am not sure what he is referring to here, though the passage implies that the Germans did take some action over the play. I conclude that the play failed not because the French critics were collaborationist, but rather from its own faults. It is significant that the revival in 1951 was also a failure. Mme de Beauvoir, and possibly Sartre himself, have been misled by memories of later attitudes to the Occupation.

XV

Literature and Life

SARTRE may be considered the writer *par excellence*; the award of the Nobel Prize for Literature, although rejected by him, is clearly legitimate. Consequently his reflections on literature in general and on his own writing are worth examination. The main source for his general comments is the well-known and often misunderstood *Qu'est-ce que la littérature?* of 1947, for his own works the fragment of autobiography, *Les Mots*, first published in 1963. This again has been the source of misunderstandings; many have taken him literally when he says of himself: "Ten years ago I woke up, became a man cured of a long bitter yet sweet madness which will never return. A man who cannot think of his old errors without laughing and who no longer knows what to do with his life" (*LM*, 211). This remark, coupled with one which follows closely, that he will continue writing through habit, that his motto has been and still is *Nulla dies sine linea*, has been taken as a gesture of despair. It is not; Sartre has often painted a gloomy view, but this is not evidence of a melancholic temperament. In an interview given soon after the publication of *Les Mots* he declares that he has always been happy, and there seems no reason to doubt this.[1] There are many things that Sartre enjoys, among them deflating the overvalued, about which he is both witty and ironical. In his latest work, though not only there, the wit and irony are turned on himself.

The almost clinical detachment and objectivity with which he views his earlier life have to be understood in reading *Les Mots*. He shows no trace of compassion for the small, ugly Jean-Paul

[1] *Encounter*, June 1964, 61–63.

Sartre of 7 or 9 years old; neither does he hate him. He merely observes and records. Because there is neither sentimentality nor any attempt at justification or excuse for the later Sartre—it might be a remote ancestor whom Sartre is chronicling—this application of 'existential psychoanalysis' to himself may leave the reader with an impression different from that intended. But the ability to live in the present, to be concerned with this 'project' not with the old ones, is only the application of those theories he has sketched elsewhere. "Someone mocked the person who bore my name in 1936; should this mean anything to me in 1946?" (*LM*, 199). One of the questions raised by *Les Mots* is whether we should feel any powerful emotional links with our childhood, or whether such feelings may not be mere self-indulgence. The idea is not a new one for Sartre; he has discussed it elsewhere under the name of 'bad faith'; what is new is the application to himself. Here again, an apparent break in his thought marks a deeper continuity.

The attitude to his childhood extends also to his own writings: "My best book is always the one that I'm writing; immediately after that is ranked the last one I published, but I'm getting ready, on the quiet, to be disgusted with it" (*LM*, 200). He goes on to laugh at himself for this trait, recounting how he remembered having written a page on the topic he was then writing about, and thinking that it might be of use. He found it, but thought he could now do better. "But when I had finished, by chance I picked up the original version. I was amazed. Apart from a few commas, I had expressed the same thought in exactly the same terms. I hesitated, then threw the original into the waste-paper basket, and kept the new version; it had something superior about it" (*LM*, 201). From Sartre's own point of view, then, it would seem as if his life and work must appear as a series of breaks. Hence we need not take too seriously his own statement that the year 1954 is particularly important in this respect. He says of that time: "As a result of political events, I was deeply preoccupied with the Communist Party. Thrown into the atmosphere of action, I suddenly understood the kind of neurosis that had dominated all my previous work" (*Encounter*, 61). From the purely political aspect, his decisions at this time may have been vital, but I have already argued that there is not such a break as he now suggests, at least so far as his philosophical attitude is concerned. The actual views on literature presented in the same interview seem to differ only in minor details from those set out in *Qu'est-ce que la littérature?* The notion of *engagement*, a word which has generally been translated 'commitment', remains central. As this theory of 'committed literature' has had wide currency, both in the Sartrean and other forms, I will examine it briefly.

The theory of commitment, as put forward by Sartre, is primarily concerned with literature, with the written word. Though he has written about both contemporary painters and Tintoretto, he has never considered their works in connection with this theory. The justification for making a sharp distinction between literature and the other arts rests, for Sartre, on the fact that the former uses as its material language, or words of a language, which are things that signify something other than themselves. A painting or a piece of music "has meaning", but this meaning cannot be translated into other terms (cf. *S.IV*, 29–30). We can be indifferent to the actual words by which a piece of information is conveyed to us; we may even have forgotten them whilst still remembering the information. It is impossible thus to extract the 'meaning' from a painting while ignoring the painting itself. Given such a distinction, it is clear that much modern poetry falls on the 'artistic' rather than the 'literary' side of the dividing line. For a poem is also a thing in itself in the way a painting is, an expression rather than a description. The poet takes words as objects in themselves and builds a poem in a way analogous to that of a painter constructing a picture 'out of' brush marks on canvas (cf. *S.II*, 64–70). "This being so, it is easy to understand how stupid it would be to ask for poetic commitment" (*S.II*, 69). Curiously enough, Sartre nowhere discusses the place of drama in his division; in spite of having written so many plays, he has written little about the drama. Literature for him means above all the novel, the specific contribution of bourgeois society to the Arts.

But the range of his interest and concern is narrower even than the novel: "I am told that bananas taste better when just picked; similarly, works of literature ought to be consumed on the spot" (*S.II*, 122–3). Sartre is contesting the notion, widespread in France, but not unknown elsewhere, that there is a body of 'literature', the fruit of the best minds, membership of which is open only to the works of defunct authors. It is said that, on the morning after Gide's death, there was a queue of students at the Sorbonne to register theses on him; death had made him a sufficiently respectable subject. Sartre himself earlier suffered from a similar attitude; his first dream of being a writer involved posthumous fame, he tells us in *Les Mots*. The corollary of such a view is that the writer's message is one for all time; the temporal accident of lack of appreciation during his life has no significance. Indeed, it is impossible to determine the message or the value of a living writer because he may embark on a new course with his next work. Only with death can the critic be certain that his judgment will not be falsified. Sartre compares libraries with cemeteries (*S.II*, 77) where critics commune with the dead, with fixed essences who are freed from the sin of existence. From this view of literature, only a sophisticated form of the doctrine of 'art for art's sake', comes a view of what a writer should concern himself with. He should deal with what is of eternal interest to mankind, not with the ephemeral, the flaws of the world in his own time. There is no place for a writer who wishes to change things in the Pantheon of literature. Sartre feels that this has been the attitude of many who attacked his doctrine of commitment. What they wanted from literature was the intellectuals' equivalent of the "good book" which the housewife demands from a lending library.

The error of such a view springs, in Sartre's opinion, from the fact that the controversies and protests which motivated some of the great works of the past were, at the time of writing, real and important both to the writer and his readers, even though no longer so for us. We can read one of Dickens' attacks on the abuses of his time merely *as literature*, that is to say considering the style without reference to the content. We cannot do the same with the novels of Richard Wright or James Baldwin. Our indignation against the workhouses of the nineteenth century is only literary; they no longer exist. But our feelings about the colour-bar are necessarily of a different order; the emotion it rouses is real because it is possible to do, or to try to do, something about it. The danger of such talk is that it leads to the identification of literature and propaganda, of measuring the success of a book by the extent to which it causes men to act. On this criterion, *Uncle Tom's Cabin* would be one of the greatest novels of all time. Most of Sartre's critics have assumed that this is the position he, in fact, wishes to take, and have attacked him accordingly. But Sartre's call for commitment in literature is for something rather different, as an examination of his own practice or of the novels he has praised would show. As so often, he is attacked from both sides; by the Communists for his explicit rejection of 'socialist realism', by bourgeois critics for his attacks on them and his apparent espousal of the Communist view. The commitment Sartre talks of is not to a political doctrine, but rather to literature itself. To write is to be committed to a certain type of enterprise which makes certain demands on the author; if, I must add, he is to be authentic. Sartre's prescription is for an authentic literature; in most of the places where the word 'committed' occurs, 'authentic' could be substituted without changing the meaning. This will enable us to understand his remark that he could not read Robbe-Grillet in an underdeveloped country. This is not because the author does not preach revolution; his failure is of a different kind, which can be seen by the fact that Sartre goes on to say that he could read Kafka in such a place. In his terminology, Kafka is committed in a way Robbe-Grillet is not, though there is nothing of the revolutionary in Kafka.[1] This difference can be crudely expressed by saying that Kafka is concerned about man's place in the universe, whereas Robbe-Grillet, in Sartre's opinion, isn't. But Sartre's whole discussion of literature can only be understood when it is seen as a specification of philosophical views developed elsewhere.

[1] cf. ibid., 62–63.

The connecting link between commitment and authenticity is freedom. The authentic man is one who has a right appreciation of his own freedom, and hence respects that of others. Similarly, the committed writer understands the way in which freedom is involved in writing a novel, and hence respects the freedom that is required to read it. Sartre's changing view of the nature of freedom explains here, just as it does in the case of his ethics, the changes in his judgment of particular works; the principle of that judgment remains the same. It is for this reason that he criticizes the Soviet theory of art: ". . . it is a matter of ordering didactic works from civil servants to be produced in accordance with the Party's directions. Because the artist has imposed upon him a conception of the future, instead of having to find it for himself, it doesn't matter that, politically speaking, this future is still to be made; for the writer it is already made" (S.IV, 37). If the conclusion of a novel is given before the author starts, then there can be no room for genuine freedom; the reader is in some way tricked. I think that the same reasoning lies at the basis of Sartre's controversial assertion that "No one would imagine for a moment that it is possible to write a good novel in praise of anti-semitism" (S.II, 112). Unfortunately such an example involves our emotional sympathies, or else makes us want to say that there is no reason why such a novel should not be written. Sartre, however, wants to argue for this as a matter of general principle: "Thus whether he be an essayist, a pamphleteer, a satirist or a novelist, whether he deals with only the passions of an individual or attacks the whole of society, the writer, a free man talking to free men, has one single subject: freedom" (ibid.). The remainder of this chapter will be devoted to elucidating this remark.

Sartre argues for his position by considering both what it is to write a novel and what it is to read it. It is surprising that so little attention has been paid to the question why people enjoy reading stories; it is normally accepted as a datum, an original fact about human nature. But a philosopher should surely, if he is to consider literature at all, find this something which calls for explanation. Sartre does not provide a full solution, but he at least raises the problem and attempts to answer it. One thing that many writers on aesthetics have agreed about is that the object of any work of art is not to raise in the spectator the same emotion that would be aroused by the actual event represented; a stock figure of fun is the yokel who reacts to the stage murder or seduction as he would to real events of those kinds. Nevertheless, works of art do arouse emotions: ". . . even men renowned for their hardness of heart shed tears over stories of imaginary misfortunes" (*S.II*, 101). The problem lies in the relation between this 'aesthetic' or 'distanced' emotion and the real ones that are felt as a result of contact with the real world, and, further, why the former should normally be enjoyed. (We do sometimes say that a story or a play is "too painful to bear", but this is normally when the action becomes too close to reality; compare Sartre's own trouble with the scream in *Morts sans sépultures*, quoted above, p. 231.) To say that reading and similar activities involve the "pleasurable exercise of the imagination" is only to put the problem in other words; why should such exercise be pleasurable? The word 'imagination' itself in this context is only a means of referring to the fact that men can and do read stories, etc. There is a type of book which is often called 'escapist', where the pleasure of the reader lies in identifying himself with the hero and enjoying his adventures vicariously. Serious critics ignore such books because they are too like the activity of day-dreaming, where we make up our own stories. Even if such things are not worthy of serious examination, they still give rise to the same problem. It is not clear why such an activity should be pleasurable. (Sartre's own childish day-dream of becoming a posthumously famous author is interesting in this connection.)

As I have said, Sartre does not provide a complete solution to this problem, but his remarks point to one. He first likens reading to dreaming: "At any moment I can wake up and know it, but I don't want to: reading is a free dream" (*S.II*, 100). There might seem a certain circularity in Sartre's views; in *L'Imaginaire* he has characterised dreaming as being like a story in which the reader is "trapped" (*Ire*, 225, quoted above, p. 33); each activity is explained in terms of the other. But it is for him the freedom that gives reading its enjoyable quality; dreams are unpleasant when we feel ourselves trapped, when difficulties pile up and there seems no way out, or rather every way out we find is promptly closed to us. In real life such situations would often yield to a few moments' calm consideration; in a dream we are not free to consider. There are some books about which the reader may feel something of the same sensation; he does not want to read them and yet he cannot put them down. In these cases it is the loss of freedom to stop as well as the intrinsic unpleasantness of the subject itself which destroys the pleasure of reading. Sartre's claim that reading is a free activity is not fully adequate to account for its pleasurableness. It is clear that lack of freedom destroys enjoyment—how often is a story spoilt for school children because they are made to read it?—but this is not enough to allow us to argue that freedom produces the pleasure. It may, however, help to render the fact less surprising. At the moment, I cannot see what else can be said to explain this, and it is clear that neither can Sartre. What he does do is to go on to show how this freedom operates. It is generally thought that the situation presented in the novel is the cause of the reader's emotions. If this were so, then there would be nothing to distinguish him from a spectator of the actual scene. Sartre argues that it is rather the reader's emotions which give the scene whatever shadow of reality it has. "I have said that Raskolnikoff would only be a shadow if it were not for the mixture of repulsion and friendship that I feel for him and which makes him live. But, by a reversal which is a necessary feature of imaginary objects, it is not his behaviour which provokes my indignation or esteem, it is my esteem and indignation which gives texture and objectivity to his behaviour" (*S.II*, 100). It is only in so far as we lend our emotions to Raskolnikoff that he becomes real and interesting; nothing the author does can compel us to read. He may solicit or claim our attention, and he does this by means of words that we must *take* as reality for the time during which the reading continues. (Of course, not all statements in works of fiction are themselves fictional, though Sartre can easily deal with this problem.) But taking the situation *as* reality involves 'lending' our emotions to the characters, and it is only in so far as we do lend our emotions that the work becomes alive or worth reading.

It is for this reason that Sartre describes reading as an "act of generosity": "Thus the reader's feelings are never dominated by their object and, since they cannot be conditioned by external reality, they have their permanent source in freedom, that is to say they are entirely generous—for I call a feeling that has freedom for its origin and aim 'generous' " (*S.II*, 100). The emotions concerned are "free emotions" (*S.II*, 104) because they are not the result of what is happening in the world, but arise from the way in which the reader has placed himself at the author's disposal. It follows from this that the piece of writing itself must be such as to be worthy of the reader's attention. One criterion for this is that there must be an ordered imaginary universe for the reader to 're-create'; there is little enjoyment in reading a book in which anything can happen. There must be limitations on what the reader is called upon to lend his emotions to. The harmonies of nature, Sartre argues, come about by chance; in a book, we must be certain that the harmonies are the result of the author's plan. (Of course, a work may fail either by excessive planning or by lack of it; Sartre does not raise these points, because he is only interested in the general features of literature, not the details of literary criticism.)

More important for Sartre is the fact that the reader's generosity demands a similar one on the part of the author; his writing must also be an exercise of freedom. In a trivial sense this is obvious; no one is compelled to write any more than most are compelled to read. Sartre goes further and claims that the fact that the author demands the reader's freedom commits him to exercising a similar freedom. It is the recognition of this which constitutes the writer's *commitment*, not his adherence to any political creed. He argues in several ways for this conclusion. First, if a man undertakes to write, he should be aware that writing is also action, for there is no such thing as a neutral description, one

which does not involve a particular attitude to the thing described. And to publish such a description is to ask that other men
take up, even if only for the time of their reading, the same point
of view (cf. *S.II*, 72–73). The act of publication is such that the
writer cannot say to himself that only a few will read him; he
must rather ask himself: "What would happen if everyone were
to read what I have written?" (*S.II*, 74). Because he chooses to do
a public act, he cannot refuse to acknowledge the consequences.

Second, Sartre argues that in demanding one kind of freedom
in his readers the author really claims their freedom in all respects,
for freedom is 'one and indivisible'. It is in this sense that there
cannot be a "black" novel, a racist or anti-semitic one. "For
because he who writes recognises, by the very fact of taking the
trouble to write, the freedom of his readers, and because he who
reads, from the very fact that he opens the book, recognises the
freedom of the author, the work, from whatever angle it is considered, is an act of confidence in human freedom" (*S.II*, 111).
An anti-semitic novel would presumably be one which tried to
show that the Jews were inferior to or more objectionable than
other races. In so far as the author of the novel believed this, and
put his belief into the novel, he would both be refusing them
freedom and at the same time asking for their generosity as
potential readers. (There is no need to consider a piece of propaganda for anti-semitism here; Sartre has already ruled such works
out of consideration.) In writing in this way the author is being
inauthentic as a writer. For just as authenticity for ordinary men
consisted in seeing, amongst other things, that no individual was
in a special position, so in a writer it means treating all mankind
as potential readers and exercising the same generosity to all of
them, not in deliberately excluding some. In this sense, any novel
written to support a particular viewpoint will be inauthentic.
(Of course, the application of the notion of authenticity to literature raises many of the same problems that it does in Ethics; I will
not go over them again at this point.)

The authentic or committed writer must realise that he is in a
situation, and his behaviour in that situation must be authentic.

"In a word, the author is situated, like all other men. But his writings, like every other human project, at the same time include, make precise and go beyond this situation, even explain and justify it . . ." (S.II, 188). In this sense he must be 'of his time', show concern for the issues of the day in the sense of not retiring into an ivory tower of art from which it appears that they do not exist. But it does not follow that he should concentrate exclusively on such issues. The theory of commitment is the literary side of Sartre's ethics, not a detailed theory of criticism. Hence he can say that he is aware of exceptions, has only sketched an outline. Writing is a moral act, or rather, like any other human act, can be judged by moral standards, and the writer must be aware of this if his work is to be of value. Hence there can be no recipe for writing, any more than there can be for Sartre a recipe for moral action. Certainly subordination to a political party is impossible for an author. Both in 1947 and now Sartre is sure that the Communist Party is an organisation that no true writer could join (cf. S.II, 280 and interview in Le Monde). Further, commitment does not involve a style that is universally comprehensible: "I am not recommending 'popular' literature which aims at the lowest. The public, too, has to make an effort to understand the writer who, though he renounce complacent obscurity, cannot always express his new-found thoughts lucidly and according to accepted models. Take Mallarmé. I hold him to be the greatest of French poets, and I took some time to understand him! His theory of the hermetic is a mistake, but he is only difficult to read when he has difficult things to say. Besides, one should not believe that people only want reading that is easy to absorb. The recent experiences of pocket-books [paper-backs] prove this. I have changed my public since my works have been published in a smaller format. Now I receive letters from workers, from secretaries. They are the most interesting ones" (Encounter, 62).

It may seem strange that Sartre's views on literature have aroused such fierce resentment among some critics when they are such as I have expounded. The explanation seems to be that he assumes that writing, although an important human activity, is by no means the most important. This view is implicit in *Qu'est-ce que la littérature?* and explicit in the interview with *Le Monde*, where he argues that there are times when it is the duty of an educated man to teach rather than to write: "In a country lacking leaders, in Africa, for instance, how could a native educated in Europe refuse to become a professor, even at the price of his literary vocation? If he preferred to write novels in Europe, his attitude would appear to me verging on treason. Despite an apparent contradiction, there is no difference between service to an entire community and the requirements of literature" (ibid.). The romantic ideal of the artist assumes that a literary vocation is higher than anything else open to a man, and most literary critics are committed, by their very activities, to this belief. But it does not seem to be a self-evident truth, and until good reasons are produced for placing literature above all other human activities, I shall believe, with Sartre, that at times other things are more important. It is not so very outrageous to suggest that an educated African, particularly if his education has been paid for by his 'underdeveloped country', has a duty to it which can best be fulfilled by teaching rather than writing. The African is in special circumstances; for our own society, relatively affluent as it is, Sartre thinks the needs are different: "to pose problems in the most radical and intransigent manner". Such is the limit of the writer's commitment. Sartre, in the field of literature as elsewhere, has done just that.

XVI

Concluding Remarks

MY CONCERN in this book has been to exhibit Sartre's views in a language which is more easily comprehensible to those brought up on this side of that philosophic iron curtain, the English Channel. Such an activity inevitably involves both interpretation and criticism, and, equally inevitably, these are inextricably entwined in what I have written. Consequently my Sartre appears a different figure from that of Mr Thody or Mr Cranston, to name two writers who have covered the same field as myself. Indeed, sometimes what I have said has been a result of conscious reaction against their views. But, in spite of those passages where I have shown (or attempted to show) that these or other critics have misinterpreted Sartre, my aim has never been to defend him. There are two reasons for this. First, he has no need of defence; for better or worse he represents Philosophy to large numbers of people on both sides of the Channel. I have been surprised at the number of applicants for philosophy courses who have made their first contact with the subject through the medium of his writings or plays. Nothing I say about him will alter his position as a major figure of the twentieth century. Sometimes I can even detect a thin note of envy in the voices of English philosophers discussing him; such success must be galling to those who feel that honest toil has brought less reward in terms of popularity and public influence than easy brilliance. For it is clear that success has come easily to Sartre. But this is because of the immense energy and intellectual verve which underlie all he has done. The sheer volume of his work is impressive, as a glance at the bibliography will show. In addition to his willingness to speak his mind on the issues of the day, however unpopular or dangerous that may be, he has always found time to help struggling younger writers in various ways. He has edited a successful periodical. Finally, he has conducted a long and deep love affair with a woman nearly his intellectual equal. With all that, it is not surprising that some of his work should bear the mark of inadequate revision; rather it is surprising that it is so good, that most of it is well worth reading. We whose output is less stupendous are not in a position to complain if Sartre's name is popular currency whilst ours is unknown. He has, in the words of a man who was a greater philosopher though a lesser figure, Merleau-Ponty, "a spark which we need".[1] A description of Sartre lecturing will perhaps bring out this point:

Another of my dreams is of a Sorbonne peopled by *super-agrégés* arguing against each other on the highest level with conviction as well as knowledge, as Abelard refuted Anselm, or as Sartre tussled with Camus. This dream, strangely enough, was partly realised when I heard Sartre, at the invitation of a student society, give a lecture on drama in the Grand Amphithéatre, which was packed to the roof. He turned out to be the perfect professor. His lecture had been carefully prepared. It was written out in longhand on large sheets of paper, which he turned over regularly without ever looking at them, so full of his subject he was and so intent on improvising, around his central state-ments, the qualifications and tangential hints that show how a train of thought is linked to a whole philosophy of life. He spoke simply, clearly, rapidly, yet doggedly and solidly, like an expert bricklayer building up a wall in front of your eyes. He went on and on, without a pause, for two-and-a-quarter hours, so that by the end the audience, though completely fascinated, was as collapsed and wilting as people during the final stages of a long train journey. You felt that he might have gone on all night and stopped only as a concession to frailer humanity. It was a wonderful performance—the sort of lecture that ploughs up the minds of the hearers as a tractor ploughs up a field. I sat next to an American professor, who said enthusiastically as we came out across the courtyard: 'St Thomas must have lectured like that.' . . . But I must admit that, in a long career of lecture-going, I have

[1] *Sens et non-sens*, 83–4.

never heard anything which corresponded more completely to my conception of what a lecture on a non-scientific subject should be.[1]

Any defence I could offer would be otiose. But I have a second reason to explain why I am not offering, and have not offered, a defence of Sartre. To defend is to claim discipleship, to imply that there is a body of views or methods which some philosopher has introduced and which the disciple regards as gospel. Perhaps the most damaging criticism that can be made of a philosopher is that he has loyal followers who devote themselves to maintaining the purity and rightness of his doctrines, who use his words as devices for putting an end to discussion. In struggling with the thought of another man for a long period it is inevitable that I should have absorbed some of his views. I am aware that my own philosophical attitudes are very different from what they were when I started on this enterprise. I hope and believe they are better. I am also aware that there are other, perhaps more fundamental, changes in my attitudes that have been brought about by the necessity of seeing myself clearly in order to understand what Sartre has said. Autobiography would be out of place here, but philosophy is "not a sterile discussion about abstract notions beyond experience". If it is not "a living effort to embrace from the inside the total human condition" (S.II, 251), then it is not worth the time we devote to it. It may sometimes seem as if little more has been said than Socrates' "Know thyself", but Sartre has I think, provided a blue-print for self-knowledge which is peculiarly appropriate to the present age. I am not a Sartrean, but then neither is Sartre himself.

Similarly, I am not an existentialist. Indeed, I have tried to avoid using the word throughout this book, though circumstances have occasionally forced me to employ it. It is now more of a term of abuse than a description, and one which it would be advisable to consign to oblivion along with all other misleading philosophical labels. Merleau-Ponty has recounted how Sartre came to adopt the term: "When some journalists first labelled him an 'existentialist', Sartre began by protesting. Then he said

[1] J. G. Weightman, in *Encounter*, June 1961, 42.

one day that after all he had not the right to refuse the label, which described what others saw in him. Thus he courageously took its side."[1] I have stated elsewhere my criticisms of existentialism as a philosophical doctrine,[2] and, in that article, I have used Sartre as one of the examples that I criticise. I concluded paradoxically that it is on the subject of ethics that the existentialists have least to say of philosophical importance. My grounds for this were that the notion of authenticity was inevitably an empty one, that it seemed to provide a do-it-yourself kit for ethics, an instruction to choose without an adequate criterion for that choice. This is much the same criticism as I offered in Chapter X of this book. I do not wish to retract those remarks here. Within the terms of my discussion, which were roughly those of what is normally regarded as philosophic ethics, they are, I believe, correct. But there is a deeper level at which I still feel doubtful about their validity.

These reservations are undoubtedly connected with those autobiographical facts I referred to earlier; in spite of all the arguments that I can put forward, I cannot bring myself to believe that the situation is completely as I have represented it, or as the majority of my colleagues think it is. Very tentatively, therefore, I raise the question of the nature of ethics and, with it, the whole question of what philosophy is. This "ultimate scepticism" arises from a number of factors. First, the rarity of genuine moral decisions, in the sense of choices based on clear analysis of reasons for and against. This is not to deny we may afterwards *defend* such a decision by stating reasons. But the natural desire of moral philosophers to construct a tidy system leads them to make the notion of moral decision more central than it actually is in our moral experience. Indeed, what is our *moral experience*? For most of us something much more inchoate than can adequately be represented in terms of those moral systems which form the staple of introductory courses on ethics. Our situation is more like

[1] *Sens et non-sens*, 84.
[2] 'Existence and Ethics', *Supplementary Proceedings of the Aristotelian Society*, 1963, 11–26.

Mathieu's or that of Françoise in *L'Invitée* than we are often willing to admit. And hence it is sometimes the case that we learn more about how to act and how to judge actions from reading works of fiction than we do from studying ethics. The answer that the philosophical study of ethics is intended to be morally neutral seems philosophic provincialism. It may be that at its earlier stages a neutral attitude is necessary, but unless the ultimate aim of moral philosophy is to help in some degree with substantive moral issues, it would seem an interesting but useless study. Even though they may not be able to justify it, I suspect that most philosophers want to claim that their thought is related to life. This relation seems more manifest in the work of Sartre than in many other philosophers, and this is partly because of his ability to exhibit, in his novels and plays, the complexities of actual moral choice.

Sartre is not the only writer to try to bring about such a synthesis; D. H. Lawrence also desired it:

It seems to me it was the greatest pity in the world, when philosophy and fiction got split. They used to be one, right from the days of myth. Then they went and parted, like a nagging married couple, with Aristotle and Thomas Aquinas and that beastly Kant. So the novel went sloppy, and philosophy went abstract-dry. The two should come together again—in the novel.[1]

My professional commitment prevents me from agreeing that philosophy can be completely absorbed in the novel; some subjects would be awkward to deal with by fictional means. There is clearly a special relation between questions of morality on one side, and the novel and drama on the other, as I have indicated. But there may also be a deeper one, in that ultimately an action may need to be judged by what can only be described as 'aesthetic' criteria. I mean by this that we may be able to see, after it has been done, that an act was right, though, beforehand, we would not have been able to advise the agent what he should do. And this case is similar to genuine aesthetic judgment, where we may be quite able to pronounce on the value of a finished work of

[1] 'Surgery for the novel—or a bomb', in *Selected Literary Criticism* (Mercury Books, 1961), 117.

art, but where no one could have been in a position to tell the artist how to go about making such a work. Of course, this 'aesthetic' type of judgment will only apply in complex moral cases, such as those involving personal relations. But the moral issues which trouble many people nowadays are complex in this way; for example, in a period in which virginity is no longer regarded as a prerequisite for marriage, and when there exist reasonably reliable contraceptive techniques, questions of sexual morality are precisely of this nature. The normal moral rules are too general to be of assistance. Neither would new rules or a detailed list of cases assist. What is required is something more akin to the development of moral sensitivity, though I am not certain whether this is a task for the philosopher. It is clear, I think, that many of those who look forward to the study of ethics in the universities are seeking something of this kind; to give them only an ability to distinguish the logical points involved will not satisfy them. I feel that philosophy ought to have something to contribute here, and that the value of Sartre lies partly in his having, by his writings, raised this kind of problem. It is

a question of knowing whether there is for every man a formula which will justify him in the eyes of others, or if, on the contrary, men are not, by their very position in the world, unpardonable each by the other and if, in this situation, moral principles are not rather a device for reassuring oneself or for disposing of questions than for saving oneself or for solving the questions. In morality, as in art, there may be no solution for the man who wants above all to make certain of his next step, to remain at all times absolutely master of himself.[1]

If this is the case, then a solution lies more in the direction that Sartre has taken than in any other, and this alone would constitute a reason for examining what he has said.

[1] Merleau-Ponty, *Sens and non-sens*, 9.

BIBLIOGRAPHY

This bibliography does not claim to be complete; I have omitted a number of letters to the Press, interviews, short prefaces and other trivia. It does include all of Sartre's major writings, those which are important for a full understanding of his views. They are listed in chronological order, with the exception of articles reprinted in the various volumes of *Situations*; in the case of articles listed only under these volumes I have mentioned the year of first publication after their titles. I have tried to include all English translations of Sartre's works.

In Part II of the bibliography I list a few works on Sartre or especially relevant to an understanding of his views. Those included have particularly influenced me.

The place of publication is throughout Paris except where otherwise stated.

I. SARTRE'S MAJOR WRITINGS

1931

'Légende de la vérité', *Bifur*, 8 (10 June 1931), pp. 77–96.

1936

'La Transcendance de l'égo: Esquisse d'une description phénoménologique', *Recherches philosophiques*, 6 (1936–7), pp. 85–123.
  TRANS. F. Williams and R. Kirkpatrick, *The Transcendence of the Ego* (New York, Noonday Press, 1957).
L'Imagination, étude critique. Félix Alcan.
  TRANS. F. Williams, *Imagination: a psychological critique* (Ann Arbor, Mich., University of Michigan Press, 1962).

1938

La Nausée. Gallimard.
  TRANS. Lloyd Alexander, *The Diary of Antoine Roquentin* (London, John Lehmann, 1949; and as *Nausea*, New York, New Directions, 1949).

1939

Esquisse d'une théorie des émotions, Actualités scientifiques et industrielles, No. 838. Hermann.
  TRANS. (1) Bernard Frechtman, *Outline of a theory of the Emotions* (New York,

Philosophical Library, 1948); (2) Philip Mairet, *Sketch for a Theory of the Emotions* (London, Methuen, 1962).

Le Mur. Gallimard. Contains 'Le Mur' (1937), 'La Chambre' (1938), 'Intimité' (1938), 'Erostrate' and 'L'Enfance d'un chef' (not previously published).
TRANS. Lloyd Alexander, *Intimacy* (London, Neville Spearman, 1949; New York, New Directions, 1952; paperback edition, London, Panther Books, 1960).

1940

L'Imaginaire: psychologie phénoménologique de l'imagination. Gallimard.
TRANS. Bernard Frechtman, *The Psychology of the Imagination* (London, Rider, 1949).

1943

L'Etre et le néant: essai d'ontologie phénoménologique. Gallimard.
TRANS. Hazel Barnes, *Being and Nothingness* (New York, Philosophical Library, 1956; London, Methuen, 1957). Extracts under the title *Existential Psychoanalysis*, trans. Hazel Barnes, were published in 1953 (New York, Philosophical Library).

Les Mouches, drame en trois actes. Gallimard. First performed in 1943; first printed in *Théâtre I*, 1947.
TRANS. Stuart Gilbert, *The Flies*, in *Two Plays* (London, Hamish Hamilton, 1946; and as *No Exit and the Flies*, New York, Knopf, 1947).

1945

L'Age de raison: Les Chemins de la liberté I. Gallimard; reprinted 1949, with pagination slightly altered.
TRANS. Eric Sutton, *The Age of Reason* (London, Hamish Hamilton, 1947; New York, Knopf, 1947; Penguin Books, 1961).

Le Sursis: Les Chemins de la liberté II. Gallimard; reprinted 1949, with pagination slightly altered.
TRANS. Eric Sutton, *The Reprieve* (London, Hamish Hamilton, 1947; and as *Reprieve*, New York, Knopf, 1947).

Huis clos, pièce en un acte. Gallimard. First performed 1944; reprinted in *Théâtre I*, 1947.
TRANS. (1) Stuart Gilbert, *In Camera*, in *Two Plays* (London, Hamish Hamilton, 1946; and as *No Exit*, in *No Exit and the Flies*, New York, Knopf, 1947); (2) M. Gabain and J. Swinstead, *Vicious Circle*. This was the translation that was used in the Arts Theatre Club production, July 1946, and also by the B.B.C.

1946

L'Existentialisme est un humanisme. Nagel.
> TRANS. (1) Bernard Frechtman, *Existentialism* (New York, Philosophical Library, 1947); (2) Philip Mairet, *Existentialism and Humanism* (London, Methuen, 1948).

Morts sans sépulture, pièce en trois actes. Lausanne, Marguerat; reprinted in *Théâtre I,* 1947. First performed, with *La Putaine respectueuse,* 8 November 1946.
> TRANS. Kitty Black, *Men without Shadows,* in *Three Plays* (London, Hamish Hamilton, 1949).

La Putaine respectueuse, pièce en un acte et deux tableaux. Nagel; reprinted in *Théâtre I,* 1947. First performed, with *Morts sans sépulture,* 8 November 1946.
> TRANS. (1) Kitty Black, *The Respectable Prostitute,* in *Three Plays* (London, Hamish Hamilton, 1949); (2) Lionel Abel, *The Respectful Prostitute,* in *Three Plays* (New York, Knopf, 1949).

Réflexions sur la question Juive. P. Morihien; reissued by Gallimard, 1954.
> TRANS. (1) Eric de Mauny, *Portrait of the Anti-Semite* (London, Secker and Warburg, 1948); (2) J. Becker, *Anti-Semite and Jew* (New York, Schocken, 1948).

1947

Baudelaire, précédé d'une note de Michel Leiris. Gallimard.
> TRANS. Martin Turnell, *Baudelaire* (London, Horizon, 1949; New York, New Directions, 1950).

Les Jeux sont faits, scénario du film. Nagel.
> TRANS. Louise Varèse, *The Chips are Down* (London, Rider, 1951).

Situations I. Gallimard. This contains:
* ★ '*Sartoris* par W. Faulkner' (1938).
* ★ 'A propos de John Dos Passos et de *1919*' (1938).
* '*La Conspiration* par Paul Nizan' (1938).
* 'Une idée fondamentale de la phénoménologie de Husserl: *L'Intentionalité*' (1939).
* ★ 'M. François Mauriac et la liberté' (1939).
* 'Vladimir Nabokov: *La méprise*' (1939).
* 'Denis de Rougemont: *L'amour et l'occident*' (1939).
* ★ 'A propos de *Le bruit et le fureur.* La temporalité chez Faulkner' (1939).
* ★ 'M. Jean Giraudoux et la philosophie d'Aristote. A propos de *Choix des Elues*' (1940).
* ★ 'Explication de *L'Etranger*' (1943).
* ★ '*Aminadab* ou du fantastique considéré comme un langage' (1943).

'Un nouveau mystique' (1943).

★ 'Aller et retour' (1944).

'L'homme et les choses' (1944).

'*L'homme ligoté*. Notes sur le Journal de Jules Renard' (1944).

★ 'La liberté cartésienne' (1946).

TRANS. Annette Michelson, those items indicated by an asterisk, in *Literary and Philosophical Essays* (London, Rider, 1955). 'Aller et retour' is also translated as 'The Journey and the Return' in *Essays on Language and Literature*, ed. J. L. Hevesi (London, Allan Wingate, 1947).

Théâtre I. Gallimard. This contains *Les Mouches, Huis clos, Morts sans sépulture*, and *La putaine respectueuse*: for translations see the individual plays above.

Introduction to *Descartes*, in series 'Les classiques de la liberté'. Geneva–Paris, Trois Collines. Though the copyright date is given as 1946 and the date of printing as 1948, the book appears to have been published in 1947. Sartre's introduction is reprinted as 'La liberté cartésienne' in *Situations I*.

1948

Situations II. Gallimard. This contains:

'Présentation des Temps Modernes' (1945).

'La nationalisation de la littérature' (1945).

'Qu'est-ce que la littérature?' (1947).

The third item was translated by Bernard Frechtman, *What is Literature?* (New York, Philosophical Library, 1949; London, Methuen, 1951).

L'Engrenage, scénario. Nagel.

TRANS. Mervyn Savill, *In the Mesh* (London, Dakers, 1954).

Les Mains sales, pièce en sept tableaux. Gallimard. First performed 2 April 1948.

TRANS. (1) Kitty Black, *Crime Passionel*, in *Three Plays* (London, Hamish Hamilton, 1949; and separately, London, Methuen, 1961); (2) Lionel Abel, *Dirty Hands*, in *Three Plays* (New York, Knopf, 1949).

'Conscience de soi et connaissance de soi', *Bulletin de la Société Française de Philosophie*, 42, no. 3 (April–June 1948), pp. 49–91, and subsequent discussion.

By a decree of the Holy Office dated 30 October 1948, 'all the works' of J-P. Sartre were placed on the *Index of Prohibited Books*.

1949

La Mort dans l'âme: Les Chemins de la liberté III. Gallimard.

TRANS. Gerard Hopkins, *Iron in the Soul* (London, Hamish Hamilton, 1950; and as *Troubled Sleep*, New York, Knopf, 1951).

Drôle d'amitié (part of *La Dernière chance*, the projected fourth volume of *Les Chemins de la liberté*, never completed). Part I in *Temps Modernes*, no. 49

(November 1949), pp. 769–806; Part II in *Temps Modernes*, no. 50 (December 1949), pp. 1009–39.

Entretiens sur la politique (in collaboration with David Rousset and Gérard Rosenthal). Gallimard.

Situations III. Gallimard. This contains:

    'La république du silence' (1944).

    'Paris sous l'occupation' (1944).

    'Qu'est-ce qu'un collaborateur?' (1945).

    'Fin de la guerre' (1945).

    ★ 'Individualisme et conformisme aux Etats-Unis' (1945).

    ★ 'Villes d'Amérique' (1945).

    ★ 'New York, ville coloniale' (1946).

    'Présentation' (1946).

    ★ 'Matérialisme et révolution' (1946).

    'Orphée noir' (1948).

    'La recherche de l'absolu' (1948).

    'Les mobiles de Calder' (1946).

    TRANS. Annette Michelson, those items indicated by an asterisk, in *Literary and Philosophical Essays* (London, Rider, 1955).

1950

Preface to *Le Communisme yougoslave depuis la rupture avec Moscou*, by Louis Dalmas (pp. ix–xliii). Editions Terre des Hommes.

Preface to *Portrait de l'aventurier: T. E. Lawrence, Malraux, von Salomon*, by Roger Stephane (pp. 9–29). Le Sagittaire.

Preface to *L'artiste et sa conscience. Esquisse de la dialectique de la conscience artistique*, by René Leibowitz (pp. 9–38). L'Arche. Reprinted in *Situations IV*.

1951

Le Diable et le Bon Dieu, pièce en trois actes et onze tableaux. Gallimard. First performed 7 June 1951.

    TRANS. Kitty Black, *Lucifer and the Lord* (London, Hamish Hamilton, 1953; and as *The Devil and the Good Lord* (with *Kean* and *Nekrassov*), New York, Knopf, 1960).

1952

'Sommes-nous en démocratie?', *Temps Modernes*, no. 78 (April 1952), pp. 1729–33.

'Les Communistes et la paix'. Part I, *Temps Modernes*, no. 81 (July 1952), pp. 1–50. Part II, *Temps Modernes*, nos. 84–5 (October–November 1952), pp. 695–763. Part III (conclusion), *Temps Modernes*, no. 101 (April 1954), pp. 1731–1819.

'Réponse à Albert Camus', *Temps Modernes*, no. 82 (August 1952), pp. 334–53. Reprinted in *Situations IV*.

Saint Genet: comédien et martyr. (Volume I of the *Oeuvres complètes* of Jean Genet). Gallimard. Fragments (221 pages out of 573) were published in *Temps Modernes*, nos. 57–62 (July–December 1950), under the title 'Jean Genet ou le bal des voleurs'.

TRANS. Bernard Frechtman, *Saint Genet* (New York, Braziller, 1963; paperback edition, Mentor, 1964).

1953

'Réponse à Lefort', *Temps Modernes*, no. 89 (April 1953), pp. 1571–1629.

L'Affaire Henri Martin: Commentaire. Gallimard. This book consists of extracts about the arrest, trial and release of Henri Martin with Sartre's comments.

1954

'Opération Kanapa', *Temps Modernes*, no. 100 (March 1954), pp. 1723–28.

'Les Peintures de Giacometti', *Temps Modernes*, no. 103 (June 1954), pp. 2221–32. Reprinted in *Situations IV*.

Kean (Alexandre Dumas, *Kean*, adaptation de Jean-Paul Sartre, cinq actes). Gallimard. The volume also contains Dumas' original play, *Kean ou désordre et génie*. Sartre's adaptation was first performed in November 1953, with Pierre Brasseur, for whom it had been written, in the title role.

TRANS. Kitty Black, *Kean, or Disorder and Genius* (London, Hamish Hamilton, 1954; and (with *The Devil and the Good Lord* and *Nekrassov*), New York, Knopf, 1960).

1956

'Le Réformisme et les fétiches', *Temps Modernes*, no. 122 (February 1956), pp. 1153–64.

'Le Colonialisme est un système', *Temps Modernes*, no. 123 (March 1956), pp. 1371–86.

'Réponse à Pierre Naville', *Temps Modernes*, no. 123 (March 1956), pp. 1510–25.

Nekrassov, pièce en huit tableaux. Gallimard. This was first printed in *Temps Modernes*, nos. 114–117 (June–September 1955). It was first performed 8 June 1955.

TRANS. S. and G. Leeson, *Nekrassov* (London, Hamish Hamilton, 1956; and (with *The Devil and the Good Lord* and *Kean*) New York, Knopf, 1960).

Preface to *Portrait d'un inconnu*, by Nathalie Sarraut. Gallimard. Reprinted in *Situations IV*.

1957

'Le Fantôme de Staline', *Temps Modernes*, nos. 129–31 (November 1956–January 1957), pp. 577–696.

'Vous êtes formidable', *Temps Modernes*, no. 135 (May 1957), pp. 1641–47.

'Le séquestré de Venise', *Temps Modernes*, no. 141 (November 1957), pp. 761–800. A fragment of a study of Tintoretto, 'to be published by Gallimard'. Reprinted in *Situations IV*.

1958

Preface to *Le traitre*, by André Gorz (pp. 11–47). Editions du Seuil.
     TRANS. Richard Howard, *The Traitor* (London, Calder, 1962). Reprinted as 'Des rats et des hommes' in *Situations IV*.

Preface to *La Question*, by Henri Alleg. Editions de la Cité, Lausanne. Sartre's preface was entitled 'Une Victoire'. Attempts were made to publish this preface as a tract in France, but owing to its attack on French torture in Algeria, the tract was seized and destroyed. The edition of *L'Express* of 6 March 1958, in which extracts from it appeared, was also seized by the police. Extracts in English were published under the title 'Almost as mute as during Occupation' in the *Observer*, 9 March 1958. Reprinted in *Situations V*.

1960

Critique de la raison dialectique, tome 1, *Théorie des ensembles practiques*. Gallimard.

Les Séquestrés d'Altona, pièce en cinq actes. Gallimard. This was first printed in *Temps Modernes*, nos. 164 and 165 (October, November 1959); it was first performed on 23 September 1959.
     TRANS. S. and G. Leeson, *Loser Wins* (London, Hamish Hamilton, 1961; and as *Condemned of Altona*, New York, Knopf, 1961).

1961

'Merleau-Ponty vivant', *Temps Modernes*, nos. 184–5 (September–October 1961), pp. 304–76. Part of a double memorial number of *Temps Modernes*. Reprinted in *Situations IV*.

Sartre on Cuba. New York, Ballantine Books. A paperback original, with no details of translator or origin, except for the last chapter, 'Ideology and Revolution', which was first published in *Lunes de Révolution*, no. 51 (21 March 1960).

Preface to *Aden arabie* by Paul Nizan (pp. 9–62). François Masperon. Reprinted as 'Paul Nizan' in *Situations IV*.

1962

Marxisme et existentialisme: controverse sur la dialectique, par Jean-Paul Sartre, Roger Garaudy, Jean Hyppolite, Jean-Pierre Vigier, J. Orcel. Plon. (Sténographie intégrale de la controverse du 7 décembre 1961, à la Mutualité, sur le thème: 'La dialectique est-elle seulement une loi de l'histoire ou est-elle aussi une loi de la nature?') Sartre's contributions are on pp. 1–26, 81–83.

1964

Les Mots. Gallimard. Originally published in *Temps Modernes*, nos. 209, 210 (October, November 1963), 577–649, 769–834.

TRANS. (1) Irene Clephane, *Words. Reminiscences of Jean-Paul Sartre* (London Hamish Hamilton, 1964); (2) Bernard Frechtman, *The Words; the Autobiography of Jean-Paul Sartre*, New York, George Braziller, 1964).

Situations IV: Portraits. Gallimard. This contains:
'Portrait d'un inconnu' (1957).
'L'Artiste et sa conscience' (1950).
'Des Rats et des hommes' (1958).
'Gide vivant' (1951).
'Réponse à Albert Camus' (1952).
'Albert Camus' (France–Observateur, 7 January 1960. An obituary notice).
'Paul Nizan' (1960).
'Merleau-Ponty' (1961).
'Le Séquestré de Venise' (1957), 'fragment d'un ouvrage à paraître'.
'Les Peintures de Giacometti' (1954).
'Le Peintre sans privilèges' (1961; on Lapoujade).
'Masson' (ND).
'Doigts et non-doigts' (ND).
'Un Parterre de Capucines' (1952).
'Venise, de ma fenetre' (1953).

Situations V: colonialisme et néo-colonialisme. Gallimard. This contains:
'D'une Chine à l'autre' (1954).
'Le colonialisme est un système' (1956).
'Portrait du colonisé' (1957).
'Vous êtes formidables' (1957).
'Nous sommes tous des assassins' (1958).
'Une Victoire' (*L'Express*, 6 March 1958).
'Le Prétendant' (*L'Express*, 22 May 1958).
'La constitution du mépris' (*L'Express*, 11 September 1958).
'Les grenouilles qui demandent un roi' (*L'Express*, 25 September 1958).
'L'analyse du référendum' (*L'Express*, 4 January 1961).
'Les somnambules' (1962).

'Les damnés de la terre' (1961).

'La pensée politique de Patrice Lumumba' (ND).

II. SOME WORKS ON SARTRE

Champigny, Robert, *Stages on Sartre's Way*. Bloomington, Ind., Indiana University Press, 1959.

Cranston, Maurice, *Sartre*. London, Oliver and Boyd, 1962.

Greene, Norman N., *Jean-Paul Sartre: The Existentialist Ethic*. Ann Arbor, Mich., University of Michigan Press, 1960.

Jeanson, Francis, *Le problème moral et la pensée de Sartre*. Paris, Editions du Myrte, 1947. Includes a short letter from Sartre commending it as an accurate account of his views.

—, *Sartre par lui-même*. Paris, Editions du Seuil, 1954.

Merleau-Ponty, Maurice, *Humanisme et Terreur*. Paris, Gallimard, 1947.

—, *Sens et non-sens*. Paris, Nagel, 1948.

—, *Les aventures de la dialectique*. Paris, Gallimard, 1955.

Murdoch, Iris, *Sartre: Romantic Rationalist*. Cambridge, Bowes and Bowes, 1953; New Haven, Conn., Yale University Press, 1953.

Thody, Philip, *Jean-Paul Sartre: a Literary and Political Study*. London, Macmillan, 1960.

III. SOURCES FOR SARTRE'S LIFE

The main sources for details of Sartre's life, in the absence of the later volumes of his autobiography, are the three volumes of Simone de Beauvoir's memoirs. These give a detailed picture of the background against which Sartre's works were written. Also of interest is the fictional account of the Sartre-Camus quarrel in her novel *Les Mandarins*. I append details of these works:

Mémoires d'une jeune fille rangée. Gallimard, 1960. Translated by James Kirkup, *Memoirs of a Dutiful Daughter* (London, André Deutsch and Weidenfeld and Nicolson, 1959; Cleveland, Ohio, World Publishing Co., 1959).

La Force de l'âge. Gallimard, 1960. Translated by Peter Green, *The Prime of Life* (London, André Deutsch and Weidenfeld and Nicolson, 1960; Cleveland, Ohio, World Publishing Co., 1962).

La Force des choses. Gallimard, 1963. Translated by Richard Howard, *The Force of Circumstance* (London, André Deutsch and Weidenfeld and Nicolson, 1965).

Les Mandarins. Gallimard, 1954.

INDEX